NATURAL RISK

COLUMBIA STUDIES IN THE HISTORY OF U.S. CAPITALISM

COLUMBIA STUDIES IN THE HISTORY OF U.S. CAPITALISM

Series Editors: Justene Hill Edwards, Devin Fergus, Bethany Moreton, and Julia Ott

Capitalism has served as an engine of growth, a source of inequality, and a catalyst for conflict in American history. While remaking our material world, capitalism's myriad forms have altered—and been shaped by—our most fundamental experiences of race, gender, sexuality, nation, and citizenship. This series takes the full measure of the complexity and significance of capitalism, placing it squarely back at the center of the American experience. By drawing insight and inspiration from a range of disciplines and alloying novel methods of social and cultural analysis with the traditions of labor and business history, our authors take history "from the bottom up" all the way to the top.

The Columbia Studies in the History of U.S. Capitalism series was founded in 2013 by Louis Hyman, Bethany Moreton, and Julia Ott to publish the best new work in the history of capitalism. In 2017, Devin Fergus joined the series board. In 2025, Justene Hill Edwards joined the series board.

Coding Capitalism: Computers and the Remaking of the Postwar US Economy, by Devin Kennedy

The Lowest Freedom: Racial Capitalism and Black Thought in the Nineteenth Century, by Justin Leroy

Faith in Markets: Christian Capitalism in the Early American Republic, by Joseph P. Slaughter

The Rise of Corporate Feminism: Women in the American Office, 1960–1990, by Allison Elias

The Dead Pledge: The Origins of the Mortgage Market and Federal Bailouts, 1913–1939, by Judge Glock

Unfree Markets: The Slaves' Economy and the Rise of Capitalism in South Carolina, by Justene Hill Edwards

Histories of Racial Capitalism, edited by Destin Jenkins and Justin Leroy

Brain Magnet: Research Triangle Park and the Idea of the Idea Economy, by Alex Sayf Cummings

How the Suburbs Were Segregated: Developers and the Business of Exclusionary Housing, 1890–1960, by Paige Glotzer

Threatening Property: Race, Class, and Campaigns to Legislate Jim Crow Neighborhoods, by Elizabeth A. Herbin-Triant

Natural Risk

A HISTORY OF OIL, POLITICS, AND THE ENVIRONMENT IN WEST TEXAS

Sarah Stanford-McIntyre

Columbia University Press
New York

Columbia University Press
Publishers Since 1893
New York Chichester, West Sussex
cup.columbia.edu

Library of Congress Cataloging-in-Publication Data

Names: Stanford-McIntyre, Sarah, author.
Title: Natural risk : a history of oil, politics, and the environment in West Texas / Sarah Stanford-McIntyre.
Other titles: Columbia studies in the history of U.S. capitalism.
Description: New York : Columbia University Press, [2026] | Series: Columbia studies in the history of U.S. capitalism | Includes bibliographical references and index.
Identifiers: LCCN 2026008285 (print) | LCCN 2026008286 (ebook) | ISBN 9780231197366 (hardback) | ISBN 9780231197373 (trade paperback) | ISBN 9780231566704 (pdf) | ISBN 9780231552134 (epub)
Subjects: LCSH: Petroleum industry and trade—Texas, West—History—20th century. | Petroleum industry and trade—Environmental aspects—Texas, West. | Texas—Politics and government.
Classification: LCC HD9567.T3 S73 2026 (print) | LCC HD9567.T3 (ebook)
LC record available at https://lccn.loc.gov/2026008285
LC ebook record available at https://lccn.loc.gov/2026008286

Printed and bound by CPI Group (UK) Ltd, Croydon, CR0 4YY

Cover design: Milenda Nan Ok Lee
Cover photo: Permian Basin Petroleum Museum

GPSR Authorized Representative: Easy Access System Europe, Mustamäe tee 50, 10621 Tallinn, Estonia, gpsr.requests@easproject.com

To Eleanor and Audrey

CONTENTS

ACKNOWLEDGMENTS

My mother grew up in the cotton town of Plainview, Texas. Her parents were Dust Bowl migrants, happy to leave behind the Oklahoma oil patch. Still, the industry's impact easily spanned state lines and crossed generations. I began work on what would become *Natural Risk* in the summer of 2013, early in the fracking boom. A close friend learned that I was researching Texas oil and connected me with her father, who had worked in the industry for over two decades. His stories of trigger-happy ranchers, cantankerous crews, and monumental paperwork combined with my father's memories of the 1980s bust to color my early archival forays in the Permian Basin. Over ten years after those informal interviews, the results perhaps speak for themselves.

Beyond personal connections, countless others have also lent their time and expertise at different points in this project. To name only a few, Cindy Hahamovitch, Charles McGovern, Alan Braddock, Andrew Fisher, Thomas Andrews, Robert Lifset, Brian Leach, Darren Dochuk, Hugh Gorman, Bobby Weaver, Erik Hintz, Roger Horowitz, Tyler Priest, Jeff Manuel, and Julie Cohn provided invaluable insights and feedback. My research would have been impossible without the help of the historians, archivists, and librarians at the Hagley Museum and Library, the Smithsonian National Museum of American History, the Briscoe Center for American History at the University of Texas at Austin, the Permian Basin Petroleum Museum, the University of Colorado Boulder Archives, the Texas State Archives, the Walter Reuther Library, and the American Heritage Center at the University of Wyoming. I would like to thank the members of the Society for the History of Science Technology and Medicine, Energy History Working Group, who read early drafts. Lastly, John, thank you for the title and for everything else.

NATURAL RISK

INTRODUCTION

Natural Risk

In 1950, George H. W. Bush took a risk. He moved his wife and three young children roughly two thousand miles from the tree-lined, suburban sprawl of Connecticut to the dusty oil town of Midland, Texas. The scion of an influential family and a recent Yale graduate, Bush moved in elite circles. However, like many other young white men in mid-twentieth-century America, he hoped to profit from oil's postwar industrial boom. West Texas was a safe investment. By the early 1950s, West Texas, especially the geological region known as the Permian Basin, located halfway between El Paso on the Texas-Mexico border and the city of Lubbock in the Panhandle, was the rapidly expanding heart of American onshore oil production. Oil had been discovered in the Permian Basin three decades earlier, and as national oil consumption ballooned in the postwar era, the region was a hub for crude oil extraction and a lucrative target for financial speculation. Crucially, Bush had money to invest. He had connections on Wall Street, making him representative of a growing class of white-collar oil speculators who flocked to Texas oil in the 1950s.

Bush's financial risk-taking led to both economic and political power, culminating in a term as president of the United States. Two of his sons, George and Jeb, would enjoy similar success—George even became president thirteen years after his father was elected. However, less well-connected risk-takers had a very different experience in the West Texas oil fields. For example, Steve Sparger grew up in Denver City, Texas, on the northern edge of the Permian Basin. A child during Bush's rise to success, Sparger was a local high school football star who graduated in 1974 and took a job with Atlantic Richfield (ARCO). He was employed as a night-shift line walker, monitoring ARCO pipelines for signs of leaks or breaks. Oil was the region's major employer, and constant labor shortages during the boom years of the 1970s meant that Sparger's lack of either a college education or industrial experience did not prevent him from enjoying lucrative pay. However, inexperience and lack of protective equipment would cost him his life. In February 1975, Sparger responded to a reported pipeline leak near a farmhouse outside Denver City. Unaware of the leak's location and lacking any safety gear, he drove his truck into a cloud of toxic hydrogen sulfide gas. Sparger suffocated within minutes.

While tragic, this story was not unprecedented. In the 1970s, oil work remained notoriously dangerous, and in the Permian Basin, hydrogen sulfide was a known, silent killer that leaked from oil wells and lingered in low-lying areas. Sparger's death shows us that, for many, working in the oil industry was more than an economic gamble.

As these contrasting examples make clear, oil employers and employees—from prospectors, to drilling crews, to maintenance workers, to engineers, to leaders of large, multinational corporations—managed varying degrees of physical danger and environmental risk, even as they participated in a balancing act that weighed the industry's notorious uncertainty against the possibility of profit. This book tells their intertwined stories. It begins with the arrival of oil prospectors in the 1920s and follows the rise of natural gas production and early fracking efforts in the 1950s and 1960s. Finally, it ends with the catastrophic industry bust of the mid-1980s. This story shows how efforts to define and manage a set of competing and interlinked risks shaped the oil industry in the Permian Basin and influenced Texas politics and regulatory policy throughout the twentieth century.

Such influence was shaped in part by the Permian Basin's environmental history. Despite an emphasis on East Texas and the Gulf Coast in Texas cultural memory, the Permian Basin was, and still is, the longest-running commercial oil-producing region in the state.[1] Further, compared to other early extractive regions in Texas, oil did not come easily in the Permian Basin. Water was scarce. Permian Basin oil was comparatively deep underground. The Permian's "sour crude" was rife with high levels of toxic hydrogen sulfide and other dangerous impurities, which made air contamination a constant problem. As oil drove Texas's economic success, the scale and impact of its infrastructure took a growing toll on the health of residents in oil communities. Through decades of oil production, the Permian Basin became what scholars have called a "sacrifice zone," a place environmentally blighted by the processes of extraction for the benefit of people in geographically distant centers of power.[2] All regional communities were impacted by this process, as seen in the maps of major towns, cities, and adjacent oilfields in figure 0.1.

Oil's expansion was inextricable from its environmental impact; however, people with money and power used the industry to profit while sidestepping its most immediate threats. Some implemented new technologies in an attempt to reduce the long-term hazards produced by deteriorating air and water quality. However, as segregation in boomtowns and regional oil cities subjected local minoritized communities to increasing environmental risk, racism in the industry stilted efforts to scale up community remediation. Similar patterns emerged more broadly as elites outside the Permian Basin, such as investors, oil executives, and Texas legislators, used their economic and political power to balance the industry's multiple, at times contradictory risks and smooth the way for oil expansion. Permian development was lucrative, and it helped fuel a ballooning Texas economy. As early as the 1950s, most American oil workers and oil money passed through Texas, and the state was central to a national energy agenda. By 1970, oil helped Texas shed its cotton-Southern roots to become a central node in a globally dominant American fossil fuel–processing and transportation empire.

However, this is not to say that oil communities in the Permian Basin made a simple trade-off between profit and environmental destruction, and this book highlights the at-times unexpected fractures within local and industrywide risk management efforts. Jobbers, contractors, union organizers, engineers, speculators, regulators, and investors all responded to oil's mix of environmental contamination and workplace hazards. In turn, priorities, concerns, responses, and analyses existed within a Venn diagram mediated by industry affiliations, workplace pressures, wealth, and political power. These perspectives can be divided into four groups.

First, big payouts and sudden wealth were rare among the industry's wage-earning workers, for whom perennial job insecurity and financial

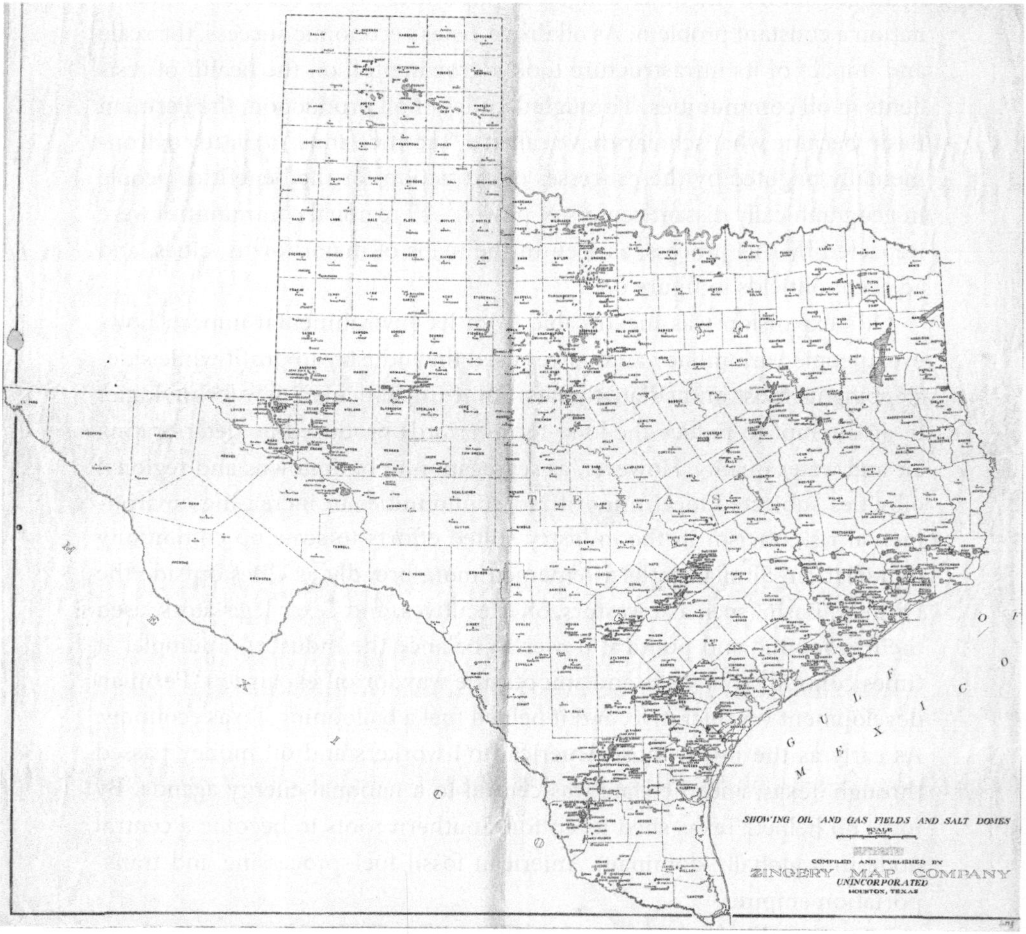

FIGURE 0.1A AND FIGURE 0.1B. Oil and gas fields and subsurface salt domes in Texas in the 1930s (a). A zoomed-in section (b) highlights major oil fields in the Permian Basin and the location of significant cities and towns in the region. Image courtesy of the Texas State Library and Archives Commission Archives & Information Services Division.

uncertainty incentivized a high level of personal risk. For many oil workers, the immutability of debt and instability of contract work overruled more amorphous environmental health risks. Oil drilling required itinerancy, and workers did not put down roots in one location for long. While this exacerbated racial and ethnic divides that hindered worker organization,

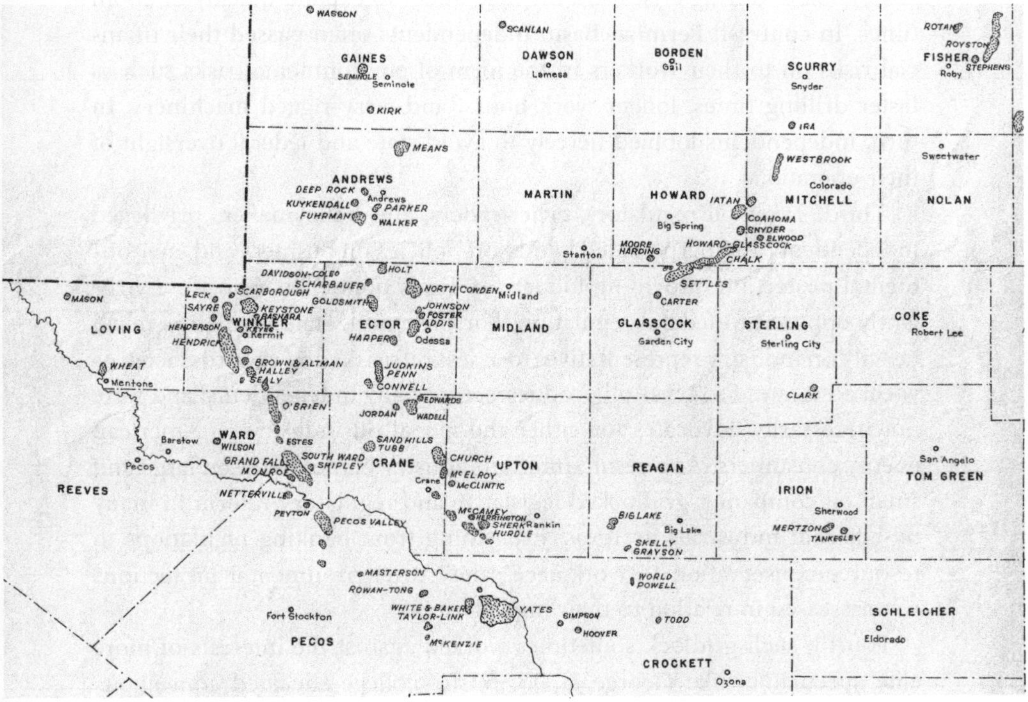

it also fostered strong industry-based ties among working-class people in oil-producing towns and cities throughout the region. While some workers avoided personal environmental risks such as air pollution or unsafe drilling practices by walking away from a job, doing so incurred a financial and social cost that many could not pay.

Second, most Permian Basin drilling was conducted by smaller, speculative operators, called "independents," that were unaffiliated with the increasingly powerful multinational American oil corporations, known as the "majors." Competition between independents and majors complicated risk management, as calls to increase safety oversight and standardize production were seen as hinderances to antimonopoly efforts. While neither American independents nor majors truly controlled oil prices after the 1950s, larger oil companies could better respond to the industry's boom-and-bust fluctuations. They had the capital reserves to take on debt or absorb losses during crises and the machinery to expand quickly in boom times. In contrast, Permian Basin independents often passed their financial risks on to their workers in the form of environmental risks such as faster drilling times, longer work hours, and jerry-rigged machinery. In turn, independents lobbied fiercely to avoid state and federal oversight of their operations.

Third, Texas oil regulators, civic leaders, and policymakers privileged independents and perpetuated hands-off policies on business and environmental protection, providing fodder for Texas politicians who were virulently opposed to federal regulation. For their part, state regulators relied heavily on industry representatives to assess oil's risks and rewards; acted as vocal advocates for Texas oil producers, especially independents; and were not necessarily advocates for either the global oil industry or American energy consumers. As a result, internal industry battles between large and small oil companies gridlocked legislative and regulatory reform in many oil-adjacent industries in Texas. Everything from banking regulations to resource conservation to workplace safety to environmental protections were assessed in relation to their impact on oil.

Fourth, such gridlock sometimes worked against the interests of more elite speculators like George H. W. Bush—college-educated consultants and credentialed engineers at larger oil companies who understood risk management as an effort to increase industry predictability. These white-collar workers developed and employed new technological fixes, internal inspection procedures, and safety protocols designed to increase efficiency and create stability in a financially and environmentally volatile industry. While industry innovation greatly extended the life of regional oil production, such technological fixes also created new problems, as illustrated by Steve Sparger's tragic death due to the failure of ARCO's experimental pipeline. Efforts to prevent future tragedies were complicated by an industry focus on further technological fixes that required engineers and industry management to see an environmental hazard as just one potentially chaos-creating variable among many rather than an urgent priority to address.[3]

While these four groups were often at odds, over time they perpetuated a prevailing industry discourse that had far-reaching impacts. At all levels of the industry, workplace safety and environmental risk management were articulated and assessed in financial terms. For these groups, the cost of a decline in environmental or individual health most fundamentally represented a drop in future earnings, collective economic success, or investment potential. However pragmatic, this study shows that such an assessment obfuscated the very material and physical consequences of extractive industry. Abstraction and quantification smoothly equated the health of communities and individuals with the fate of institutions and corporations, anthropomorphizing the industry and turning people into mere numbers on a balance sheet.[4]

Historians have shown that such practices were not unique to oil. Rather, similar equations were manifest in twentieth-century American regulatory and legal systems at all levels and were reinforced by social and cultural institutions built from decades of conflict.[5] Such debates over community health and safety manifested in competing desires: a push to preserve personal autonomy and a desire to uphold the collective good in an era of increasingly complex hazards. Before 1900, Americans used a mix of litigation, direct action, and sometimes legislation to make daily life safer and people healthier both at home and in the workplace. And in an effort to better document risks, dangers, and the consequences of accidents, institutions increasingly lumped together diverse social ills using future-projected numerical calculations. For example, federal officials calculated the impact of industrial accidents, natural disasters, pollution, and epidemics using very similar financial terms and equations.[6] Over the first half of the twentieth century, such language of future economic cost was used to support both growing legislative oversight and the consolidation of American heavy industry. Many diverse groups, including industrial unions, consumer advocates, actuaries, and insurance companies, all insisted that it was the obligation of employers, manufacturers, and governments to manage—if not prevent—negative future risks for individual workers and consumers.[7] Focusing on the dangers that such industries posed to the public good, these groups and others argued that unexpected hazards—be they sudden workplace accidents or stock market crashes—were an indication of systemic failure rather than an unavoidable part of industrial capitalism. Put another way, they argued that in a well-managed economy, growth could remain constant and was achievable without the high level of personal risk seen in previous centuries.

Industries with a high environmental impact, exemplified by oil, fit uneasily within this increasingly risk-averse system.[8] Even as the largest oil companies readily adopted financial frameworks for documenting industrial hazards and economic risks, key members of the oil industry, including many in the Permian Basin, were slow to accept efforts to actually remove industry volatility—either in the name of safety or in the pursuit of profits. There were many reasons for this.

Scholars have used the terms "extractive capitalism" and "extractivism" to describe the unique impact of ultimate resource depletion and cyclical booms and busts on the economies and social structures of extractive communities.[9] Case in point—Permian Basin oil production was contingent on the location of mineral deposits. Equipment costs and work delays were dictated by the presence of water, subsurface gases, or unforgiving terrain. As with other minerals, oil profits were inherently finite and lasted only as long as the size of geological deposits. In this way, a particular set of material risks shaped the cultural and economic institutions that both governed oil's patterns of infrastructure and technological development and set the boundaries of community cohesion and public controversy.[10]

In turn, the same set of environmental constraints that made oil jobs dangerous also made the industry as a whole economically volatile. Despite dramatic advancements in oil detection and extraction technologies in the twentieth century, such risks could never be fully ameliorated. This produced a focus on short-term, immediate risks among workers and small producers, disincentivizing paying attention to more complex environmental and public health consequences. This study shows that ironically, despite a widespread acknowledgment of inevitable oil depletion, the economic and environmental hazards produced by oil were very hard to remove once they were codified into state regulatory policy and drilled into the dirt and sand of West Texas.

This conceptual focus on risk contributes to the rich literature on oil in American history by illustrating ongoing fractures within an increasingly global and seemingly monolithic American oil industry. Scholars have shown that at key moments in the twentieth century, federal calls for industry nationalization promised to end domestic oil industry volatility and resource waste in the name of national security.[11] However, these were ultimately walked back as a result of growing partnerships between federal officials and the largest American oil companies. Over the same period, internal industry efforts to control supply and curb speculation were complicated by limited infrastructure and a global scramble for untapped oil. As the largest American oil companies became emissaries of Cold War foreign relations, local calls to improve workplace and environmental safety were marred by accusations of industry consolidation, exploitation, and monopoly. New battle lines emerged between those who understood control over the oil supply as key to twentieth-century American economic hegemony and an emerging movement to reduce domestic oil consumption.[12] This study shows that even as such external pressures made the oil industry leery of external critiques, no industrywide consensus on the best way to manage these risks truly existed.

Within such a story of internal fracture and oncoming resource depletion, how do we assess the impact of Permian Basin risk management? If we follow the industry's example and measure success in purely economic terms, we might say that the primacy of West Texas independents and their ability to prevent meaningful regulation allowed for industry innovation and greater localized control over an important resource. One might also look at the region's industry-led regulatory structures and argue that the technological fixes proposed by industry personnel creatively addressed systemic environmental problems that avoided supposedly inevitable resource depletion.

A scholar of Texas's economic history might remark that Texas oil, especially in the Permian Basin, was a crucial outlier to a national mid-twentieth-century trend toward federal management of risk assessment and environmental safety. And they also might say that by the industry's high point in the 1970s, the flexible regulatory and economic structures built by oil contributed to the rise of Texas as a Sun Belt economic powerhouse.[13] However, labor historians and scholars of Hispanic Texas would be quick to point out that oil increased already deep income and environmental inequality in the state and shored up Texas's racial hierarchies. They would highlight the suffering of Tejano landholders stripped of their land by speculators searching for mineral rights, and point to contaminated wells and municipal water systems caused by fracking operations.[14] By privileging the often divergent experiences and perspectives of those who considered themselves participants—if not decision makers—in the region's oil industry, this book attempts to explain how one industry produced such wildly different stories.

Such contradiction is key. A rich body of literature in business and economic history tells us that competing social pressures, interests, and traditions have influenced American policymakers and business leaders as they shaped twentieth-century capitalist industrial systems.[15] Building on such work, this study highlights that widespread understanding—if not consensus—that risk would be managed on economic terms united workers at all levels in the Texas Permian Basin. It shows that such understanding lasted, with key cracks and disruptions, for the duration of the twentieth century and was fundamental to maintaining the region's complex industrial and economic systems. Put another way, we know from global oil histories that oil discovery has tended to thwart economic diversification and has often cultivated dependence on a single extractive industry.[16] Such studies clearly demonstrate that oil's impact on the environment and public health is a direct consequence of industry priorities and decisions. While these top-down accounts are important, this study reminds us that complex industrial systems do not function without the participation of the thousands of people who live and work within them. Great local variability exists within nominally global systems. A focus on the perspective of the people who most viscerally experienced oil's risks and rewards paints a more complex picture of how extractive industries represent an amalgamation of specific and contingent ecologies, infrastructures, and cosmologies.

However, nuance is important here. Any place-based study runs the danger of overstating the uniqueness and importance of a single location within broader systems. It is certainly true that due to isolation from population centers and financial capital, West Texas did not displace Houston as the center of either Texas oil processing or oil wealth. Nor would the Permian's largest fields—Yates and Spraberry—ever compare with the massive Ghawar Field of Saudi Arabia or Kuwait's Greater Burgan. With such national and global context in mind, this book does not argue that West Texas oil producers were the originators of industry risk management policy, nor does it suggest that the experiences of oil workers in the Permian Basin were demonstrably unique. However, the size and longevity of Permian Basin oil deposits gave regional representatives an outsized importance in broader American discussions of supply stability, technological development, and financial risk. This also meant that most American oil workers spent at least some time in the region, experiencing locally common responses to industry hazards. For these reasons, this book does make clear that West Texas oil influenced Texas environmental and economic policy, most importantly by contributing ample data justifying state regulators' insistence that internal regulation of oil supply and production was possible and desirable.

The chapters that follow tell intertwined stories of oil industrialization and the interlocked state, industry, and individual reactions to resulting risks. Chapter 1 contextualizes 1920s Permian Basin oil prospectors as useful to West Texas ranching elites as they attempted to save a flagging agricultural economy amid national debates about speculation and industrial monopoly. Chapter 2 contrasts oil drillers' individualized responses to industrial work and risks before the Great Depression with an industrial health and safety movement at American oil refineries. Chapter 3 looks at 1930s and 1940s industry pushback against calls for resource conservation through the development of pipeline infrastructure and experiments in voluntary supply regulation. Chapter 4 contrasts efforts to manage the financial risks of oil through real estate development during a regional water crisis. Chapter 5 looks at the environmental impact of new refining and petrochemical industries in the region and the failure of labor organizing. Chapter 6 contextualizes Permian Basin wealth in the face of the 1970s energy crisis and inattention to environmental disasters within the era's national deregulatory turn. Finally, in its conclusion, the book discusses the 1980s bust and the collapse of the regional economy.

In this chronology, an ongoing discussion of risk assessment is undergirded by an interrogation of the meaning of data—both the data examined by historical actors and the data used by scholars to reconstruct past events. Scholars from many disciplines have theorized risk as a way of understanding the future, a process of imagining the possibility of prospective disaster, and a tool to assess ways to avoid it.[17] For individuals at all levels of the industry, such a predictive, future-oriented focus depended upon an expansive and complex body of industry information compiled by quickly professionalizing fields, including geology, cartography, seismology, statistics, and actuarial science.

Such data was not neutral. Rather, new data analysis trends were built from the on-the-job knowledge gained by long-term industry employees and the risk assessment industry. Such data was used to produce institutional, authoritative, and seemingly accurate sources of industrial consensus.[18] Employee manuals and insurance requirements, engineering reports, and scientific studies, as well as job specifications and management structures, provided seemingly clear numerical data indicating that industry risk management should be an internal effort. While booms and busts were considered inevitable and extraction without contamination impossible, such data seemed to support the idea that new technologies would allow the oil industry to accurately predict, if not prevent, future environmental hazards and financial losses.

However, this study makes clear that while statistical and numerical data was important, community trust in such data was crucial. Often, trust in the sources of information would prove more important than the information itself. In West Texas's oil towns and growing cities, both individuals and institutions received a constant influx of industry information. Workers, residents, and policymakers curated this against personal, individually produced knowledge gained from repetitive daily actions and personal experiences with oil's environmental and public health impacts. Oil workers maintained often visceral connections with technology and nature. They developed emotional ties to the landscape, wildlife, and geological formations and cared about the health and safety of themselves and their coworkers.[19]

Such relationships appeared in oral histories, popular accounts, and informal conversations. They mediated how individuals reacted to curated scientific data provided about industry hazards both on and off the job, and influenced how workers responded to state policy changes or federal regulators. This history attempts to avoid the internal data hierarchies that privileged numerical or statistical data over personal accounts—in both form and function avoiding a reproduction of the internal industry hierarchies and divisions identified in this book.

To this end, working at the confluence of culture, policy, and the histories of technology and daily work practice, I use the term "natural risk" in this volume to describe how understandings of economic success, public health, and environmental risks changed, overlapped, and merged throughout the twentieth century. Risks were contingent and constantly changing. They were also indicative of economic trends and personal material circumstances. Case in point, a loan officer tasked with approving George H. W. Bush for a business loan might have said that oil speculation had a high level of "natural risk." Oil prospecting was a gamble, and the chance of failure was often high. Similarly, an actuary pricing a midcentury oil worker's life insurance policy might have concluded that this worker would likely become injured or incapacitated on the job. This worker, then, also embodied a high level of natural risk. Either the bank or the insurance company might have concluded that such risks were ill advised and attempted to shield these institutions with high interest rates or insurance premiums. In either scenario, risk assessment professionals would have made decisions based on a set of personal standards, previous evidence, and institutionalized best practices.[20] Their decisions would have reflected a cultural consensus about oil's inherent and unavoidable unpredictability and the appropriate role of markets, the state, and private actors as a social safety net but would also still be contingent on personal opinion, instinct, and experience.

This study shows that, at different moments, an array of industry actors formed assessments of particular risks and then deployed them beyond oil, creating policy and shaping infrastructures. Such analysis is not intended to reproduce work done in the cultural history of oil, in which examination of the national political and cultural discourse surrounding petroleum, extraction, and consumption under capitalism is nuanced and thorough.[21] Rather, "natural risk" is intended as a shorthand descriptor that articulates the important role that the workplace experience of oil production played in determining how certain overlapping environmental, economic, and public health risks came to be accepted as inherent and unavoidable by members of the industry and their advocates.

With this said, it is appropriate to problematize semantics. Environmental and social historians have long documented that there is nothing "natural" or inevitable about industrial capitalism and its consequences.[22] The dangers of a faulty gas pipeline were hardly the products of evolutionary biology, and communities sickened by water contaminated with petrochemicals were not doomed by unavoidable fate. Instead, oil's twentieth-century industrial risks were the result of cascading decisions made by individuals working within complex technological and social systems. They displayed the possibilities and limitations of particular and contingent cultural imaginaries. We might instead say, then, that Permian Basin oil produced an array of "naturalized risks"—risks that became so ubiquitous within local economic and social systems that they seemed inevitable, unavoidable, and therefore socially acceptable.

Whether natural or naturalized, this study shows that over the course of the twentieth century, West Texas roughnecks, drillers, contractors, and engineers accepted the ongoing risks of resource depletion and industrial contamination, at times putting them out of step with national trends. At midcentury, Permian Basin oil workers rejected organizing efforts from industrial unions and a rising environmental movement, and at the industry's height in the late 1970s, they embraced deregulation and further reliance on a financially shaky industry to protect community health and safety. While this ultimately spelled environmental catastrophe for many of its most ardent adherents and only exacerbated rifts between local leaders and federal regulatory agencies, it also led to alliances between Permian Basin oil producers and national sources of power. This story reveals that oil workers were not gullible dupes, unaware of the consequences of their actions. Neither were they villains. Instead, their decisions to assume some risks and reject others depended on a deep understanding of the industry, the environment, and efforts to benefit themselves and their communities. Such actions set the trajectory of their lives and built the Permian Basin oil industry.

Chapter One

REIMAGINING SANTA RITA

The story is printed on two pages of yellowed paper. An excerpt from a 1958 book manuscript by Martin W. Schwettmann, it is preserved in the archives at the University of Texas at Austin.[1] On a dark summer night, Frank Pickrell climbed to the top of a wooden oil derrick, leaned far over the drilling floor, and dispersed a handful of rose petals sent to him by a group of New York nuns. The nuns had pooled their scant spending money on a long-shot oil investment in Reagan County, on state-owned land ninety miles south of Odessa. The nuns had blessed the roses, handing them to Pickrell as a good-luck charm.

He needed a miracle.[2] Pickrell's money was about to run out. According to Schwettmann, he prayed for help from his perch, naming the well Santa Rita in honor of "the patron saint of miracles." Soon after, Pickrell's dogged persistence was rewarded with divine intervention. Pickrell and the Texon Oil and Land Company finally struck oil on May 28, 1923, after twenty-one long, dangerous months of drilling in the hot sun, battling sand, an influx of brackish water, and hard, unforgiving rock. Once tapped, the Santa Rita No. 1 well gushed oil across the desert for over a month, blackening the makeshift road leading to the rig.[3] "Pickrell Strikes Oil!" proclaimed newspapers across Texas, generating national acclaim for both Pickrell and the Permian Basin. Profits from the well filled the coffers of Texas public schools for the next hundred years.[4]

During Texas oil's post–World War II boom years, this story was retold in books, industry publications, and the regional press. Into the 1970s, images of Santa Rita No. 1 appeared on postage stamps, postcards, and post office murals throughout Texas. Most recently, the scene was reimagined in the opening minutes of the 2013 Hollywood film *The Rookie*, starring Dennis Quaid.[5] While the story is compelling, many aspects of it are apocryphal. Pickrell probably climbed a derrick at some point in his career, but he was not responsible for daily drilling. Although Pickrell did sell stock certificates in New York, it is unclear if nuns ever invested in the wells. However, retelling this story exemplifies the narratives about Texas oil that were shared, remembered, and dispersed by different groups in the twentieth century. It illustrates a prevailing tendency to paint oil prospectors—distinct from oil companies—as heroes. While oil transport and sale monopolies were understood as a rising industrial evil, oil discovery was an individual achievement and the result of personal sacrifice and triumph over great physical danger. Such accounts paved over a profession fraught with social complexity and financial risk in 1920s America and reduced years of collective risk-taking to one instance of seemingly spontaneous effort. With this in mind, Pickrell's story of divine intervention can be expanded to reveal a more complex picture in which the timing and location of his discovery was the result of a confluence of decisions, pressures, and events, including the needs and desires of a powerful regional ranching elite, a set of financial relationships between individuals in the Permian Basin and across the nation, and a set of shifting and contradictory priorities within the Texas legislature. Let's start again.

American oil production ballooned over 7.5 times between 1889 and 1914, expanding westward and southward out of the already depleted fields of western Pennsylvania and into eastern Oklahoma, southern California, and Texas.[6] As the West and the Midcontinent, an industry-described oil region including Texas, Louisiana, Oklahoma, Arkansas, and Kansas, became the most important American oil producers, production was pushed forward by exponential increases in oil consumption in the industrial East and Midwest. Kerosene replaced whale oil as the primary fuel for lighting and cooking, and the popularity of cheaper automobiles created a new market for gasoline. This was augmented, in turn, by an exploding global market for American oil, which was increasingly central to European energy systems, both domestic and military. By 1918, American yearly output had reached roughly 356 million barrels and American oil companies dominated the brisk international commodity trade in oil.[7]

The 1901 discovery of oil at Spindletop, near Houston, began the first Texas oil boom, with the first gusher well producing over 100,000 barrels in its first nine days.[8] Other booms at Burkburnett, on the Texas-Oklahoma border, and Sour Lake, outside Beaumont, followed, and oil began to seriously compete with cotton as the state's most lucrative export. By 1920, Texas had outstripped other oil-producing states in both product quantity and total profits. Such rapid growth put Texas oil producers on the national stage, adding fuel to statewide debates over how to manage financial and physical risk in an industrializing economy. One big problem was infrastructure. While oil was abundant in Texas, the equipment and infrastructure needed to extract and transport it did not exist, and money for such construction was lacking. One solution was railroad speculation, initially promoted by the state of Texas. However, these new railroads quickly earned public ire and accusations of corruption.

This was part of an old problem. Texas was deep in debt when it joined the United States in 1845. Despite the initial hopes of Texas's white planter class, annexation did not immediately boost cotton prices. Capital investment for basic infrastructure like roads, dams, and rail lines did not materialize. Cash-poor and industry-starved, the state had land, and later minerals, as its biggest assets. Texas's first governor, James Henderson, and his early successors gave land as a financial incentive to railroad companies that were willing to lead infrastructure-building projects.[9] In an arrangement common across the American West, railroad speculators received a grant of sixteen sections of land, each approximately one square mile (640 acres) apiece, for every mile of completed track, as well as control over all land within two hundred feet of any new railroad. This trend continued after the Civil War as Texas's ex-Confederate political leaders attempted to use cheap land, especially in arid West Texas, to attract both white settlers and investors. This gambit saw some success. In the 1870s, Texas joined a national railroad speculation boom that would last into the twentieth century.[10] Hoping to speed up this process, the legislature enacted the Fifty Cent Law in 1879, in which the state of Texas sold over two million acres of public land, mostly in West Texas, to any comers for fifty cents an acre. All told, between 1835 and 1942, the state of Texas sold approximately eighty-six million acres—more than half the area of twenty-first-century Texas—to private interests. Some of these sales were to individuals. Others were fraudulent. The designation "public land" referred to any land for which residents could not prove current, legal proof of ownership. This meant that many residents, especially in South Texas, whose land claims dated to Mexican or Spanish statehood lost property because they could not produce papers for it. Others, mostly Tejanos, African Americans, or Native Americans who maintained occupancy based on custom or tradition, also lost some of or all their land.[11]

In the Permian Basin, successive battles between the Apache leader Victorio and US army troops led by Benjamin Grierson ended in 1880, resulting in tentative Anglo control over the region. The Texas legislature hoped to solidify both political and economic power and encouraged railroads to be the first large-scale land promoters in the region. Such speculation built early transportation infrastructure. The Texas and Pacific Railroad, completed in 1881, was the first rail line to come through West Texas. The line, established by federal charter and funded by railroad financier Jay Gould, ran from the stockyards of Fort Worth, near Oklahoma, to the growing industrial trade center of El Paso on the Mexican border, cutting directly across the center of the Permian Basin. While commander of the District of the Pecos, Grierson himself became a railroad speculator in 1882, organizing a local railroad promotion company. By the 1890s, railroad companies owned over half the land in West Texas. This was part of a wider trend, and by 1900, Texas was ranked first in the nation for the total amount of railroad track constructed in a single year.[12] In figure 1.1, we see the expansive nature of such development across the state.

Railroad companies advertised dry West Texas as ideal for commercial agriculture and enticed settlers with low freight prices. One such company, the Odessa Land and Townsite Company, advertised in newspapers throughout the Midwest promising potential farmers a land of flowing water and rich soil. While some were skeptical, others found the low prices hard to pass up. Prominent West Texas rancher John Alexander explained that his father moved to West Texas in 1909 after hearing a rumor that there were "five sections of cheap land near the Pecos Mountains," which the state of Texas would sell to homesteaders for 1.25 cents an acre.[13] Longtime resident J. J. Amburgery remembered the prices being higher: "Land was pretty cheap out there. I bought seven section[s] of school land [Permanent

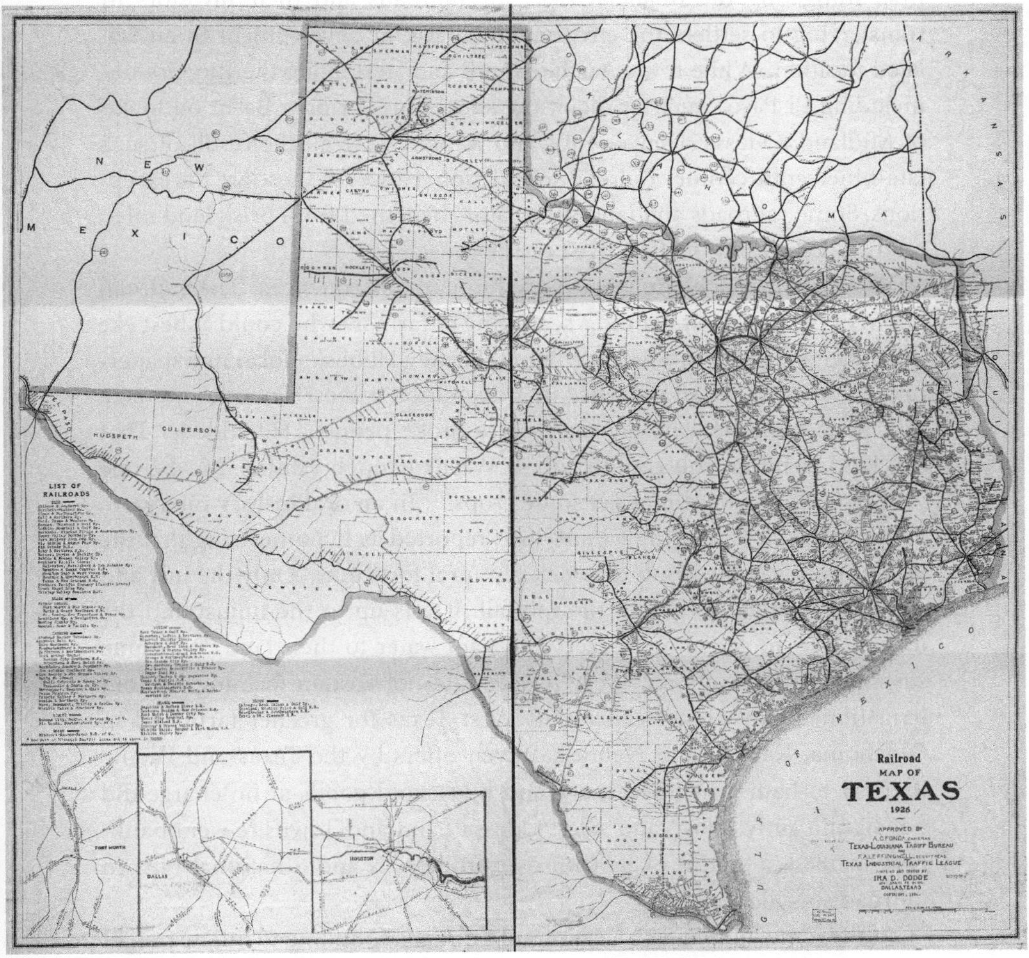

FIGURE 1.1. 1926 railroad map of Texas. While Texas experienced a railroad-building boom during the period, West Texas, and especially the Permian Basin, experienced exponentially less growth. Image courtesy of the Library of Congress, Geography and Map Division.

University Fund land] for $1 an acre."[14] The still-low price enticed him to settle in the region.

West Texas railroads made a profit in two ways. First, they transported passengers and goods for a fee. Second, they sold or leased land that they owned at prepared town sites to their passengers. The second fueled the first, mitigating the financial risks for railroads and their investors by transferring to settlers the environmental risk of development in an isolated location. While towns farther south and west along the Rio Grande, including El Paso, were far older, the successful Permian Basin oil towns of Midland, Odessa, Denver City, and Rankin were all the result of such late-nineteenth-century railroad speculation. However, these are the exceptions. Some railroads and land speculators benefited from brisk land sales; many failed within the first five years.

Such failed speculation had very human consequences. The railroad boom of the 1880s left behind a scattering of farmers who could at best eke out a rough, largely subsistence living. Barney Hubbs, a local newspaperman who spent his adolescence in a dugout on a West Texas homestead, said that "homesteaders generally were broke people." He added, "That dry land farming, you couldn't do it. Wasn't enough rainfall. Maybe one year out of ten, you might get some crops."[15] In an oral history interview, Harry Tweedle of Sterling County was reported as hypothesizing that the lack of rain was the result of a lack of moral fortitude: "Only the just and righteous seemed to get all the rainfall. It was up to the unjust and the unrighteous to get some buckets and haul water to their land."[16] Despite sustained booster efforts, West Texas could not sustain farming without irrigation. Many homesteaders left West Texas for greener farmland in Oklahoma, Kansas, and Nebraska. Even offers by the Texas and Pacific Railway to haul farm machinery and household goods at no charge did not significantly boost land sales. Odessa Land and Townsite went bankrupt in 1889, a victim of its own overpromotion and a national bust in railroad speculation.[17]

At the same moment, accusations of railroads colluding to inflate freight rates and mislead passengers led to state action. Texas passed an Anti-Trust Act in 1889, aimed at curtailing rate fixing. One year later, in 1890, James Steven Hogg successfully ran for Texas governor on a promise to devise local measures to regulate railroad monopolies. As one of his first actions, he passed a series of laws, colloquially called Hogg's Laws, to limit collusion within speculative industries. Railroads and insurance companies were particular targets of the legislation. As part of this effort, Hogg founded the Texas Railroad Commission (TRRC) in 1891 to ensure fairness in rail transportation. Although it would later become internationally relevant as the regulatory agency for Texas oil producers, in its early years the TRRC was a weak organization, led by political appointees with close ties to Texas railroads who performed little meaningful oversight.[18]

Texas industrialization was off to a shaky start. Numerous politicians continued to blame railroads for rural hardship, and railroads quickly developed a statewide reputation for mismanagement, fraud, and monopoly. For some Texas voters, especially Anglo ex-slaveholders located in South and East Texas, this represented a bigger problem. For them, industrialization was a symptom of post–Civil War Northern overreach and the erosion of Texas autonomy. In this context, efforts to curtail monopoly also worked to thwart outsider control over Texas's resources and economy. After oil was discovered along the Gulf of Mexico, such resource nativism continued to govern the Texas political landscape and shape industrialization.

However, it did not halt attrition out of West Texas over the first decades of the twentieth century. Disillusioned homesteaders either leased or sold their land to a dwindling number of regional ranchers. John Alexander remembered that the town of Mentone, founded by a community of Mormons on the east side of the Pecos River, declined from between 50 and 100 people in 1909 to complete abandonment by 1912.[19] Porterville met the same fate, shrinking from a town of settlers from central Texas and Oklahoma to abandonment by the 1920s.[20]

While railroads and commercial agriculture failed to make Texas an industrial power, oil slowly changed the game. In the 1890s, John D. Rockefeller's Standard Oil had consolidated power over oil production and transport in the Midwest and in California. However, after 1900, Texas independent companies grew fast. By the 1910s, Houston was a growing hub for oil processing and export. Gulf Oil and the Texas Company—later Texaco—were two Houston-based oil giants born from the Spindletop discovery. In 1911, Ross Sterling founded the Humble Oil Company to process the expansive Humble Field on the Gulf Coast. Magnolia Petroleum was founded in 1911 to consolidate growing East Texas refining and pipeline operations.[21]

Over the next two decades, others expanded into oil detection as well. In 1930, geologist Everette DeGolyer provided the money to start Geophysical Services Incorporated (GSI), which competed with the rising geophysical industries in Oklahoma, California, and abroad. Following a pattern set by Standard and others, all these new Texas oil companies quickly began international exploration, especially in Mexico, securing leases and building early transport and refining infrastructure. By the end of the Great

Depression, Texas's convenient, central location was key to its industry importance. Most oil was shipped via either rail or water during this period, and Houston's proximity to the Gulf of Mexico made it a hub for Mexican oil exports as well as providing easy access to East Coast and European markets. Such long-term growth of key Texas oil giants was, in part, the result of federal regulatory action.

Spurred by competition between majors and a growing number of independents, and exacerbated by existing debates over railroads and trusts, US oil majors, especially Standard Oil, faced national criticism at the turn of the century, gaining a label as a source of monopoly and freedom-killing control. During an 1888 congressional investigation, representatives for Standard Oil had attempted to justify their control over oil transport markets. They argued that due to high fixed costs and unpredictable profit margins, combining operations into integrated monopolies linked financially through trusts was simply the best way to shield a vitally important industry against the inherent risks posed by global commodity markets. They maintained that shielding their operations and their investors from high risk helped to keep oil supplies and oil prices stable.[22] Such arguments foreshadowed the perspective of oil majors for the next century. However, this contrasted with Progressive-era fears that monopoly stifled general economic growth and individual autonomy and, despite the best efforts of large industrial leaders, a consensus was emerging among policymakers that federal regulation was necessary to rein in Big Oil's bad actors.[23] President Benjamin Harrison signed the Sherman Antitrust Act in 1890. In 1903, the newly elected President Theodore Roosevelt formed the Bureau of Corporations, within what would become the US Labor Department, to investigate Standard Oil on charges of monopoly. In 1906, the Hepburn Act extended the power of the Interstate Commerce Commission specifically to regulate oil transport rates. The Standard Oil Trust was formally dissolved in 1911 by enforcement of the Sherman Act.[24]

In Texas, Democratic leaders also attempted to balance the central importance of oil to the state economy against perennial concern about monopolies. As with the railroads, political rhetoric focused on unfairness and corruption. The Democrats were joined by representatives from Humble Oil, the Texas Company, and others who argued that integrated oil companies unfairly usurped profits from smaller operations that took the real risks while engaging in dangerous oil exploration. Hoping to appease these groups, Texas legislators rode an at-times impossible line between promoting strictly local industry and supporting large-scale industrialization in the years before the Depression.

Significantly, while remaining rhetorically ambivalent about federal oversight, the Texas legislature filed a lawsuit against Standard Oil subsidiary Waters-Pierce in 1889, signaling state support for the passage of the Sherman Act.[25] This enforced a state-level antitrust law that forbade Standard Oil and any other oil company organized through a trust agreement from doing business in Texas. This decision was ultimately upheld by the US Supreme Court in 1909. While public fanfare during the lawsuit won the hearts of Texas independents, the breakup of Standard in 1911 did not end popular debate, nor did it make it significantly easier for individual prospectors to succeed in the oil industry.[26] In 1920, several of Standard's largest competitors, including Sun Oil, were engaged in oil exploration in Texas and benefited from the state's very lenient taxation policies and nonexistent workplace safety or environmental regulation.[27] Ultimately, Texas's efforts to keep Standard Oil out had a limited long-term impact on local oil development. Case in point—both Humble and Magnolia ultimately merged with Standard subsidiaries in 1925.

In such a landscape, key cards were stacked against Frank Pickrell when he began his search for oil in 1919. Texas's antimonopoly laws were designed to keep resource wealth in Texas, but detractors argued that they only exacerbated the industry's financial hazards by slowing oil infrastructure development, increasing resource waste and pollution, and contributing to the oil industry's notorious market volatility.[28] Pickrell was not independently wealthy, nor was he affiliated with a large oil multinational. He had no background in geology or previous experience in oil exploration. Still, he was confident that he understood the local geography and geology better than his predecessors. He probably knew that the first exploratory oil drillers had arrived in the Permian Basin in the late 1800s, and he watched as more came immediately after Spindletop. His parents were transplants from Ohio and Mississippi, but Pickrell was born in Pecos County and had grown up in the border city of El Paso, probably both listening to news of fantastic oil wealth coming out of East Texas and reading popular children's novels and pulp serials such as *Young King Brady Detectives* (1907) and *Nick Carter Stories* (1912), which valorized oil speculation and romanticized oil prospectors as dangerous, glamorous men.[29] His decision to eschew affiliation with oil majors might suggest a belief that big oil companies were not to be trusted.

Whatever his personal motivations, Pickrell's efforts were helped in perhaps unexpected ways by the state of Texas's conflicted response to business regulation, infrastructure construction, and risk management. Pickrell bought his oil leases from a World War I acquaintance named Rupert Ricker, a local attorney who had lived in Reagan County since childhood. He had hoped to attract investors to fund speculative drilling, but with few takers, he was ready to cash out. Crucially, Ricker's leases were on a swath of state-owned land in the Permian Basin known as the Permanent University Fund. In 1839, the government of the Republic of Texas set aside land to fund a public university.[30] By 1876, further allocations had increased this amount to half a million acres of prime North Texas farmland. Later that year, the legislature swapped these parcels for one million acres of less valuable land in West Texas. For decades, the land had sat largely vacant, arid and worthless for commercial agriculture. Case in point—until 1923, the land generated only $1,000 a year from West Texas ranchers in grazing fees. Crucially, while this land was seemingly mineral deficient, the state opened it up to oil speculation in an attempt to attract prospectors, setting favorable lease terms that allocated to the state only one-eighth of gross production profits on a successful well, with initial drilling fees set at only ten cents per acre.[31] Some took the state up on its offer. John Alexander remembered that his neighbor, George Champion, was "sucking oil away from Continental Oil that had leased all the other lots" in 1916, west of the town of Orla in far West Texas.[32] Probably based in part on such accounts, Ricker convinced Pickrell to buy out his leases at cost, for $43,136—significantly below the price of proven leases in other parts of the state.

Despite the good price, this remained a big financial risk. Pickrell did not have the experience or capital to do this alone. He enlisted the financial and logistical help of Haymon Krupp, a Lithuanian immigrant and wealthy El Paso dry goods merchant who borrowed the money to cover the initial lease payment.[33] They named their operation the Texon Oil and Land Company. Krupp made his money selling dry goods amid the growing industrial and rail transportation economy of El Paso. He was wealthy, but not on the level of Standard Oil. Krupp relied on Texas's precarious state banking and finance industry to fund the operation. Many of the state's largest banks, such as the First National Bank of Dallas, and growing regional banks like the First National Bank of Midland were very involved in oil. This represented a sea change.

By the 1920s, the Texas banking industry represented a protracted and contradictory effort to balance monopoly, speculation, and industrialization. It was central to the rise of Texas oil. Texas's 1845 state constitution had prohibited the establishment of state banks, leaving a mix of nationally chartered banks, unregulated private banks, and under-the-table lenders to fill any gaps. Rather than stifling all commerce, such a free-for-all environment, coupled with the push to build resource infrastructure, had fueled the steady-if-precarious growth in Texas banking and finance by the late nineteenth century. In 1900, there were approximately 330 national banks operating in Texas, servicing cotton farmers in East and North Texas. The number of Texas national banks increased to 450 by 1905.[34] Also, approximately 250 private banks were chartered in Texas during this period.

While they varied wildly in size and solvency, these banks were historically vital to the agricultural economy. Cotton farmers, as well as West Texas ranchers, and later oil speculators all relied heavily on credit. Those who did not have capital or access to banks still depended on informal and unregulated credit lenders that were run out of bars or dry goods stores. This old, largely informal system was centered in the old South Texas port city of Corpus Christi and was insufficient for oil speculation. By the twentieth century, Texas legislators sought to encourage the local speculative economy. State regulators backpedaled to allow state-chartered banks, easing the way for locally sourced mineral speculation with more flexible lending and capital requirements. These new state banks did have some oversight. They anticipated regulations under the new Federal Reserve Act, which would come in 1913, and required deposit protection beginning in 1909. In 1913, Texas set up a state oversight board for bank charters. However, loans with these banks remained otherwise unregulated. Loan officers retained much discretion, with many deals requiring only a simple application and a handshake. Despite the risks, the amount of money in Texas state banks increased sharply after 1918, dovetailing with an explosion in oil speculation.

Haymon Krupp probably benefited from such comparatively lax loan requirements as he attempted to put together $43,136 to buy oil leases, pay drillers, and lease equipment. However, like the region's homesteaders and railroad speculators before him, his efforts required more than financial liquidity and smooth talking—they also depended upon the successful assessment and manipulation of a harsh, unforgiving environment.

OIL'S (UN)NATURAL HISTORY

In 1921, Pickrell and Krupp hired experienced driller Carl Cromwell and tool pusher Dee Locklin to drill their Reagan County wells. Cromwell and Locklin led multiple crews in the search for oil. Cromwell knew that oil discovery depended on patience and an ability to understand and manipulate minute clues about the subterranean world. He was a longtime oil driller and had followed the job through previous oil booms in Pennsylvania, Illinois, and Oklahoma. Cromwell promptly moved his wife, Luella, and young daughter, Carlene, to the desert camp in Reagan County.[35]

The local climate made life in the camp harsh. The Permian Basin in Texas was mostly treeless and flat. Temperatures were mild relative to other parts of the desert Southwest, but water was scarce and of poor quality. The region's low-lying mountains pushed precipitation out of the area, with rainfall ranging between ten to twenty inches per year.[36] The same geological processes that produced oil trapped fresh groundwater hundreds to thousands of feet below the surface. Much of this water was mineral heavy and salty, at best unpleasant and sometimes toxic to drink. Local farmers called it "gyp water" and warned that it caused stomach upsets. The region's vegetation reflected these conditions. Most of the Permian Basin was made of short-grass prairie, interrupted by sparse timberlands of ash, juniper, scrub oak, and mesquite. The two significant exceptions to the region's monotonous topography were small mountains in Pecos County far to the south and stretches of full desert, called the Sand Hills by 1920s homesteaders and ranchers, along the New Mexico border. Life in the Cromwell tent camp was hot, dirty, and monotonous. Presumably, Luella was used to life in an oil camp, but the isolation was probably a hardship for her. In figure 1.2, a photograph of workers and their families at a similar oil camp illustrates the rough conditions. At only 377 people, Reagan County was one of the least populous counties in the isolated and rural Permian Basin.[37] Cromwell and Locklin drilled steadily for the next two years.

Such a timeline was not unusual. In 1921, even experienced wildcatters like Cromwell relied largely on an industry tradition of trial and error, drilling at times randomly in the hopes of striking oil. However, the profession was changing fast. During the first two decades of Texas oil exploration, the "oil smellers," "mediums," and "doodle bugs" of Central Texas's Sour Lake

FIGURE 1.2. Undated image of the Abrams No. 1 discovery well in Mitchell County, Texas, the first significant oil well in the Permian Basin. The well was spudded in 1920 on the Texas & Pacific Land Trust. Archival records state that pictured are driller L. R. Dan Lewis and tool dresser R. G. Bob Thompson, as well as two other men and an unknown child. Photo courtesy of the Petroleum Museum, Lee Jones Jr. Collection.

and Spindletop, so named for their supposedly mystical knowledge and supernatural luck, received much press attention.

The story of Frank Pickrell hedging his bets with an appeal to saintly intervention speaks to this tradition. However, it does not represent reality. As in the mining industries, geology and engineering professionalized quickly after 1900, standardizing processes of surveying, mapping, and analyzing the physical world both above and below ground. By the 1920s, Cromwell and most other oil prospectors consulted reports, surveys, and maps produced by the growing field of petroleum geology. Although oil did not seep out of the ground in visible pools as it did in eastern Oklahoma or along the Gulf of Mexico, prospectors in the Permian had found the fossilized remains of prehistoric plant and animal life throughout the region, and some, such as Swedish geologist Johan August Udden, publicly argued that the presence of marine fossils greatly increased the likelihood of oil deposits in the region.[38] Limitations still existed. Some drillers had access to early seismic testing techniques, but the machinery remained heavy and time-consuming to use.[39] The era's aerial photography was expensive and often inconclusive. Because roads were nonexistent, surveyors and geologists had to instead travel by foot or on horseback to examine potential drill sites. Down-hole drilling analysis techniques such as core sampling, in which portions of rock and mud were analyzed during the drilling process, were in their infancy.[40]

With such limited knowledge, it is perhaps unsurprising that, like Rupert Ricker before him, Cromwell's first efforts yielded only a series of empty, nonproducing, dry holes. However, in 1920, a year into Cromwell's search, the Rio Grande Oil Company struck oil in Mitchell County near Colorado City, roughly one hundred miles to the north. This was the region's first producing commercial well, and it signaled that Cromwell was on the right track. However, the simultaneous collapse of American cotton prices, which made up 70 percent of state agricultural revenues, caused a wave of bank failures in Texas. By 1925, 17 percent of rural state banks in Texas had failed.

Pickrell began to run out of money as early as 1921 and feared that he would be unable to pay for his leased equipment or pay Cromwell and the rest of his drilling crew. The wave of local bank failures only exacerbated this problem. Unable to secure backers in Texas, Pickrell took Texon Oil and Land public, traveling to several East Coast cities to attract investors. After multiple failures, he finally managed to raise over $100,000 through the sale of approximately 685 stock certificates to individual New York City investors, each valued at $200.

Pickrell returned to Reagan County with enough cash for another effort. However, there was no guarantee of success, and the harsh environment only made the task more daunting. Pickrell was probably spurred on by his sunk costs and the knowledge that he had invested years of his life in the assumption that there was oil under Reagan County. Key people in the area also probably encouraged him to continue his search. While homesteading and commercial agriculture had failed in the region, some large-scale ranchers had enjoyed success in the late nineteenth century. These very large landholders watched Pickrell's efforts closely. While they controlled the most land in the region outside of railroads or the state, by the 1920s, these local elites were sinking into increasing debt. Like oil prospectors, they had long looked to the speculative economy to reduce very harsh environmental risks. While these ranchers did not finance Pickrell's operation in 1921, his ultimate success would represent an answer to their prayers that ensured their economic and political importance in the region.

Competition for scarce resources, especially water, had long been central to ranching in the Permian Basin. The failed history of West Texas homesteading should make this no surprise. For example, the career of prominent local rancher William Henry Cowden was defined by efforts to control the local water supply and manage access to subsurface resources. Cowden established his first herd of approximately one hundred cattle in 1883, allowing them free range over the 150 miles between Midland, Texas, and Carlsbad, New Mexico. In an oral history interview, Cowden's son Elliott remembered that even though land was cheap and the region was largely unfenced, his father still had trouble providing water for his cattle.[41] This was a perennial problem. According to historian Walter Rundell Jr., a full section of land—one square mile—in Loving County, Texas, on the New Mexico border, could sustainably feed and water only four of the animals. Oral histories tell similar stories. Many ranchers drove herds for miles across sand hills and scrub to the Colorado River to drink.[42] However, both the Colorado and the Pecos rivers could be treacherous. The Pecos was known for its quicksand banks, which could trap cattle, and it was lined with scrub oak forests that would poison cows if eaten in large quantities. In 1886, Cowden fenced in his range to prevent theft and control his access to precious water. The year before, he had expanded his herd to approximately 7,000 cattle and needed to protect his investment. Such fencing was expensive to maintain, but success or failure depended on having proprietary control over good-quality water. Fences also enforced property boundaries that prevented competitors from gaining easy access to stock pens along railroad lines.[43]

The pressure to secure resources only increased as agricultural prices remained volatile in the early twentieth century. According to one estimate, West Texas cattle sold for $15 a head in 1915. Therefore, thousands of acres were required to support a successful West Texas ranch.[44] Case in point—Cowden and his business partners tapped the region's deep network of subsurface aquifers under his fenced land, drawing water up via windmill from deep underground into large tanks. Such control over land and resources paid off. Cowden's operation continued to expand through the 1890s. When Cowden sold his ranch to his son in 1917, he owned forty-eight sections of land (totaling 30,720 acres) in Ector County, west of Odessa.

By the 1920s, several other families owned over 20,000 acres each. This included Edwin Giddings, originally of Colorado. In 1884, he bought the Elsinore ranch, which crossed Brewster, Pecos, and Reves counties on the southern edge of the Permian Basin. Similarly, "Uncle" John Scharbauer raised sheep, cattle, and horses in Midland and Ector counties and in 1914 founded the Scharbauer Cattle Company. At its height, Scharbauer Cattle encompassed approximately 500,000 acres. Scharbauer seeded the land with more hardy, nutritious grasses. He experimented with selective breeding programs, crossing longhorn cattle, which were more resilient to heat and aridity, with Hereford and later Angus cows. He also experimented with raising desert-bred sheep along with cattle, with the hardier sheep acting as insurance against cattle dying due to disease or starvation.[45]

Despite diverse efforts by Scharbauer, Cowden, and others to control nature, Permian Basin ranchers lurched from one environmental catastrophe to another. Along with ranchers from Wyoming to South Texas, the closing of the open range put pressure on resources and encouraged ranch consolidation.[46] Later, three decades of cyclical drought between the 1890s and 1920s kept ranching enterprises mostly in the red. Even as the largest rangers compensated by raising yet more cattle, the growing herds contaminated local streams. Lakes were contaminated or dried up altogether. Later, mass cattle death in the hard winter of 1918 reduced ranchers to selling hides stripped from the frozen carcasses. By the 1920s, steam-powered cable tool drills allowed ranchers to reach the deep Edwards Aquifer or the even deeper Ogalala. However, hard times culminated at the same moment with the crash of farm prices and the worsening of already bad cyclical drought patterns. Many smaller ranches failed, and those ranches that held on were heavily mortgaged, leveraging cattle for credit.

In this environment, Cowden, Scharbauer, and other large Permian Basin ranchers sought to manage environmental risk by further diversifying their investments. Many speculated in local banks, placing them deep within the era's national flow of speculative investment, infrastructure construction, and commodity sales. They benefited from Texas's lax banking laws. Christopher Columbus "C. C." Slaughter epitomized efforts to use financial speculation, especially banks, as a safety net. In 1873, Slaughter bought the Long S Ranch in Garza County, Texas, north of the Permian Basin. By 1877, it was one of the largest ranches in Texas. A lifelong rancher, Slaughter knew that profit hinged upon not just animal husbandry but also both land and capital, and he worked hard to acquire both. Slaughter steadily expanded his holdings, and by 1905, he owned approximately 40,000 cattle and several million acres on various properties in West Texas.[47] Key to Slaughter's success, in 1884 he merged his existing banking interests into the American National Bank of Dallas, of which he became vice president.[48] Slaughter moved to Dallas to oversee this operation. By 1930, the bank had deposits exceeding one hundred million dollars, many from speculative oil companies. By the end of his life, Slaughter was the richest man in Texas through a combination of continued ranching profits and the success of his banking ventures, and he became known as the "Cattle King of Texas."[49] The town of Slaughter in Midland County was named in his honor in 1883.[50]

Others had a similar story. In 1890, John Scharbauer founded the bank that became the First National Bank of Midland, which thanks to oil would become the largest independent bank in the United States.[51] Similarly, John Moore Shannon arrived in West Texas in 1883 from New Orleans, hoping to make money in the livestock industry. Shannon worked a series of jobs, as a railroad laborer, sheep herder, and fence builder. After building his savings, he ultimately made his money by raising sheep. Several years later, he owned approximately 125,000 acres in Crockett and Archer counties.[52] Like Scharbauer, Shannon augmented his extensive properties with real estate speculation but made his money in banking.[53] Riding the region's oil boom, he invested in a series of small, local banks, including the Ozona National

Bank, the First National Bank of Snyder, and the Central National Bank of San Angelo.

Although known simply as "cattlemen" in the local press, these elites were linchpins in the construction of the region's speculative, extractive economy. Along with banking, they invested in local dry goods sales, hotel management, agricultural production, and residential construction in and around oil towns.[54] They donated land to build trade depots. They built roads. They hired law enforcement officers. And they were West Texas's major employers before oil, hiring a multilingual, multiracial swath of failed homesteaders, out-of-luck ranchers, landless cowboys, and sheepherders into a system that reinforced their power and control. They were in turn joined by many other smaller players. For example, Cecil Bickley, a local dry goods and grocery salesman, founded the first bank in Denver City.[55]

Such efforts to temper the unpredictability of nature and pragmatically diversify financial holdings shaped the trajectory of oil development in the region. The ranching economy, already deeply imbedded in a global system of natural resource sales, eased the way for oil. Ranching depended on managing the region's harsh and variable climate, and large ranchers used twentieth-century scientific approaches to carefully control desert energy systems—from the life cycles of plants, cattle, and sheep; to the movement of people and the daily rhythms of work; to the extraction of water, oil, and gas deposits. They participated fully in the national speculative economy, investing in everything from dry goods to banking. They quickly leased their land to oilmen, using one form of speculation to offset the risks of another. Later, as the full scope and size of West Texas oil deposits became clear, their acceptance of Texas's solidifying racial hierarchies and their pragmatic approach to land management determined that they would most benefit from the Permian's mineral wealth, consigning landless agriculturalists and small-town residents to bear the largest environmental cost.[56]

Case in point—while vital to the region's commercial development, such combined financial and commercial dominance made the region's largest landholders into bitter enemies for those without access to such capital. Especially in the 1920s, the region's environmental pressures exacerbated hierarchies of wealth and power. For example, the First National Bank of Pecos gained local infamy for foreclosing on homesteaders and small ranchers during successive environmental catastrophes.[57] Further, in the town of Alpine, located south of the Permian Basin, such financial inertia contributed to political and economic power shifting away from a multiethnic, multinational coalition of sheep-herding families with roots on either side of the US-Mexican border to a select few Anglo ranchers who managed vast herds.

AFTER SANTA RITA: OIL AND RISK IN THE PERMIAN

In this environment, Pickrell's 1923 gusher inspired a flurry of excitement. Curious spectators traveled from as far away as Fort Worth, near the Oklahoma border, to watch the big show. Savvy entrepreneurs sold railroad excursions to see the flowing oil and marketed small vials of "Santa Rita" oil as good luck charms.[58] Soon after the discovery, Mike L. Benedum and Joe Trees, two Pittsburgh, Pennsylvania, wildcatters, bought many of Texon's leases for $200,000 and formed the Big Lake Oil Company, with Frank Pickrell as vice president. Benedum and Trees held a quarter-share in the company. Big Lake Oil built the town of Texon to house its drilling teams, and the company enjoyed significant profits. In 1926, Big Lake Oil opened an office in nearby San Anglo, operating sixty producing oil wells.

Reports of that success sent a new wave of oil prospectors to the Permian Basin and the land controlled by the Permanent University Fund. As in ranching, the individual risks posed by oil prospecting were both physical and financial, which quickly discouraged some. Unprepared fortune-seekers trapped their Model Ts in sand dunes along the sparse network of unpaved roads. They dotted the desert with abandoned, dry holes and derelict drilling equipment. Securing potable groundwater for drilling crews was crucial, and the inexperienced obtained water at prices well exceeding crude oil. Many of these early oil speculators—and their investors—simply ran out of money before they struck oil. They cut their losses and moved on to wetter regions or less risky industries. Some of them, such as C. G. Watson of Fort Stockton, put out newspaper ads, hoping to recoup their losses by selling unused or no-longer-needed drilling equipment.[59] Many left empty-handed, saddled with mounting debt and severed business relationships.

For the more systematic prospectors, Pickrell's discovery revealed a crucial detail—oil in the region lay very, very deep underground. Serious speculators needed better equipment and highly skilled drillers. This took money. The first significant American oil discovery in Titusville, Pennsylvania, came in at only 70 feet, and the famously prolific Spindletop was tapped forty years later, at 1,139 feet. In 1923, Frank Pickrell's Santa Rita No. 1 was almost three times as deep, striking oil at 3,050 feet. Later that year, Karl Cromwell and the Texon Oil and Land Company would drill the deepest well in the world at the time at Big Lake, with a depth of 6,350 feet. While technologically exciting, the need for such deep wells made prospecting in the Permian Basin both more expensive and more time consuming than earlier American booms. By the late 1920s, Permian Basin drillers began to replace their cable tool equipment with newer, more versatile rotary drilling tools. These were equipped with diamond drill bits and better suited to the region's mix of sandy soil and hard rock formations. Better drilling technology brought further success.

Between 1923 and 1926, an array of independents made big discoveries throughout the region. In 1925, the Continental Oil Company struck oil in the Howard-Glasscock Field, at a depth of 2,081 feet. That same year, the Republic Production Company struck oil near the town of McCamey, at a depth of 2,100 feet. In 1926, the equally deep Hendricks Field was discovered on the Hendricks family ranch in Winkler County.[60] Still, the expense of drilling at these depths was prohibitive for some. According to the American Petroleum Institute (API), 25,623 American speculative wells were dug in 1925. Of these, 16,559 produced oil.[61] While these numbers are probably inflated, this figure means that 62 percent of American wildcat wells struck oil that year—seemingly good odds for speculators looking for new investments. However, these numbers did not indicate whether oil was produced in profitable quantities. Nor did it demonstrate the extreme cost of a single drilling operation, which, at approximately $22,000, was almost sixteen times the average American annual income in 1925.[62]

Despite the costs, drillers set new depth records in 1928 in the region. That year, the V. T. Bolin Company discovered oil near the town of Kermit. The Texon Oil and Land Company once again set a producing well-depth record near Big Lake, drilling to 8,523 feet. And oil was discovered on the Cowden ranch near Odessa at over 4,000 feet underground. By the end of the decade, the largest Texas oil companies, including the Texas Company, the Gulf Oil Company, Humble Oil, and Magnolia Petroleum, were heavily involved in the region. In 1930 alone, the Permian Basin produced 50,725,000 barrels of oil. By comparison, the better-established Gulf Coast fields did not produce much more, reaching a total of only 69,676,000 barrels.[63]

Despite these impressive statistics, oil prospectors were still subject to many of the same constraints as ranchers and homesteaders. West Texas geography and lack of infrastructure meant that oil discovery was not always a fortune maker for prospectors. Both the Hendrick Field and the large Yates Field, discovered in 1926, were particularly isolated. According to industry historians Roger Olien and Diana Hinton, "Both fields, however, had the liability of being in regions that were isolated, bleak, and underpopulated even by West Texas standards."[64] These fields were in Pecos and Winkler counties, both with populations of less than one hundred, and they were prohibitively far from railroads, pipelines, refineries, and oil markets.[65] Multiple drillers found themselves in the unfortunate position of filling in their newly tapped wells, absorbing their overhead costs, and hoping that pipelines would someday be built to make their discoveries profitable.

Indicative of the era's railroad bust and resulting debates about industrialization in the state legislature, the lack of infrastructure meant that oil reinforced established hierarchies of land ownership and use. An 1866 amendment to the Texas Constitution gave all mineral rights to surface landholders. While in other states, especially California, most oil leasing took place on public land, almost all of Texas land was held by private entities by the 1920s. The Public University Fund Land was the exception, not the rule. Private landowners negotiated hard, pushing for any possible advantage. In a standard 1920s oil lease, the rights holder agreed to allow a drilling company exclusive drilling access to the land for a set amount of time.[66] The lease was considered void if a prospector failed to begin drilling within the specified period, usually six months. If oil was found, the rights holder received a percentage, often 12.5 percent, of all profits earned from that oil as well as a cash bonus.[67]

While the state of Texas received a small percentage of all mineral profits after 1919, oil royalties were a specific boon to West Texas cattlemen. National production data reveals their sometimes hefty size. In the early 1930s, the average production from an American oil well was eight barrels per day. If rights holders had only four producing wells on their property, they could expect to receive approximately $949 ($14,230.99 in 2018 dollars) per year in oil royalties.[68] Sometimes royalty payments were larger depending on the lease location and the value of the property. For example, more was paid if the lease was located within a town or city limits.[69]

As a result, when Pickrell announced that he had struck oil, an increasing number of local ranchers entered negotiations with speculators. They were quick to embrace oil exploration as another form of financial risk management and private infrastructural development, similar to banking or breeding hardier cattle. Carl Estes exemplified the popular sentiment. He fully credited oil with the region's economic survival: "Before the discovery of oil, there were a number of old pioneers in this country—my father was one of them. . . . This was primarily a ranching country. . . . I don't think there was a rancher in this country who could have survived without the discovery of oil here."[70] Ranchers' existing familiarity with speculation was tinged with urgency, as decades of drought had bleached the land dry.

However, it was the largest ranchers who reaped the most reward. Ira Yates's story is illustrative. In 1915, Yates traded his Rankin County grocery and dry goods store for 16,640 acres of failing ranchland in southern Pecos County. He bought more land over the next several years, expanding his cattle holdings in an attempt to hedge against drought. This effort sunk him into increasing debt. In 1926, fearing foreclosure, Yates offered up his land for oil drilling. Due to his large landholdings, he was able to play oil companies off each other to negotiate the most lucrative royalty terms. Drilling began that year under a partnership between the Mid Kansas Oil Company and Transcontinental Oil. Drillers struck oil on October 28, discovering what would become the Yates Field, one of the largest and most prolific oil fields in the region at the comparatively shallow depth of 1,310 feet.[71] By the spring of 1927, the first five wells produced an average of 9,009 barrels per day, and several thousand barrels more were gathered from skimming runoff oil out of the nearby Pecos River.

Ira Yates and his wife became millionaires.[72] Before his death in 1939, he personally negotiated dozens of favorable lease agreements with Magnolia, Humble, and Phillips Petroleum.[73]

The Scharbauers and the Cowdens also found significant oil deposits on their land in the 1920s and 1930s. They divided their holdings into small sections, negotiating competing leases with various oil companies and profiting from multiple bonuses and regular royalty checks.[74] Sometimes landowners were able to demand whatever prices they wanted from equally desperate wildcatters. According to an oral history interview, E. N. Beane, of Crane County, negotiated with oil companies over the right not only to drill, but also to secure separate payments for any groundwater wells dug by drillers and their crews.[75] In such ways, speculative drilling made ranchers wealthy, surpassing banking and other investments as the most common safety net for the risks inherent in the region's cattle business.[76] As the number of wildcatters increased in the region, a pattern emerged. Cowden, Scharbauer, and others could rely on oil royalties from successful wells as a secure way to pay off their debts, even as they enlisted new payments from exploratory drilling leases to hedge against future variability.

Before World War II, this ad hoc system of extractive management would make West Texas geographically and politically distinct from other oil-producing regions in Texas.[77] West Texas's network of large landholders made the processes of oil discovery, extraction, and processing comparatively more orderly and less prone to waste than other oil-producing regions at that time. Duplicitous practices such as drilling into adjacent leases were less likely since one surface owner was more likely to own the mineral rights to most or all of an oil deposit and would often have negotiated with a single company for drilling on their land. As a result, while oil towns like Big Lake, Rankin, and Denver City did experience waves of wildcatter overcrowding and a subsequent rise in petty crime, in contrast to East Texas or Eastern Oklahoma, West Texas drilling crews were less worried about armed robbery or violent well takeovers. John Alexander, who was employed as a driller near the oil town of Wink from 1927 to 1928, explained that "Wink was a pretty tough little town . . . some highjacking [robbing workers on a drilling site at gunpoint] but nothing like Ranger and Burke."[78] Further, in the West Texas oil fields, strategic spacing during this early period kept the well pressure higher for longer and the number of unproductive, dry holes relatively low.

This is not to say that oil arrived without pushback. Court disputes between Permian Basin landowners, homesteaders, and oil prospectors demonstrate that this system did not always work as advertised. Some people simply did not believe in the oil industry's long-term sustainability and vocally predicted that negotiating leases with oil companies was a waste of resources. Others in scenes that fueled state and national debates about predatory industrialists, turned against the industry after dishonest oil companies signed contracts and then did not drill as promised. Yet others, mostly homesteaders or poor farmers, had already sold their mineral rights to their neighbors or directly to oil companies for the immediate cash payout during the lean 1920s. This act of desperation meant that they had forfeited any potential profits and, even worse, had little control over the location or duration of drilling on their land.[79] While drillers were legally obligated to pay surface landowners for damages to their property, oil drilling was fundamentally destructive to the immediate area surrounding the rig. A single cash payment, even if it were fairly allocated, did not offset long-term damage.

This said, surviving oral histories insist that the region's landowners understood the oil business as a bid for survival.[80] Elliott Cowden put it bluntly: "Most of them [ranchers] welcomed anything they could get out of an oil company. They felt like it was a gift."[81] This is probably not surprising. Under extreme economic pressure, large landholders were perhaps less dismayed by the prospect of damage to their land. Crucially, instead of disrupting existing power structures through environmental means, oil sustained regional elites during a time of prolonged crisis.

Whether extractive speculation was a strategic act of desperation or an exciting adventure, the decisions made by men such as Elliott Cowden, John Sharbauer, Frank Pickrell, and Karl Cromwell represent an effort to manage multifaceted risks. As in any industry, many aspects of success were beyond their individual control. Neither ranchers nor oilmen could control the harsh regional climate or predict the location of oil deposits. However, success at finding and extracting oil was governed not merely by the limitations of the human senses or an ability to innovate new drilling technology. Instead, it also depended on the limitations of logistical and infrastructural networks and hinged on national and international commodity markets.

Environmental and financial risks were overlapping and contingent. In West Texas and across the nation, the speculative economy provided little in the way of a financial safety net for individuals, although many tried to use this system to their own advantage. Especially for small agriculturalists, risk management took the form of an individual's ability to manipulate the environment to make a profit. However, such ability was limited at best. Many of the Permian Basin's environmental risks were the product of millions of years of geological change and beyond the knowledge or control of turn-of-the-century farmers and ranchers. Ironically, it was the same long environmental history that contaminated groundwater, produced the region's dry, unforgiving terrain, and created the region's expansive oil and gas deposits.

While infrastructure development and the expansion of commodity markets were intertwined at the turn of the century in the United States, there were clear winners and losers in this system. In the case of oil, the potential to make money from money was high—but so were the risks. Risk begot further risk as one form of speculation backstopped another. Banks, especially small, unregulated Texas banks, were swift to provide credit to speculators who either struck oil or lost everything.[82] The largest farmers, ranchers, and oil producers used this system of futures markets, bank loans, and stock sales as risk reducers to curb environmental risk such as aridity, drought, or disease. Land management strategies—from crop choices to grazing patterns to the speed and amount of resource extraction—required resources that also were gained through the speculative system. Speculative investments could pay debts, credit could be taken out to build infrastructure, and diversified markets could hedge against local environmental catastrophe. However, few in Texas had the ability to manipulate such markets, and many understood outside capital as exploitative, roping extractive peripheries into a financial and contractual web of debt and legal obligation. This made local political leaders ambivalent about how to manage speculation as its presence ballooned.

Still, they kept coming. Pickrell's dramatic success would help to inspire a new wave of oil prospectors. Numerous small drilling firms set up offices and advertised job openings. In one week in 1927, for example, the Eastland Oil Company, Church and Fields, the Weekly Oil Corporation, and Shira & Davidson drilling contractors all opened offices in Odessa.[83] The number of lease permits for West Texas "wildcat wells"—exploratory wells dug on land not already proven to hold oil—increased into the 1930s, and such exploration would help build the economic, cultural, and technical infrastructure to sustain long-term oil production. However, this process would take decades. In the interim, just as the development of railroads, agriculture, and ranching made visible the constraints and boundaries of the speculative economy, oil prospecting did not make many instant millionaires.

As much a product as a creator of this speculative whirlwind, Frank Pickrell would spend the next two decades bouncing from prospect to prospect, attempting to use his oil success to launch new speculative ventures. In 1927, the El Paso city directory listed him and his wife, Arlene, as residents. That year, Pickrell was the vice president and treasurer of the Farmers Cotton Finance Corp. Three years later, the 1930 census showed him as a resident of the prestigious Hotel Biltmore in Manhattan and listed his occupation as simply "investor." Pickrell later returned to the industry where he made his first money; in 1940, he was living in Fort Worth and listed his occupation in the census as "Independent Oil Operator."[84] However, he continued to migrate in search of industry and investment opportunities. At least for a time, Pickrell moved back to El Paso and was living there, in a rented apartment, in 1947.

Chapter Two

A TOUGH, GREEDY, BRAWLING TIME AND PLACE

On the afternoon of January 28, 1928, an oil storage facility in the Permian Basin oil town of McCamey exploded. Twelve tanks owned by the Humble Oil and Refining Company suddenly caught fire, igniting between 6,000 and 36,000 barrels of crude oil, gasoline, and other petrochemicals. The results were catastrophic and received national press attention. Reports described "a billow of yellow and orange flame shooting upward into a sea of boiling black." Initially, it was impossible for locals to accurately estimate total casualties because the town was engulfed in a "mile high wall of smoke." In the immediate aftermath, Humble Oil, represented by Superintendent R. X. Cook, pinned fault for the explosion on chemist Fred Hendricks, a new employee tasked with climbing onto Tank No. 15 for steam cleaning. According to Cook, Hendricks lifted a hatch on the tank, igniting the flammable liquid inside: "The only theory advanced to account for the explosion was that a spark had been struck in the opening or closing of the test hole by Hendricks, igniting the gas in the tank."[1] Humble dispatched representatives from Houston to investigate and, depending on the source, damages to the facility were estimated to be between $100,000 and $1 million, unadjusted.[2] While homes and other businesses in the makeshift oil town were spared due to quick action by the local volunteer fire department, Hendricks was unable to admit or deny his role in the accident—he had been killed in the explosion. Thrown in the air by the blast, his body was burned beyond recognition in the ongoing fire. However, despite initial reports of widespread fatalities, only five other workers were injured, slammed to the ground by the force of the explosion.[3]

Like many who arrived in the Permian Basin oil fields, Fred Hendricks had probably been attracted by the Humble refinery's high pay, and he probably did not have previous experience working in oil. He was probably given little specific safety training and was wearing no protective gear at the time of his death. Hendricks grew up in the agriculture town of Wichita Falls and had spent only a few months working in McCamey before the explosion.[4] His father was a local railroad engineer.[5] He was twenty-six years old and left behind a young wife and an extended family.

The explosion in McCamey was not unique. Nor was the fact that Hendricks was blamed for his own death. The Texas oil industry expanded rapidly between 1925 and 1930, led by discoveries in the Permian Basin. As the industry grew, oil companies hired a range of new employees for an array of temporary, dangerous jobs. Often one paycheck away from poverty, many of these workers were injured, maimed, or killed on the job. The oil industry's extreme physical dangers were well known—local and national press took any opportunity to report on oil's fiery catastrophes. However, while other heavy industries began to implement insurance-backed guardrails on workplace dangers and appeased their most valued workers with incentives like pensions and hazard pay during this period, oil speculation lagged. Instead, the drilling industry's primary risk creator and reducer—financial speculation—fundamentally shaped how Permian Basin rig workers, the speculators who hired these drilling crews, and local and state officials responded to harsh working conditions in the emerging oil industry.

For Texas's many small-time oil speculators, a stable, fully employed workforce made little economic sense in a constantly changing industry.[6] As a result, for workers, almost all oil jobs were temporary operations, and most workers did not bring their families or build lasting financial or social connections in a particular place. Many of these men worked only seasonally in oil, moving between ranching, agriculture, or other industrial work as needed in a system that shielded property owners, rather than workers, from fluctuations in commodity markets. In such a system, the best-case scenario was that workers bet life and limb—took on a high level of physical risk—in the hope that they could put together the funds to also become financial speculators in oil, land, and other industries. Such risk-taking dovetailed easily with the state's existing system of itinerant agricultural labor and was financially advantageous to Texas elites, who were otherwise uneasy about the prospect of industrialization. As speculative drilling developed its own standard practices and safeguards, acceptance of natural risk was baked into Texas regulatory policy.

OIL'S NATURAL RISKS

Far removed from Texas's oil refining and processing hubs in Houston, the town of McCamey was only two years old in 1928, organized immediately after oil was discovered in Upton County. Located sixty-seven miles east of the Pecos River in the far-western reaches of the Permian Basin, the town was a stop on the Kansas City, Mexico, and Orient Railway and was a waypoint for supplies headed to the oil fields. Humble constructed its McCamey refinery in 1927, one of the first in the Permian Basin.[7] The refinery was a bid for permanence in a region in which entire oil towns appeared and disappeared within a decade. For example, the small boomtown of Crossett, located seven miles to the northwest of McCamey, was founded in 1925 with a population of two hundred, which declined to fifty by 1930. In McCamey itself, the population had peaked at 10,000 in 1927, the result of an influx of oil prospectors and would-be rig workers looking for employment. Less than ten years later, however, the population had declined by half, falling with a reduction in exploratory wells in the area.[8]

For workers in these and other upstart boomtowns throughout the region, oilfield work was notoriously dangerous. While 1920s oil prospecting was fraught with financial risks for prospectors and represented a strategic gamble for rights-holders, oil jobs required workers to accept an at-times catastrophically high level of immediate and long-term physical danger. Much of this danger came from the drilling process itself.

In the nineteenth and early twentieth centuries, slow but relatively simple cable tool drills dominated the industry, and oil discovery was the job of a two-person team of driller and machinist. Cable tool drills used a cantilever system and brute force to slowly punch a hole through subsurface rock. Its operators were often assisted by crews of specialized "shooters," men who used nitroglycerin or dynamite charges to break up subsurface rock strata and ease the way for the fragile and cumbersome drills. These workers transported dangerously volatile nitroglycerin in horse-drawn wagons into the 1930s. Stories of shooting accidents and tales of nitroglycerin blasts used to burn off already flaming well fires were common.[9] Canisters often blew up in transit, ripping apart both transport wagons and their occupants. Sometimes charges detonated early, sending shooters, drillers, and their rigs plummeting hundreds of feet into the muddy drilling hole.

However, the technology did improve. Permian Basin crews adopted the rotary drill as early as 1924, and by the 1930s, most Permian Basin wildcatters invested in a rotary drill. Operating a rotary drill was more technically complex and required between two and five workers to perform.[10] Led by a driller, a typical 1920s team might include a derrick man to attach cables to pipe, firemen to run engines and boilers, tool dressers to assist the driller, and a team of laborers and roustabouts who assisted the others.[11] While this division of labor meant that speculators needed to pay more workers to operate more expensive machinery, rotary drills were lighter, faster, and more efficient than cable tool drills. Further, rotary drills were easier to haul around in the Permian Basin's roadless terrain. They were also more precise at deeper well depths.[12]

Still, they were not necessarily safer than cable tools. These rotary drills were powered by a steam engine, later by fuel oil or diesel. This engine rapidly turned a hollow pipe with a serrated drill bit attached to one end. As the rotary drill bored a hole through friction, it rotated the drill bit, which slowly ground down the subsurface rock. As the bit sank into the expanding hole, "drilling mud," high-pressure water mixed with clay and other chemicals, was pushed through the drill pipe. This flowing mud forced rock cuttings and other debris to the surface. As nitroglycerin was phased out, rotary drillers augmented their search with crews hired to detonate subsurface dynamite explosions within the drill hole, measuring the resulting vibrations and finding oil via the variations in rock strata. While safer than nitroglycerin, these blasts continued to cause well-publicized injuries.[13]

For both cable tool and rotary teams, drilling and blasting into unknown subsurface geology required experience and skill to navigate without disaster. Heavy, constantly moving machinery could produce horrific injury to vulnerable human bodies. Oral histories described drill bits broken due to undetected subsurface phenomena. Others described drill holes collapsing underfoot while workers drilled into unstable ground. Folklorist Mody Boatright described mistakes made by the inexperienced driller: "[The driller's] hole was seldom truly vertical—indeed, instances are on record of bits from rigs hundreds of yards apart meeting hundreds of feet under the ground."[14] Such mistakes could destroy both the bodies of workers and their equipment, costing oil prospectors time and money. William Joseph Philip described a driller named Bert Rambeau, who was killed after his drill pipe became stuck in a well. Rambeau reversed the drill engine and the rig collapsed, crushing him.[15] Similarly, another driller's memorable account described hitting a gas bubble underground. The resulting explosion collapsed the rig and killed several other workers.[16]

Oil drilling also required contact with an array of flammable and corrosive liquids and gases, often encountered unexpectedly and at high pressure. Famously, gushers were the result of a drill pipe penetrating a high-pressure, underground oil deposit. Visually stunning and advertised as local tourist attractions, gushers were also incredibly dangerous. One worker remembered, "We've seen many of those places blow out. . . . [Oil comes] in and just absolutely [obliterates] the surface and [blows] a hole in the ground twice as big as the platform that the derrick was setting on and just [makes] a mud pie out of it. . . . We saw many, many of those happen."[17] The resulting explosion of oil turned the drilling pipe into a fountain that shot both oil and debris hundreds of feet into the air. James Riggs remembered a similar scene working a gusher: "We were working under, we were just saturated with oil. Just a gusher going to the top of the derrick and falling back on us. . . . At the same time, we didn't realize it was so dangerous. We even had the boiler firing, a boiler within seventy-five yards of us. And today they wouldn't think about doing a thing like that, but we did at that time."[18] After the initial explosion, each gusher became an oil spill. Gushers destroyed surrounding wildlife habitats, cattle forage, and agricultural production alike. And, as oil poured overhead, workers operated steam boilers powered by open flames. As Riggs ominously implied, such proximity to open flame at times ended tragically.

Oil drilling was known for its spectacular conflagrations, sometimes the result of gushers or blowouts. In the Permian Basin, without access to large quantities of water or sufficient transportation equipment for fire brigades, these well fires went largely unchecked, sometimes sparking wildfires that swept across the desert. Such fires were alternatively the result of unexpected geological conditions, worker mistakes, or simply bad timing. In 1929, Martin Smith, Albert Helms, and R. C. Jackson were burned alive and two others were wounded after a gas heater exploded next to them in the bathhouse of the Republic Oil Company camp near Odessa, Texas. They used gasoline to wash off their crude-oil-soaked skin, all of which ignited catastrophically when the heater caught fire.[19]

Other fires were much larger, caused by insufficient waste storage at drilling sites or hastily constructed oil storage facilities. In a vivid prologue to the McCamey fire, Jack Knight described a disastrous 1919 fire in which lightning struck several oil storage tanks and quickly spread to a nearby town: "And, this electric storm that afternoon, lightning struck that tank and just burst it wide open. That oil, just solid flame, spread out on that water, just enveloped those houses and drilling rigs and shacks of all kinds, clear down to Main Street and into this creek, burnt up so many people before they ever knew that there was a fire."[20] Once burning, crude oil provided a constant source of fuel. Oil fires could burn for weeks, quieting only when oil reserves were exhausted.

Drilling companies had no standardized safety protocols to prevent fire, let alone avoid simple worker injury. In the Permian Basin, desert climate and local geology exacerbated hazards caused by isolation and limited equipment. As a rule, workers attempted to cap gushers quickly to prevent waste and reduce fire danger, but in inaccessible West Texas, gushers could continue for weeks at a time. For example, the blowout of the 1912 Lucas well at Spindletop famously lasted for nine days and spilled more than 500,000 barrels of oil. In contrast, the Santa Rita reportedly gushed more than a million barrels during the three months that it took to cap the well.[21] By comparison, workers wore no protective clothing, and gushing crude oil burned and irritated skin and eyes, leaving rashes and sores. Curt Hamill described the difficulty in cleaning up after oil work, which was up to worker discretion: "We first rubbed the rough oil off with sacks or cloth of different kinds. . . . And then, after we'd rubbed it off, we would bathe in warm water or water as hot as we could stand it."[22] Many of these risks, epitomized by the pain caused to skin saturated with crude oil, were less spectacular and did not make news reports, but they still affected the lives of workers. Case in point—deep rotary drilling in West Texas required working with longer, heavier pipes, and at well depths that had higher subsurface pressure. Workers broke bones and sometimes lost limbs when their hands or feet became trapped by the chains used to direct the spinning drills. John Alexander, who spent forty years working in the industry, remembered 1920s rigs as particularly dangerous, saying that rigs

FIGURE 2.1. A 1939 photograph by Russell Lee depicting the rotary drilling process. Here, workers are removing a length of pipe from an oil well in Kilgore, Texas. Clamps are being removed from a rotary table, and the pipe will be elevated by the links and clamp of the elevator. Photo courtesy of the Library of Congress Prints and Photographs Division.

had "chains slamming all day and banging, nothing covered up."[23] Other workers sustained mobility-limiting injuries or damaged their hearing by working alongside the shrieking and grinding of the drilling machinery.[24] The proximity between workers bodies and heavy, moving equipment can be seen in figure 2.1.

Rotary teams, drilling to extreme depths over a period of several months, were met with other subterranean hazards. They had little choice but to consume the unpleasant and unhealthy West Texas groundwater, which caused both intestinal discomfort and logistical challenges. Workers hauled water over long distances to operate their drills and for personal consumption and, according to firsthand accounts, water for bathing or toilet facilities was a luxury.[25] Most insidiously, toxic sulfur and other gases common to the region were released during deep drilling. John Alexander put it succinctly: "I got a whiff of that sulfur one time at Wink and didn't like what it did to me."[26] Sulfur gas poisoned drillers. Richard Mason also encountered the gas when dressing tools in the Wink field, saying, "I got gassed there—went blind for several days."[27] While he recovered, such exposure compounded with the inhalation of methane and other gases and took a cumulative toll on workers' respiratory and nervous system health.

While many of these hazards were the result of specific geography and regional isolation, they were compounded by a contract-work system that incentivized risk-taking, corner-cutting, and inattention to long-term risks. Bill Ingraham blamed worker injury and death on insufficient safety equipment, but he also implied that workers took unnecessary risks: "Lots of people got hurt. . . . Lots of men got killed or crippled up, uncalled for. Through ignorance, a lot of it, and through unsafe equipment too, you know. Most of the accidents could be avoided, but people were ignorant of the danger and they'd just take chances."[28] As he indicates, worker injuries were exacerbated by a lack of uniform safety laws. For example, firefighting tools such as asbestos suits and breathing masks were not required in the region until World War II. According to former oil worker O. J. Lawson, other personal safety gear such as hard hats, steel-toed boots, sparkproof tools, and gas masks were not required, so they were not used.[29] Despite their frustration at absent regulations, Ingraham's and Lawson's understandings of workplace risk also paralleled Cook's announcement after the McCamey fire. All articulated an expectation of personal competence and a culture of individualized hazard management, placing ultimate blame for accidents on the workers themselves. Nationally, pushback against this perspective was growing.

WORKPLACE INJURY AS FINANCIAL RISK

In the waning years of the 1920s, the national popular press breathlessly reported on the dangerous conditions in West Texas oil fields. Such accounts took place amid a growing national discussion about acceptable workplace risk and industrial hazards.[30] Reports from the oil fields provided new fodder for a vocal workplace health and safety movement that was backed by the era's most powerful labor unions. By 1930, "safety first" had gained supporters among both workers and management in Texas's largest oil-refining and processing centers.[31]

In contrast to speculative oil drilling, other American workers in industries from textile manufacturing to hard-rock mining during the first decades of the twentieth century were increasingly vocal in their collective efforts to reduce workplace injury. This was a long time coming. As early as the 1850s, industrialization meant that more and more Americans worked alongside heavy and fast-moving machines. Repetitive work and long hours increased the likelihood of injuries due to human exhaustion or simple mistakes. Case in point—railroad brakemen became renowned in the nineteenth century for navigating a constant wave of crushing or maiming injuries.[32]

While the courts agreed that something should be done, they were often reluctant to rule that employers were responsible for the actions of their employees, and recompense for truly unjust injuries was deemed appropriate only as a moral reward for wronged individuals. However, as the number of industrial accidents only increased later in the century, a coalition of unions, muckrakers, and social reformers pushed for new federal regulations to curb what they saw as systemic employer negligence. Many of these lawsuits steered the problem away from moral culpability. Instead, more and more American industrial workers sued their employers based on their lost future economic potential. Such a shift won compensation for many American industrial workers and, after the passage of the Federal Employers Liability Act in 1908, legal precedent fully shifted, making employers liable for worker injuries regardless of their moral context or the employers' intent to harm.[33] However, such a new system also inscribed a financial rather than moral impetus for safety and health into the American legal system, with ramifications well beyond injured workers.

Standardizing worker compensation, perhaps unintentionally, monetized the value of human life and limb in worker contracts, workplace policy, and the US legal system.[34] It also helped to create entirely new industries. Workers increasingly turned to unions and fraternal organizations, which provided insurance policies against lost wages or death. Employers built a competing employee insurance system. Both supplied workers with compensation based on the value of future labor lost, not as a moral reward for employer negligence. In turn, such policies fed the increasingly powerful insurance industry, in which actuaries developed a standardized system of economic restitution for hazards or accidents in workplaces, homes, and transportation systems. Such numbers were institutionalized within new workers' compensation laws and made worker payouts for accidents or death a predictable risk for employers. In turn, large industrial employers bought hazard insurance in the hope that predictable payouts would be less costly than the courts, whose rulings were seen as friendlier to injured claimants. These large employers, including oil companies like Standard Oil and others implicated in the trust-busting shake-ups of the 1910s, built financially acceptable numbers for worker injury or death into their business models. Crucially, this system was not necessarily designed to shield workers from harm, but rather to buffer employers against financial risk of unplanned lawsuits, reducing a previously unpredictable financial hazard.

Starting in the early twentieth century, the largest American industrial employers also implemented some preventative workplace safety measures as a further shield against the unpredictable financial risks created by workplace injury. Part of a national "safety first" movement, industrial employers from Carnegie Steel to Anaconda Copper standardized industrial safety equipment and developed safety regulations for both management and workers. However, such efforts remained uneven.[35]

As detractors pointed out at the time, safety regulations worked only if they were rigorously enforced, and Texas legislators, sensitive to the agricultural lobby and the state's need for industry and infrastructure, followed such trends only anemically. Texas enacted a statewide workers' compensation law in 1913, but it was an at-will law that allowed employers to decide whether they would participate. Similarly, in response to a 1917 US Supreme Court ruling that clarified that states could force employers to participate in state workers' compensation programs, Texas again articulated its commitment to the voluntary system.[36]

In Texas and beyond, smaller companies were less successful at risk reduction, and independent inspections at industrial facilities were hampered by insufficient money and personnel.[37] Mechanical failure, lack of training, or simple inattention, coupled with the ballooning size of the American industrial workforce, meant that the total number of accident payouts continued to skyrocket into the twentieth century. As workers organized under the banner of health and safety, industrial employers, exemplified by coal mine bosses, attempted to use brutal violence to suppress such discontent.[38] As a result of these factors, industrial fatalities, if not injuries, began to fall rapidly across the United States in the 1910s.

Still, by the time oil exploration kicked off in the 1920s Permian Basin, the level of responsibility that American industrial employers assumed for workplace safety had increased, as had the level of recompense that most workers could expect in the event of workplace injury or death. Across the nation, there was growing popular support for the idea that an industrialized society was obligated to provide a social safety net for its workforce and legislation, the courts, and industry leaders should work together to boost worker safety.[39] This was codified by further waves of workplace safety legislation, such as the Longshore and Harbor Workers' Compensation Act of 1927, which codified compensation for workers injured in all navigable US waters. Such legislation was pushed forward by union organizers and state agencies, both of which sought to make industrial spaces safer.

It was in this context that Texas's integrated oil distributors and processors emerged in the newly important oil transport hubs along the Gulf of Mexico. Cities such as Houston, Beaumont, Texas, and Baton Rouge absorbed a wave of new industrial jobs. Larger Texas oil processors such as Humble and the Texas Company, as well as multinationals such as Socony-Vacuum, quickly integrated Texas's industry and resources into a national and global system of industrial risk management. As early as the 1910s, legacy branches of the old Standard Oil, including Jersey Standard, Humble Oil, and Socony-Vacuum, as well as Sun Oil, Union Oil, Magnolia, and others, began building refineries and chemical plants along the Gulf Coast. Following national trends, these companies set the tone for Texas oil's earliest industrial health and safety programs.

Safety efforts at Houston's Socony-owned Magnolia Petroleum refineries were indicative of the norm. Socony implemented a multipronged approach that included new employee rules, manuals, and training, as well as a strictly bounded hazard compensation plan. Joined by the American Petroleum Institute (API) and oil companies, Socony published an array of new safety manuals during the 1920s, all couched in the language of advice and individual self-help. In 1921, for example, Socony Mobil distributed safety manuals billed as "a book of information designed to help employees." Half job training manual and half hazard awareness text, it encouraged workers to follow company protocol and avoid risks.[40] While the manual did provide a needed set of procedures for employees engaged in hazardous work, the language of these refinery risk management programs placed the burden of hazard awareness and prevention squarely on workers. To this end, Socony and other oil companies simultaneously developed internal safety departments that provided worker surveillance even as they assessed workplace hazards. For example, the Socony Mobil Oil company hired its own safety inspectors beginning in 1925.[41] Vacuum Oil also maintained a separate safety and employee claims department throughout the 1920s and 1930s, and Magnolia Oil set up a safety and fire protection department during this period. As early as 1922, Socony's company magazine, the *Socony Flash*, began publishing accident reports, divided by plant. Such publications indicated that the new safety programs did seem to have real success in reducing worker injury and death. However, workers, including members of the International Association of Oil Field, Gas Well, and Refinery Workers of America, argued that these inspectors were biased on behalf of management and independent inspections were needed.[42] These groups argued that such internal safety programs, paternalistic at best, simply pushed workers to follow an arbitrary list of safety protocols rather than prompting oil companies to invest in safety gear or effective hazard detection systems.

While widely touted in company publications, actually invoking insurance policies or receiving injury compensation was often a challenge for refinery workers. For example, an employee policy manual from the General Petroleum Company reminded workers that going back to work too soon after injury or not following doctor's orders could "prejudice your right to medical treatment and wage compensation." In more extreme cases, worker death would prompt a company safety team investigation to determine whether it was caused "by the workman's own negligence." If so, survivor benefits would be cut in half. If a worker's death was found to be due to his own intoxication, the company was not liable.[43] Similar to analogous programs in the American manufacturing, steel, and textile industries, these policies were designed to shield employers from the financial risks posed by worker accidents, not protect workers from physical harm.[44]

Such internal safety departments and hazard insurance programs were part of a wider response by oil management to the national "safety first" movement. While also promoted by unions and worker fraternal organizations, safety first also felt the influence of Progressive-era social management and hygiene programs, which were top-down efforts to teach urban industrial workers—often immigrants—how to act in an inevitably hazardous industrial world. If the hazards of modernity were immutable, it was up to educated elites to help individuals protect themselves. Indicatively, safety first pushed an underlying assumption that under such newly safe conditions, accidents must be the result of worker inattention or lack of training. The language in these publications was telling. An article from the company periodical *Magnolia News* stated, "The refinery men have learned the value of caution and how to avail themselves of the safeguards at their disposal," and added, "Magnolia men and women are learning that it pays to keep well and play safe."[45]

Tellingly, these programs sidestepped traditional labor complaints, such as speed of production or length of work hours, and instead placed the responsibility for accidents onto the workers themselves. They also reassured readers that the company was acting in the workers' best interest. For example, another article stated, "Throughout the property evidence of safety work is apparent, suggesting to the stranger that it must be a very dangerous place to work. But we conclude otherwise when we learn that the equipment is for prevention."[46] In rhetoric and in practice, such a management-led "safety first" focus was not altruistic. Rather, it attempted to shift the onus for risk reduction onto employees instead of employers.

Although Humble built its McCamey plant in 1927 and the Burford Oil Refining Company built a 5,000-barrel capacity refinery in the town of Pecos in 1928, the Permian Basin remained on the physical and administrative periphery of such safety-first trends.[47] However, the drilling industry did adopt key components of them. Like oil refiners during this period, speculative oil companies in Texas and across the United States also monetized the value of worker life and limb. Nationally, speculative oil companies employed actuaries to assess risks and industry leaders embraced the primacy of statistical data and information. Drilling data, geological information, financial statistics, wages, work stoppages, and technical capacity were all carefully analyzed by the largest US oil companies.[48] However, on the ground, the Permian Basin's speculative drillers did not codify safety regulations and only rarely produced contracts stipulating hazard or injury pay. This was not the result of absentee, trust-fueled greed, although such decisions were not necessarily benevolent. Instead, a mix of expediency and convention meant that a more informal and ad hoc system of personal risk management continued to be enforced by both drilling crews and their employers.

Speculative drilling was an industry based on contingency. Industry pressures and the many specific, localized dangers produced by the job encouraged decentralized hazard management, strategic risk-taking, and personal autonomy. As a result, drillers casualized the risks faced by individual workers through a contract labor system and then turned to technological fixes to increase efficiency and reduce work stoppage and resource waste. While West Texas oil drillers were not unique in experiencing a high level of workplace risk, the drilling workforces' itinerancy, isolation, and links to the region's ranching economy further limited how far workplace safety efforts could penetrate local speculative operations. Crucially, while environmental risks such as geography, climate, and hazardous materials remained problems, individual risk assessment decisions in the oil fields were shaped by employer debt and the logistics of worker itinerancy. This made an already hard job even more dangerous.

In West Texas, most drilling operations were small and staffed by contract labor. Larger independents like Humble, Magnolia, and Phillips, as well as small operations like Frank Pickrell's Big Lake Oil Company, extended contracts to small drilling crews for a fixed fee that would be paid upon completion of the job. These drilling companies owned or leased one or two drills and, once they got their money, paid their workers by the job. While a 1920 survey of US drilling employment lists hourly pay for oil workers, this was probably less common in the Permian Basin. One estimate, from 1935, estimated that 68 percent of drilling work was done by contractors.[49] While this percentage probably increased over time, it is safe to estimate that at least half of speculative jobs were contract work in the 1920s and 1930s. While rig workers like Clarence Bryan and John Alexander were probably paid comparatively well for the era, oral histories record that few drilling crews actually had formal job contracts; instead, they were hired through informal verbal agreements. This made them vulnerable to sudden layoffs or unscrupulous bosses.

Especially for small-time prospectors, the financial risks in oil production remained very high. These employers had few tools to respond to global commodity prices, complex supply chains, and variable technologies. As a result, both prospectors and drilling contractors held very high levels of debt and, with limited options, passed this risk to their employees. For example, according to John Alexander, he was simply laid off rather than paid for his time and labor after drilling a 4,500-foot-deep dry hole near Porterville, Texas.[50] Further, most undercapitalized prospectors were simply unable to set aside money to pay for on-site medical care or compensation for worker injury or death, let alone invest in hazard insurance or reserve funds to hedge against lawsuits from injured employees.

Even for fully employed oil workers, the inherently temporary, speculative nature of drilling operations discouraged the construction of initial infrastructure, further exacerbating industry hazards. According to former oil worker E. N. Beane of Crane, Texas, by the late 1920s, a single drilling operation typically lasted anywhere from thirty to one hundred days.[51] Once drilling started, the process would stop only due to accident or upon well completion. Federal reports from this period record workers being paid for either eight-, nine-, or ten-hour days and described either six- or seven-day pay periods. However, West Texas oral histories emphasized the physically exhausting nature of the work, with drills running twenty-four hours a day, 365 days a year.[52]

Fred Jennings described his experience: "Well, we had no vacations. We didn't know what that was. I ran a drilling rig for twelve months, seven days a week for one year to a day without loss of a day. That's right. No overtime [pay]. We didn't know what that was. No."[53] Such nonstop drilling took place far from existing communities, and the sandy, rocky terrain made swift transportation arduous, if not impossible. In such conditions, repairs, emergency services, or even second opinions on drilling practices took days if not weeks to arrive. Throughout the 1920s, lack of reliable roads or telephone lines made communication intermittent at best. According to E. N. Beane, "When we first started this thing out here [oil exploration], you would start from Odessa to Crane and there were several alternate roads that you could take, but maybe you wouldn't get through on any of them without getting stuck in the sand."[54] The region's network of dirt roads was often flooded, drowned in sand, or overgrown by thorny scrub forest.[55] This was a particular problem for early automobiles, with simple engines and rudimentary transmissions.[56] E. E. Brackens, a former driller for Gulf Oil, described using horses and oxen to move pipe and heavy machinery after roads became impassable.[57] As seen in figure 2.2, well into the twentieth century, most supplies or visitors arrived on horseback, on mule trains, or via oxen-led wagons. Such isolation and intermittent access to supplies incentivized accuracy and speed.

Similarly, worker housing for West Texas drilling crews was minimal to wildly insufficient, adding yet more workplace risks. In the short term, drillers slept on the derrick floor or in hastily constructed tents or cabins near the drilling site. For more established operations, larger oil companies built temporary, on-site work camps to house drillers, their assistants, and

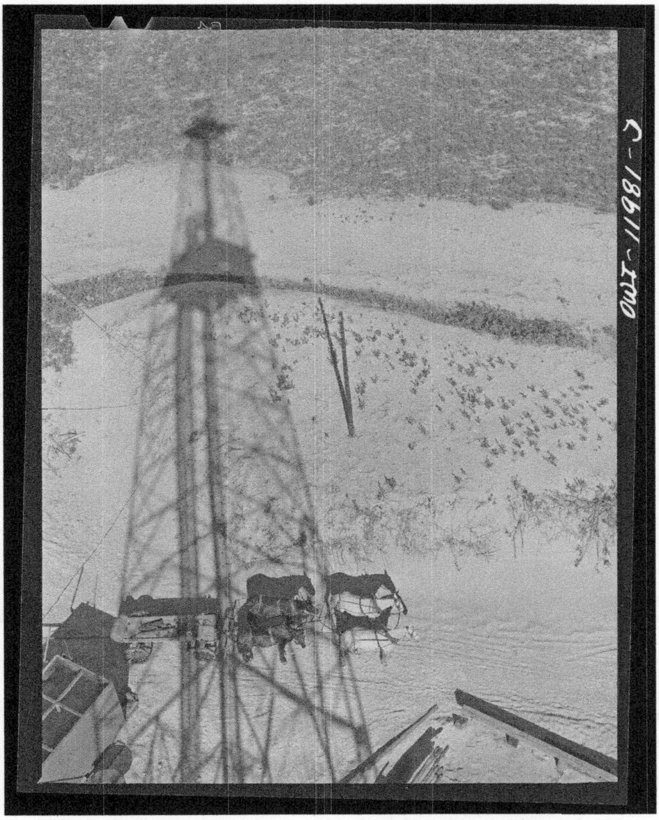

FIGURE 2.2. A 1942 image of an oil derrick in Andrews County, Texas. Due to lack of road infrastructure, oil maintenance workers and residents continued to travel by horseback in what was known as "Sand Hills Country." Photo courtesy of the Library of Congress Prints and Photographs Division.

any engineers, surveyors, and geologists. For example, after Pickrell's initial discovery, the Big Lake Oil Company established a camp between the towns of Big Lake and nearby Rankin to house the influx of their workers. Similarly, Gulf Oil, Humble Oil, and Phillips Petroleum also set up work camps in West Texas.[58] As seen in figure 2.3, when employers did not provide housing, members of drilling crews built their own shelters from any available materials, including tin, cardboard, canvas, brick, and the region's limited supply of wood. While workers who brought families were sometimes provided with private shacks or tents, this was unusual,

FIGURE 2.3. A 1937 Dorthea Lange photograph of the outskirts of an oil boomtown in Texas. In many such towns, as hundreds of workers poured into town for jobs, living quarters became scarce. Some built their own shelters using any available materials. Photo courtesy of the Library of Congress Prints and Photographs Division.

and unmarried workers often bunked together in groups. In larger camps, the oil company provided food and the camp residents ate together in communal dining halls.[59]

While exacerbated by the logistical challenges of construction and lack of materials, the industry's financial risks shaped oil companies' priorities when developing such infrastructure (or not). While roads, electricity, and worker housing might increase well completion speed, they were also major expenses for fundamentally temporary operations that carried a significant chance of failure. Most oil drillers chose to avoid construction and accept the resulting work delays. The region's deep wells already produced unusually long drilling times and comparatively high production costs.[60] Further, the ticking clock on drilling leases and the need to drill until oil discovery counterbalanced the possibility of breaks or time off due to worker exhaustion, illness, or injury. Looming lease deadlines and limited funds encouraged drillers to cut corners on equipment maintenance and avoid work stoppages.

Despite the many hazards, oil companies easily attracted workers with high wages, especially compared to other work available in the region. Drillers, the leaders on a speculative job, enjoyed the highest pay. In a 1920 US Bureau of Labor Standards report, American oil drillers were paid approximately $12 per day, an attractive sum at the time.[61] Drillers in West Texas, where skilled labor was scarce, could expect even higher pay. F. Arthur Stout remembers that he received $14 per day working on a Texas oil rig that same year.[62] A labor or roustabout, the least skilled job on a rig crew, earned around $4.90 a day, roughly sixty cents more than the national average, during this period.[63]

Texas oil companies advertised nationally, and these industry wages were the source of much rumor and excitement. Scholars have shown that while many potential oil workers had no previous experience in industrial work—let alone oil production—the slow mechanization of farmwork over the previous several decades gave rural migrants an edge over those arriving from urban areas.[64] Accordingly, throughout the 1910s and 1920s, boosters spread the word that there were lucrative oil jobs in Texas. For example, Clarence "Flappy-Jaw" L. Bryan, who was born in Georgia and worked for several decades in a Magnolia Oil machine shop, remembered his parents receiving a promotional letter in 1917 saying, "In Texas the money grows on trees. A man can get a job working twelve hours a day and make more money in a day than he could in a week in Georgia." His family moved to Port Neches, Texas, that same year.[65]

Such hyperbolic ads were not completely without substance. Despite the dangers, high oil wages were conducive to upward mobility, and there was a general consensus that hard work and learned skills would result in more responsibility and more pay. According to Mody Boatright, "From the beginning, a man could work his way up—from tool to driller, from boil weevil to pusher, to owning a rig, a well, a producing field."[66] According to John Alexander, "You start working in oil and making good, you go to a new field, you just about always know someone working that new field so you can go right to work."[67] Alexander started in the industry as a roughneck and rose through the ranks as the "West Texas district superintendent over both drilling and production" for the state of Texas. According to him, this "was quite an accomplishment for someone who had the amount of education I had." However, he tempered this by arguing, "All it takes is using your head and hard work."[68] Fred Jennings described a more modest upward advancement in the industry: "Well, I started in as a roughneck, December 27th, 1916. And I worked on the floor as a roughneck . . . for a short while, about three months. And then I worked derricks. . . . Well, a derrick man got twenty-five cents a day more than the men on the floor got . . . he had more responsibility in the derrick than he had on the floor. He was supposed to know more than the men on the floor. That's why he got that big twenty-five cents more."[69] Other reports describe those with greater technological or machinist skills as recognized elites who were able to pick and choose their rig crews and the most desirable jobs.[70]

Even further, while movement all the way from wage worker to speculative investor was relatively rare, some drilling personnel made this jump, seen as the ultimate payoff for the industry's itinerancy, instability, and dangers. For example, Frank Pickrell's head driller, Carl Cromwell, went on to many more drilling jobs and was ultimately appointed as drilling superintendent for Big Lake Oil's Reagan County fields. He would retire wealthy in San Angelo. In September 1931, Cromwell was killed in a Pennsylvania car accident. At the time of his death, he owned properties throughout West Texas, in San Angelo, in McCamey, and in Hinton, Oklahoma, and Hobbs, New Mexico. He received royalties from numerous oil leases and held stock in multiple oil companies, including the successful Oklahoma independent, Phillips Petroleum. Cromwell's estate, left to his wife, included two small airplanes and was valued at $69,800.[71] Cromwell—a well-paid, upwardly mobile driller who used slowly accumulated wealth and good professional reputation to make the jump from wage worker to oil speculator—was representative of an industry ideal.

OIL LABOR AND THE RANCHING ECONOMY

While Cromwell's success was the aspirational goal, many oil workers were moving into oil from agricultural labor and ranch work as conditions declined in those industries. They could expect more modest returns on their investment of life and limb.

In West Texas and throughout the state, agricultural and ranching operations consolidated and mechanized during the first decades of the twentieth century. Unable to compete in an era of rock-bottom farm prices, many smaller producers were pushed into cotton sharecropping. These farmers were not employees of a particular landowner, but rather tenants who paid a percentage of their total annual crop as rent.[72] Sharecropping was an option born of desperation, and many of these workers quickly became trapped in a cycle of unending debt that could not be paid off. As a result, these sharecroppers, the shrinking population of small West Texas farmers and ranchers, and wage-earning agricultural and ranch workers were all eager to take seasonal oil work when they could get it.

Easing this transition was the fact that farmwork and ranch work presented many of the same physical risks as oil work, but oil paid much better. Indicatively, John Alexander understood the danger in ranching and oil work to be similar: "Close calls? I was in two nitro explosions while I was in there . . . had close calls on [the] ranch also, so it was all just everyday life for me."[73] Historical accounts back his assessment. Due to fears of price inflation, agricultural work had been largely excluded from turn-of-the-century increases in American safety legislation and formal worker injury compensation.[74] Injuries incurred using farm machinery, working with unpredictable animals, handling early pesticides, and sickness caused by simple exhaustion and heat were common. For these workers, as in the oil industry, informal and contract labor placed the burden of workplace risk squarely on the shoulders of the workers themselves. This was useful in the agricultural economy.

Large landowners employed expanding crews of farmhands and ranch hands, often working without a contract and paid under the table.[75] According to Barney Hubbs, West Texas cowboys were paid $30 a month.[76] Laborers on an oil rig made five times as much over the same period. As a result, these agricultural laborers made up the majority of Texas's workforce in the early twentieth century and, perhaps unsurprisingly, most often moved in and out of oil drilling in the Permian Basin. Crucially for landowners, oil's temporary, contract-based labor system did not significantly disrupt patterns of work in either ranching or agriculture.

Oral history interviews with Permian Basin homesteaders, smaller ranchers, and cowboys who worked for John Scharbaurer, William Henry Cowden, and others all describe working in oil at different times but never fully putting aside ranch work. Joe Conger, whose father was the foreman on C. C. Slaughter's ranch, was a cowboy. He had three younger brothers, one of whom worked in the oil fields. According to Conger, his brother strongly preferred oil jobs, reflecting that "he'd been a driller for a long time when he died. He died at fifty years old."[77] Similarly, John Alexander founded the Screwbeam Ranch but later alternated between ranch and oil work near the town of Orla.[78] According to Alexander, "Every now and then, I run into a lot of old cowboys who worked the oil fields down there at Wink. . . . Guys I'd punch cows with back in the day."[79] Many describe oil work as producing dramatic upward mobility, if not stability. Some used their time working in oil to save money to get married or to buy a house. For others, oil provided a way to hedge against the risk of unemployment or failed agricultural speculation. Alexander remembered one of his neighbors, E. O. Olds, who tried to make a profit breeding mules near the Pecos River, but instead "he came [to Texas] from Arkansas and went back and started working in oil as driller. . . . His five sons were roughnecks in Arkansas during the Depression."[80] As these interviews indicate, most oil contractors followed migratory patterns, alternating between farmwork, ranch labor, and oil work when they could get it.

Of course, some stayed in oil. However, these workers still moved from job to job, following new discoveries. Folklorist Moody Boatright explained, "The workers—the drillers, the tools, the roughnecks, the roustabouts, the pipe liners—were necessarily wanderers, for it required many fewer men to maintain a field than to develop it."[81] For example, George Bentley worked in oil jobs across Texas during the 1920s and 1930s. He worked as a laborer in an oil machine shop in Brackenridge, Texas. Then he moved to the Humble Oil and Refining Company in Throckmorton County. He left for the Kellogg Drilling Company and then worked as a tool dresser in Iraann, in Pecos County, Texas, for the Red Bank Oil Company. Bentley was then employed by C. L. Dittman in McCamey and later found oil work in Grandfalls, Texas, and yet again in New Mexico.[82] While head drillers might be known and sought after due to reputation, the lower ranks of roughnecks did not linger with a single company. This atmosphere did not cultivate formal ties or records. As former oil-field worker William A. Owens tellingly put it, most workers knew each other by short nicknames only.[83]

The Permian Basin's intertwined ranching and oil labor systems worked together, reducing financial risks for regional landowners. They also provided much-needed income for some ranch workers and small farmers. This combination also solidified racial segregation and growing economic disparity between West Texas's white and nonwhite communities. Ranch work had long been a source of employment for the region's Mexican, Tejano, Black, Native American, and mixed-race residents. For some, ranch work was an avenue for wealth, and possibly land ownership as well. For example, sheep ranching had long been a staple for West Texas's Mexican and Tejano landowners. However, beginning in the 1880s and 1890s, many of the region's largest ranchers were also ex-Confederates who benefited economically from racial hierarchies that provided cheap labor and limited competition for land and resources. This was a wider trend. In the early twentieth century, segregation and racial panic solidified previously porous distinctions between white and Hispanic Americans in the US Southwest, with assumptions based on skin color, language, citizenship status, and a need for a steady supply of agricultural workers hardening into a system of legal segregation and enforced labor. Throughout the region, cotton, vegetable, and fruit growers increasingly recruited workers with no clear immigration status, who were therefore dependent on their employers. In South Texas, for example, control over a largely immigrant workforce contributed to lax safety regulations and stifled workplace safety disputes in both agriculture and industrial food production.[84]

Throughout Texas, such systems increased the physical, legal, and economic distance between white and nonwhite communities. In particular, it blocked access to oil and its profits from nonwhite populations. Oral history interviews and historical accounts document that this distance was reinforced by numerous instances of racial terror, including lynchings and race riots in oil towns throughout Central and North Texas in the 1910s and 1920s.[85] Such violence dovetailed with similar incidents in Oklahoma and Louisiana, designed to push nonwhite residents out of lucrative, oil-rich land. By design, segregation prevented nonwhite workers from enjoying the economic benefits of oil industrialization.

It is no coincidence that well-paying oil jobs were largely unavailable for nonwhite workers during the same period. In interviews, longtime residents of Odessa, Texas, remembered that Black workers were barred altogether from oil employment.[86] However, oral histories from Central and North Texas mention Black workers digging ditches and slush pits and moving heavy machinery. They record Chinese men cooking camp meals.[87] Further, after oil was discovered in North and Central Texas in 1927, newspapers reported that oil companies were quickly building worker housing, including a "negro hotel" and a "negro school."[88] Despite such conflicting accounts, it is reasonable to assume that West Texas oil operations followed statewide trends. This is supported by scholarly accounts that document segregation as barring nonwhite Texas workers from all but the lowest-paying, least desirable jobs and allowing employers to underpay workers in other oil-producing states.[89] Such tactics were documented in industries from railroads to mining during this period. For example, in El Paso, it is clear that the mining giant American Smelting and Refining Company benefited from segregation, only ending separate wage categories for Anglo and Mexican smelters due to sustained worker agitation. Similarly, historical accounts record similar pushback against low wages among Black and Hispanic refinery workers along the Gulf of Mexico.[90]

Despite the presence of such contextual histories, it is clear, however, that as white oral history informants in the Permian Basin recalled it, the region's Tejano and Mexican residents lived and worked in distinct communities, separate from the daily practices or financial orbit of speculative oil work. Indicatively, while multiple oral histories referred to "Mexicans" in New Mexico who provided the best and most reliable bootlegged alcohol, and yet others described "brawling" with Mexican farmworkers in Grandfalls, Texas, there is no discussion of working alongside Hispanic drillers or Mexican oil laborers.[91] Such absence probably hides nuance. More likely, some nonwhite laborers, roustabouts, and ditch-diggers were hired to drilling crews throughout the region. While most of, if not all these workers probably held jobs on the lowest rungs of the drill team ladder, they all navigated an array of physical dangers with varying degrees of success. In taking oil jobs, they took a calculated risk, and while they probably did not strike it rich, they turned to oil hoping to maintain a level of personal safety and autonomy within an industry and a regional economic system that had clear hierarchies but few guardrails.

THE USE OF TECHNOLOGY TO MITIGATE OIL'S WORKPLACE DANGERS

West Texas oil work produced numerous entertainers who made a living by embellishing oil's dangerous and itinerant lifestyle in their art. For example, the Texas country-and-western singer Slim Willett, looking back fondly on his time working in the West Texas oil fields, romanticized the lack of job security in his lyrics. He sang, “I'd rather have me a young girl or two and a job on a rig I can quit when I choose.” Similarly, the colorful cowboy personality Bell Cord moved between working on ranches and roughnecking in the oil fields. He also transformed a rosy version of this lifestyle, drinking, fighting, and gambling between jobs, into a successful country music career.[92] Such descriptions glossed over the harsh living and working conditions in oil, instead idealizing itineracy and a lack of long-term responsibility. Crucially, such songs also failed to immortalize the careful work of oil drillers and the sustained, coordinated effort required for successful drilling. While perhaps less exciting to put into song, the industry's temporary workplace conditions, isolation, and uncertain payouts during this period incentivized individual drillers' speed and precision. In the 1910s and 1920s, individual Texas machinists and tinkerers produced key technological fixes that increased drilling accuracy, cut drilling time, and reduced waste. Sometimes, these innovations also had the happy result of reducing instances of catastrophic equipment failure and worker injury. Crucially, although 1920s Texas drilling crews were out of step with Progressive-era safety brigades and did not join the industry's emerging unions, they did not actively court disaster. Instead, they attempted to personally control the industry's most extreme physical risks, making oil work safer by cultivating personal technical competence and knowledge of hazards, both human and industrial.

While the rise of the rotary drill was oil's most publicized technical advancement during the 1920s, others were just as important. By the time of the Santa Rita discovery in 1923, newer rotary drills were less likely to become stuck in hard rock formations, and therefore were less likely to collapse into the drill hole. However, they could still destroy engines when attempting to drill through hard rock. In 1909, Walter B. Sharp and Howard Hughes Sr. developed the twin-cone roller rock bit in Texas and Louisiana oil machine shops. The bit significantly increased the power and speed of the rotary drill.[93] Over the next two decades, Hughes's son, Howard Hughes Jr., perfected this design, the three-cone drill bit, and patented it in 1934. During the same period, rotary drills switched from steam-powered to either electric- or diesel-powered engines (figure 2.4). This was costly, but it produced more power and utilized a smaller, less accident-prone engine that could operate in remote locations. Similarly, as rotary drills became the norm, drilling mud became its own industry, with various chemical

FIGURE 2.4. A maintenance man works on a steam-powered drilling engine at an oil well in Kilgore, Texas, in 1939. Photo courtesy of the Library of Congress Prints and Photographs Division.

combinations developed to interact differently with distinct rock formations. Easing the process of mixing environmentally specific mud, Walter B. Sharp patented the Sharp Machine while drilling in Corsicana, Texas. This machine replaced teams of cattle or mules used to mix drilling mud, increasing drilling accuracy and safety.[94]

Perhaps most important for worker well-being, several oil machinists filed patents for blowout prevention equipment in the 1920s. For example, the independent Texas driller James Abercrombie and his machinist-business partner, Harry S. Cameron, patented the first ram-type blowout preventer in 1926. The device attached to the top of a drill pipe and allowed workers to use wrenches to seal the well hole quickly in the event of a blowout, thus reducing unrecoverable oil waste and preventing both fire and sudden rig collapse.[95]

These and other technical innovations made men like Abercrombie, Hughes, and Sharp into rags-to-riches success stories in the industry. However, the safety and accuracy provided by such technologies varied based on geology and geography. Crucially, it remained up to head drillers to use these new technologies correctly, wielding them alongside their personal experience and expertise to anticipate subsurface content and activity.[96] With exploratory drilling operating on a knife-edge, balanced between the potential exhaustion of funds and the possibility of workplace catastrophe, savvy prospectors hired drillers who knew how to balance competing environmental and technical factors. These drillers would enjoy semiautonomous control over workplace decision making, dictating things like the kinds and quantities of casing pipe used and whether there were expected problems with cave-ins based on the type of rock formation penetrated and the age of the drilling system. Drillers would assess the presence of water or gas in strata and estimate how this would affect drill time and the cost of labor, fuel, water, equipment, and other resources.[97] Fast, accurate, and safe drilling required precision, which could be gained only through years of practice.[98] Drillers gained geological knowledge on the job and used sensory knowledge to predict subsurface phenomena. George Abel described a head driller working east of Abilene, Texas, as he visualized the layout of subsurface geological strata and the presence of oil as follows: "Sometimes [the location of oil] would depend on the direction of the dip, sometimes the oil accumulation there would be in those wrinkles due to the closed end of the wrinkle being on the up-dip side . . . In other instances of oil accumulation in such wrinkles would be a sand condition where oil would be accumulated in sands found in these little wrinkles."[99]

Abel's references to "wrinkles" and "dips" portrayed an otherwise unmapped subterranean landscape of sand, rock, and oil. He did this without the aid of visualization technology. Instead, Abel and other drillers in the 1920s mapped the subsurface world by examining buckets of discarded mud from drilling slush pits. Drillers flushed discarded mud with water, examining the types of rock and sand expelled and testing for the presence of oil. Plummer M. Barfield explained, "There was quite a few old timers and that came from West Virginia and Pennsylvania that were exceptionally good looking at those cuttings in that mud bucket and telling you what it was and where it was at. There was any number of them that were gifted with the ability to take that mud up there and run that sand through their fingers, and some of them could tell you what it would do and what it wouldn't do. That's what made a driller, was the ability to read his mud."[100] For these early drillers, knowledge of the earth and its contents came from sensory analysis and workplace experience. By the late 1920s, some augmented these efforts with analysis of "core samples" taken from the mud and debris at the bottom of the drill pipe. This provided an uncontaminated look at down-hole conditions and helped drillers further predict changes in subsurface geology in advance of a blowout or an encounter with explosive or toxic gases. Such sampling devices were particularly useful for identifying salt domes, or pockets of subsurface salt, that often capped oil deposits and were particularly common in the Permian Basin.[101]

Such efforts to better understand and react to subsurface geology hastened the process of finding oil. It also helped prevent accidents. Head drillers made hundreds of daily decisions, and any of these could go wrong midway, making much of early drilling work an exercise in constant troubleshooting. Case in point—even the seemingly inauspicious process of mixing drilling mud required specific knowledge and experience. Nominally a waste by-product of the drilling process, correctly mixed drilling mud had to be sticky enough to collect debris from the rotary drill pipe and coat the sides of the hole to prevent cave-ins, but fluid enough to avoid clogging the pipe. Mud helped to maintain stable well pressure and to prevent blowouts that could damage equipment and kill anyone working the drill.

In the early twentieth century, drilling mud was made on site using the head driller's personal specifications. Typical drilling mud consisted of a specific mixture of water, local clays, acids, and other chemicals.[102] Drilling mud was stored in a pit next to the drill and later discarded in a series of "settling pits," where it could be examined after use.[103] This process is depicted in figure 2.5. Drillers chose the viscosity of the mud, the type of drill bit, and the size of the drill pipe, all based on their understanding of the type of rock and consistency of the earth being drilled. For example, Permian Basin wells were comparatively far underground, with oil deposits surrounded by limestone and sandstone rock. While they were relatively soft stone, these materials were much harder on drill engines and drill bits than the shallower wells dug into East Texas mud or Gulf Coast sand. This harder rock required less viscous drilling mud because the hole was less likely to cave in, but it also required the more technically challenging fishtail bit to chew through the hard surfaces.

Piecing together such divergent factors, drillers guided their teams of workers through dozens of complex and dangerous operations in the search for oil. For example, derricks, originally made of wood but increasingly

FIGURE 2.5. An oil-field worker probes an oil-drilling slush pit in Kilgore, Texas, in 1939. He balances on sections of pipe crossing a pit filled with mud, saltwater, and other detritus from the drilling process. Photo courtesy of the Library of Congress Prints and Photographs Division.

made of less fire-prone steel after 1930, were on average between seventy-two to eighty-two feet high depending on the well depth. These massive structures required on-site construction, as well as regular repair and reinforcement as drilling evolved. As they did with derricks, workers had to maintain the boilers, steam engines, drawers, rotary machines, and water pumps or else risk catastrophic failure. If the driller decided to change the drilling direction, several workers used heavy chains and brute force to turn a man-sized lever on the base of the drill, changing the angle of the pipe within the hole. Drill pipes often became packed with dirt, mud, and other debris, so roustabouts helped drillers keep water circulating through the pipe at all times to prevent clogging. When a drill pipe needed to be added as the hole got deeper or removed due to a break or clog, the driller instructed derrick workers to pull the pipe out of the hole by hand using a network of pulleys anchored midway up the derrick. These pipes ranged from four-and-a-half to eight inches in diameter and were cut into sixty-foot lengths. Workers twisted the pipes, screwing them together in a process that took both time and experience to complete safely.

Throughout this process, head drillers kept logs detailing everything from the daily distance drilled, the presence of saltwater, any core samples taken from the well, the schedule used to shoot nitroglycerin or dynamite into the well, and the estimated well pressure. As a result, using an array of numerical data such as drilling speed and amount of wear on the drill bit, along with visual analysis of drilling mud derived from core samples taken during drilling or scooped from slush pits, a skilled driller could piece together a fairly accurate picture of subsurface rock strata. Once the drill struck oil, sometimes indicated dramatically by a gusher rushing up the drill pipe, a hollow casing pipe was lowered into the hole, a pump was attached, and controlled oil extraction began.

At the region's isolated and autonomous work sites, drillers and other workers had a high level of control over both the collection and application of data. Head drillers directed machinery, navigated environmental hazards, and made swift judgments about safety. However, a driller's ability to read mud and navigate the drill through uncertain subsurface conditions was only as good as the team's ability to repair rig machinery and keep engines running. This took teamwork and an array of technical skills that were gained only through long experience. As indicated by oral histories, many workers took pride in their personal skills at oil detection and lamented those who took unnecessary risks. They worked within an informal and localized system that privileged individual action and eschewed the type of standardized, external reviews pushed by unions and national industrial health and safety advocates.[104] However, individuals could control only so much. Neither personal competence nor the industry's high pay could fully remove environmental variability or the dangers posed by temporary, ad hoc infrastructures. This was a fact that Fred Hendricks learned too late.

In 1928, when Humble officials arrived in McCamey to assess damages after the storage tank explosion, they were met with a community buffeted by competing changes. Like other refineries in Texas, the superintendent at Humble's McCamey operations had probably implemented standardized employee handbooks and set up internal safety inspections. Case in point—the immediate blame placed on Hendricks for the blast suggests an assumption that he should have known to avoid producing sparks near flammable petrochemicals. However, McCamey was not a growing industrial center like El Paso or Houston, and such programs were probably limited at best. A temporary extractive outpost, McCamey's roads and sanitation, let alone urban safety infrastructure, were simply left undeveloped. This was a conscious decision.

Oil folklorist Mody Boatright lamented that in boomtowns like McCamey, "neither public agencies nor private capitalists would or could make the investment necessary to provide what we now call a decent standard of living for the temporary population."[105] This assessment was echoed by oral history informant Anne Wolfe: "Most people when they came in, they thought they would only be here a month or so. If you are going to be that temporary, you are not going to put much money in a house."[106] Whatever the personal risks or rewards, industrialization still sat very uneasily in the Permian Basin for both individuals and oil producers like the Humble Oil and Refining Company.

Chapter Three

THE INFRASTRUCTURE OF MODERNITY

Born in 1868, just three years after the Civil War, Daisy Miller Bradford was sixty-two years old in 1930. She owned 976 acres of farmland in swampy pine forests approximately 500 miles to the east of McCamey, near the Texas-Louisiana border. A widow since 1901, Bradford was reported as having a predilection for helping others. Case in point—she had spent the previous five years cooking, cleaning, and housing a team of exploratory oil drillers, led by the charismatic Columbus Marion "Dad" Joiner. However, this was not simple altruism. She had contracted Joiner to drill for oil on her land and was determined that it would not be a wasted effort. She quickly became not just a rights-holder, but also the financial benefactor for the operation. Bradford extended lease times well beyond contract norms and loaned Joiner thousands of dollars to keep drilling. Her determination paid off, as Joiner struck oil with his third well, Daisy Bradford No. 3, on October 3 of that year. He struck oil again in January 1931.[1] While Bradford had hoped that oil would result in funding for public schools, parks, museums, and other amenities, the discovery produced a chaotic oil rush that drew an influx of both small speculators and large oil companies to the historically large East Texas Field.

Such chaos produced an environmental disaster. In the early 1930s, East Texas was mostly populated by a network of Anglo and African American tenant farmers mixed with a patchwork of small, largely subsistence agriculturalists, who owned just a few acres. All these landowners hoped to strike it rich by securing oil wells on their land. Many prospectors were less than honest. Landowners were defrauded by drillers who signed agreements but never arrived or signed leases, and then promptly sold them at auction. Some lease agreements were verbal, leaving no official records and no way to enforce broken promises. All this contributed to lack of coordination and massive oil waste. Drilling teams constructed derricks just feet apart. Oil gushed from uncapped wells, saturating the local pine forest and ruining farmland and pasture. It disrupted crops and polluted rivers and streams. In at least one case, an entire town was forced to relocate due to the contamination.[2] Untold barrels of oil were lost to uncontrolled gushers, evaporation, and insufficient storage. Along with reports of such gratuitous resource waste, stories of fraud, theft, violent crime, disease, fire, and overcrowding appeared in newspapers across the nation.[3]

This localized chaos took place amid a backdrop of growing national panic. The stock market crash one year earlier, in late October 1929, had rippled through US industry. As investors sold off all they could, banks failed, industrial production declined, workers were laid off, and oil company shares withered. While Dad Joiner might have been distracted by the heady rush of discovery, the crash exacerbated the boom's atmosphere of chaotic urgency for others. Joiner and other speculators were joined by out-of-work drillers, roustabouts, tool pushers, and derrick men, some traveling from far West Texas in search of work. These men competed with ousted sharecroppers and itinerant farmhands for the shrinking supply of oil industry jobs.[4] It was clear that Texas had an overproduction problem. However, for industry insiders, this was not a new revelation.

By the late 1920s, American oil production had already begun to outpace demand. Pundits and national economic forecasters called for coordination and supply reduction, especially in California and the Midcontinent.[5] As early as July 1929, even small West Texas newspapers like the *Abilene Reporter News* prophesied that a drastic reduction in oil production was necessary to stave off full market collapse.[6] By the summer of 1930, the oil market was glutted, in part due to ongoing discoveries in the Permian Basin, and prices started to decline. The East Texas discovery that fall could not have come at a worse time. The influx of oil sent crude prices plummeting from a little over $1 per barrel in 1930 to 2 cents per barrel in 1931.[7]

This devastated the Texas oil industry and dramatically exacerbated a growing, global depression.

Oil company leaders, speculators, state officials, and politicians all agreed that overproduction, waste, and lack of coordination were obvious problems, but it was less clear how to fix them. The situation was complex on the ground. Speculation meant that even the smallest oil prospectors owed money to someone. Despite the catastrophic drop in prices, East Texas oil prospectors still had lease agreements to honor, interest due on loans, and drilling crews to pay. Landowners were desperate to cash in while they could. Drilling could not just stop. By the summer of 1931, the East Texas Field was producing approximately 900,000 barrels per day, three times what Permian Basin wells had produced in 1929.[8] On August 17, under a threat of full industry nationalization by President Franklin D. Roosevelt's administration, Governor Ross Sterling called in both the National Guard and the Texas Rangers to enforce oil extraction quotas at gunpoint. However, while a dramatic symbol of the times and cast in the Texas press as a major blow to industry autonomy, production quotas were only partially successful. Oil prices did stabilize and rose briefly to 60 cents per barrel in 1932. However, they dropped again to 40 cents the next year and steadily declined until 1941, when the United States entered World War II.[9]

During the Great Depression, Texas was the locus for problems that had plagued the US oil industry since its inception. According to a 1934 US Bureau of Mines report, "Rapid depletion of reserves and wasteful utilization of petroleum . . . are clearly recorded throughout the history of the oil industry."[10] This was an ominous generalization, but the report made no attempt to estimate the total amount of oil lost due to waste. Similarly, state actors and industry officials during this period differed in their understanding of exactly how to define, let alone calculate, oil waste. This was in part due to the word's ambiguity. With its definition in oil and gas laws differing from state to state, waste was an abstract and fluid category, similar to the concept of risk.[11] If all risks were bets on the future, a focus on the waste produced due to blowouts or oil spills framed long-term environmental costs in terms of negative short-term future potential—as economic opportunities missed due to faulty decision making or insufficient information. In the 1930s, amid the human-caused ecological crisis of the Dust Bowl and discussions about the role of state agents in regulating interlinked economic and environmental risks, resource waste and environmental exhaustion were framed by many as optimization problems. For key state and federal actors, oil wasted due to overproduction, like wasted landscapes or out-of-work drilling crews, represented resources used incorrectly.

Similar to the industry's response to workplace safety calls, both large and small oil producers initially preferred to address such a resource allocation problem in house. Industry professionals developed and heavily promoted engineering and logistical solutions that better moved people, machinery, and oil between sites of production and consumption. The ability to implement such efforts made West Texas oil important to how Texas oil leaders and political pundits met the Depression era's linked challenges of overproduction, economic depression, and war mobilization. However, this effort exacerbated existing tensions. The industry's most heralded waste reduction technologies, in particular pipelines and tank farms, were capital and resource intensive and construction of such networks were left up to the integrated majors. As a result, the problems of environmental contamination and resource waste were worsened by the jockeying for power between big and small oil producers and between the state of Texas and the federal government. The competing desires to build infrastructure but avoid monopoly control turned the linked problems of waste, overproduction, and price control into a complex logistical, economic, and political problem that required an intricate and reliable storage and transport network. It also necessitated negotiation and cooperation among competing and often antagonistic actors.

BUILDING THE NETWORK

Historically, gratuitous, ecosystem-ruining oil spills were endemic to oil discovery. Indicatively, in the nineteenth century, American oil transporters developed financial mechanisms for recouping lost profits due to oil waste. Similar to the insurance-based system developed to shield oil producers from the monetary cost of worker injury or death, oil lost during storage and transport was estimated mathematically, and such calculations were built into premiums and sometimes noted in the balance sheets for oil transporters and distributers. Over time, however, these losses were seen as too large and unpredictable, and as technology improved, oil companies readily adopted better storage technology and transport infrastructure. As a result, West Texas was the source of much oil infrastructure development in the years leading up to the East Texas discovery. Nominally billed as "resource conservation," the development of such networks had cascading environmental impacts, with efforts at waste reduction creating new problems.

On paper, pipelines were one of the industry's oldest and most successful waste reduction tools. In the 1840s, oil was transported in leaky wooden barrels loaded onto wagons or railroad cars. Even after the invention of the steel tanker railcar, the threat of depletion or sudden conflagration remained high.[12] Pipelines nominally fixed these issues. Reinforced steel casing and careful pressure controls meant that pipelines could carry oil and chemicals across longer and longer distances. This reduced transport costs from isolated drilling locations, addressed supply instability, and decreased waste. They also increased profits. Better pipelines allowed transporters to store and then pump more oil and accept more payments from producers. For the largest American oil companies, this meant that both oil supply and prices could be better predicted, covering the cost of risks such as line breaks, lawsuits, or drops in commodity prices.

In practice, the results were more complex. For example, the Permian Basin's first two oil pipelines were built in the 1910s. They were small, inefficient by the standards of the day, and prone to leakage.[13] As a result, speculators continued to ship oil via the region's only railroad, the Texas and Pacific, which was quickly overwhelmed by oil shipments and the commercial needs of local boomtowns. Accusations of predatory freight prices and collusion dogged the rail company.[14] Desperate for better infrastructure, local producers scrambled over a full year in 1927 to develop a pipeline system that connected the Permian Basin to El Paso refineries. Two years later, in 1929, a small pipeline-building boom began, peaking in the spring and summer. Pipeline construction was covered heavily by the local press. The cover of the April 14, 1929, *Abilene Reporter News* proclaimed that the Shell Pipe Line Corporation had completed a ten-inch-diameter pipeline that stretched five hundred miles from the small oil town of McCamey to Houston's rising refining hubs. The paper also proudly reported that pipeline transport out of West Texas was expected to reach 350,000 barrels a day within the week.[15] Also in 1929, Texas-based oil companies, including Gulf Oil and the Texas Pipe Line Company, constructed several pipelines in Winkler and Pecos counties. The Humble Oil Company constructed two three-inch lines from Kemper Station, near Big Lake and the Santa Rita discovery, to the growing town of San Angelo.[16] Many of these newer pipelines were bigger (anywhere between four and ten inches in diameter) and could carry more oil—a gift to the region's nascent oil boom. However, like drilling, the pipeline construction process introduced new risks, both for the crews who built them and for surrounding ecosystems.[17]

Work on early West Texas "pipeline gangs" was brutally hard, manual labor. It was also reportedly one of the few oil jobs consistently open to the region's Black and Hispanic residents. Before the 1940s, the unsteady terrain meant that pipeline gangs most often dug pipeline ditches by hand, without excavation equipment. Gangs built pipelines in sections, with each pipe either welded together or screwed together using heavy tongs. Pipeline gangs were much larger than rig crews, each made up of approximately forty men and directed by a single "laying boss." Gang members had specialized jobs. "Stabbers" wielded pickaxes to dig ditches. "Tongsmen" employed large sets of tongs to screw pipes together. "Ropemen" helped to hoist pipes into place, assisted by "barmen" and "jackmen." Once laid, these workers covered most pipelines with a layer of dirt and gravel.[18] However, in the warm Texas climate, the pipe was left open to the elements at times if the cost of digging was too high or if the surrounding soil was corrosive.[19] While initially cheaper, these exposed pipelines were at greater risk of being punctured by human error, extreme weather, or animal disruptions. Reports of workers injured in fiery pipeline explosions during servicing or maintenance operations appeared in the local press during this period.[20]

Other less obvious risks emerged after construction. Once installed, these new pipeline networks reduced waste but also encouraged more extraction. As a result, they increased the scope of the industry's environmental contamination, as well as the size and frequency of oil spills. Beyond contaminating grassland, such spills also affected the local cattle economy. For example, in an oral history interview, former pipelayer William Wolfe remembered a pipeline leak that made a nearby herd of cattle sick, with some rendered infertile by ingesting crude oil.[21] In this case, he explained that the rancher who owned the cattle informally negotiated monetary compensation for the livestock's bad health.

Other times, such battles ended in court. In 1934, Elliot Cowden, one of the region's largest landowners and the owner of extensive oil leases, won monetary compensation from the Humble Pipeline Company for property damage.[22] In another case, farmers in West Texas and Carlsbad, New

Mexico, brought a collective lawsuit against the US Potash Company for contaminating the Pecos River with salt, but they lost the case.[23]

Intermittent lawsuits did not either dissuade the construction of large-scale transportation infrastructures or reduce the industry focus on technological fixes. In turn, the creation of the requisite oil storage facilities increased the size of spills. In the nineteenth and early twentieth centuries, extracted oil was stored in clay-lined, open pits that were prone to leakage, evaporation, and catastrophic fire. To reduce these risks, the industry developed "tank farms," which included fully enclosed oil storage containers, most often built of wood or metal. At the beginning of the century, such steel tanks could hold approximately 5,000 barrels of oil. Tank farms were constructed in centralized locations within an oil field, storing oil before pipeline transport. For example, Clyde Barton, of Kermit, Texas, remembered that such tanks sat in clusters near the small boomtown of Wickett to the east of El Paso: "There must have been fifteen or twenty of those big tanks in the heart of the field; they built them between these wells. . . . They had a big farm down at Wickett, and they would run those pipelines. It was a busy outfit for a while. They did all that drilling, 600-some wells, from the early part of '27 up to the last quarter of '29."[24] By 1929, the average oil storage tank could hold 100,000 barrels or more.[25] Tank builders in Winkler County and local boomtowns experimented with liners, roofs, and cooling systems to combat corrosion, avoid leakage, and reduce evaporation. They built dikes around each tank to prevent the spread of fire and attached lids to reduce evaporation and prevent cattle or other animals from drowning in the collected crude oil. However, leaks remained common. Like pipelines, tanks reduced key risks, allowing oil companies to accumulate an easily accessible oil supply to hedge against an unexpected demand or drop in prices. However, as such storage facilities got bigger, so did the size of spills.[26]

In 1928, the same year that multiple storage tanks at the Humble Refinery exploded at McCamey, the Shell Oil Company, a largely independent subsidiary of the European multinational Royal Dutch Shell, launched a plan for consolidated oil storage outside McCamey. This experiment in tank size stretched the limits of both engineering science and the credibility of those who would point to technological solutions as the best way to manage oil waste.

Shell engineers envisioned a single, enormous storage reservoir, hundreds of feet wide, which could hold upward of one million barrels of oil.

According to news reports, the pit was too big to dig by hand. Shell workers used steam shovels to dig a massive, circular basin and lined it with concrete, a cost-effective way to increase durability and reduce fire risk. The basin was fitted with a removable cover made of wood, cut from old-growth California redwood timber and shipped to West Texas via rail.

On paper, the risk should have paid off. Shell was building a new pipeline connecting the Permian Basin to refineries in Houston, and it expected a swift flow of oil and quick return on the investment. However, despite buoyant fanfare in the local press, this massive tank was doomed from the start. The concrete liner was designed to hold extreme weight. However, engineers had not accounted for the weak limestone bedrock underlying the pit. Cracks immediately formed in the concrete, and the tank began leaking crude oil, and Shell's profits, into the ground. Efforts were made to drain the reservoir and patch the leaks, but the massive project was ultimately abandoned just one year later—a casualty of the national stock market crash of 1929 and lack of a long-term engineering solution.[27]

A source of both professional embarrassment and local curiosity, Shell's failed McCamey storage tank joined a growing network of dry holes, abandoned pipelines, and empty storage pits that lingered after production declined in an area. Such detritus was indicative of the priorities, excesses, and failures of West Texas oil producers during this period. Shell engineers turned to engineering solutions to hedge against financial risks that depended on global price and supply contingencies. When these engineering solutions failed, the environmental waste caused by such problems was widespread and long term.

Far from deterred by the failure of the McCamey pit, as more oil was discovered in the Permian Basin, the region's tank farms and pipeline network only grew. This was part of a national effort. All new pipelines in the Permian Basin were "feeder lines" that connected the region to a network of larger "trunk lines" that stretched between national refining centers along the Gulf of Mexico and to the East Coast.[28] These new lines connected the Permian Basin with tanker ships in Houston, natural gas producers in New Mexico, and refining and oil shipping networks in Pennsylvania.[29] Such interconnection encouraged Permian Basin extraction and increased the American oil supply at a breakneck pace. In the Permian Basin alone, on March 30, 1929, seven months before the East Texas discovery and the crash of global oil prices, the average Permian Basin oil production was

363,187 barrels a day, of which only 8,291 were stored locally. Pipelines immediately transported the majority of this oil (238,242 barrels) from West Texas to either East Coast refineries or ports where it was shipped abroad via tanker ships.[30]

As these transportation and storage networks became more technically and geographically complex, they required a growing maintenance infrastructure and continuous capital investment. The region's new, high-pressure pipelines required pumping stations equipped with diesel engines, and later electricity, every forty miles. If the terrain was rough or the line was carrying particularly heavy oil, the pumping stations were more frequent.[31] For example, a 1929 pipeline traversing the relatively flat desert terrain between Winkler County, Texas, and Jal, New Mexico, was serviced by a single 55,000-barrel storage tank and two seventy-horsepower engines attached to two Gould pumps.[32] Similar storage tanks can be seen in figure 3.1. Transport companies employed technicians at pumping stations who

FIGURE 3.1. Oil storage tank farm near Midland, Texas. Steel tanks replaced earthen pits or wooden vats and were more resistant to fire and corrosion. Photo taken by Russel Lee in 1939. Photo courtesy of the Library of Congress Prints and Photographs Division.

monitored gauges for pressure loss, indicating a break in the line. "Line walkers" patrolled pipelines on foot and later by plane, searching for leaks.[33] Tank farms at pump stations supplied crude oil to the pipeline, allowing the line to maintain pressure—and continue operations—even if there was a break in the line. Even bigger than their 1920s predecessors, these tank farms could hold anywhere between 10,000 and 55,000 barrels of oil. Electricity was required to run pumps as well as drills and pump jacks, and to light drilling platforms as work continued well into the night.[34]

This infrastructure required recruiting and retaining skilled workers. For example, David Henry Levy was contracted away from the electric utility company Texas Power and Light Company (TP and L) in 1926 by Magnolia Oil to run electric lines to the Panhandle to power pump stations along newly installed pipelines. Magnolia hired a growing number of electrical engineers, with Levy joining a five-person Electrical Engineering Division at Magnolia. By the 1950s, 60 percent of Magnolia pipelines would run on electric power.[35]

Indicative of at least some local pushback against the growing presence of such oil transportation infrastructure, accounts of oil industry leaders and policymakers attending public hearings and listening sessions begin to appear in the local press during the Depression.[36] One issue was a sticking point: The growing pipeline system was indicative of the deepening power imbalance between large and small oil companies. This was a source of constant consternation for locals and the topic of regular Texas debates about oil waste. Small producers increasingly chafed under the control of larger oil companies that built, maintained, and profited from such infrastructure.

Case in point—in newspaper opinion pieces throughout the Permian Basin, local pundits argued that much of the oil price problem in 1930 was not about insufficient demand, but rather about price gouging by large producers and an inability to get oil to market.[37] One account from 1939 described the Humble Pipeline Company's "monthly safety meeting" in the Ector County courthouse. At the meeting, Humble representatives argued that pipelines were risk reducers, already safer than tanker trains, depicted in figure 3.2. They reassured listeners that the technology was constantly improving, reducing waste and increasing royalty payouts. Responses from the audience were not recorded. However, some probably expressed concern that all this new infrastructure was built and owned by either the largest Texas independents or oil multinationals.[38]

FIGURE 3.2. 1948 oil tanker train makes it way east along the Texas and Pacific Railroad loaded with Permian Basin crude. Photo courtesy of the Petroleum Museum, Lee Jones Jr. Collection.

Big oil companies, not local independents, built pipelines. Like railroads, construction of infrastructure such as tank farms and pipeline pump stations was prohibitively expensive for smaller operations. Pipeline companies made money in different ways during this period. Oil producers either paid a contract rate to pipeline companies for their transportation services or sold crude oil directly to pipeline operators. Sometimes pipeline companies acted as middlemen between producers and processors. As the industry became more sophisticated, oil-purchasing companies—intermediaries who bought crude oil from a producer and sold it to refineries based on fluctuations in market prices—became more common.[39] These entities hoped to profit from an increasingly integrated system. They knew that pipeline builders and operators were deeply invested in constant, steady increases in both oil supply and demand. However, due to sunk costs, pipeline companies were particularly sensitive to any price fluctuations.

Even further, the technological sophistication of the pipeline network made them inflexible. It was technically unwise to quickly reduce the amount of flowing oil in a particular pipeline. A drop in pressure could cause the entire line to stop flowing. Therefore, rather than acting as a storage safety valve or quick transporter for local oil producers in times of crisis, pipeline companies preferred to sign contracts with the largest and most reliable oil producers that controlled whole oil fields. Often, larger oil-processing companies spun off their own pipeline companies, such as the Texas Pipe Line Company, a subsidiary of the Texas Company. Such relationships shielded corporations from the financial uncertainty associated with pipeline construction and operation. This also cut off small producers from the market and made pipelines the source of constant corruption accusations that echoed protests against their railroad predecessors.

Beginning immediately in 1930, newspapers described independent control over pipelines as a needed solution for bringing up cratered prices.[40] In this context, local oil companies lobbied for the expansion of the oil pipeline network to bypass both railroad and oil-processing monopolies, democratize pipeline transport for small oil companies, and reduce resource waste. However, such a stance was seemingly counterintuitive. How could an industry plagued by too much oil need *more* pipelines? However, because oil producers addressed waste as a sign of badly allocated resources, the logic followed. This perspective was shaped by the US Doctrine of Correlative Rights, a key piece of US oil and gas law that received extensive scrutiny during this period. Under the doctrine of correlative rights, oil producers were entitled to access to both common resources and consumer markets. Under this doctrine, interstate oil pipelines were ruled "common carriers" and pipeline companies could not prioritize some potential customers over others—at least on paper.[41] Whatever their status, the Texas pipeline system remained extremely limited during this period, as illustrated in figure 3.3.

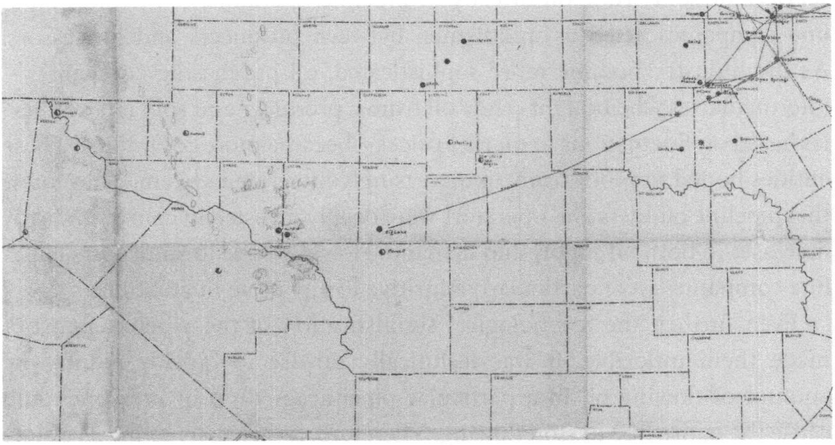

FIGURE 3.3. 1926 map of Texas Oil and Gas Fields and Trunk Pipeline System. While quickly expanding on the Oklahoma border and on the Gulf, in 1926 pipelines in the Permian Basin were virtually nonexistent. Image courtesy of the Texas State Library and Archives Commission Archives & Information Services Division.

For such reasons, among others, small producers in West Texas were angry in 1930. Blamed, along with the entire Texas oil industry, for the crash in oil prices, they were ill equipped to weather the storm. In an oral history interview, Permian Basin resident E. N. Beane explained: "The depression hit us real bad. It really started in October of '29 but didn't affect Crane until the latter part of 1930, then it was pretty severe. Oil, of course, went to a dime a barrel, and there was no progress at all during the latter part of '30, '31, '32, and then in '33 when Roosevelt took office, he came in with NRA, WPA, etc., it started back to prospering very slowly. It was real slow because people just didn't have any money."[42] Even the largest multinationals simply fired workers after 1930. According to John Alexander, the Depression "just hit overnight," and Shell laid off 15,000 workers in three days.[43]

Small producers met calls for resource coordination and waste reduction with protests that corruption had crippled the industry and locals needed greater control over oil transportation systems. As the Depression deepened and both demand and prices stagnated, small producers continued to bemoan large-company control over this transportation network. Some criticized Texas's oil regulatory agency, the Texas Railroad Commission (TRRC), for failing to intercede on their behalf. However, the TRRC was ill equipped to enforce any form of cooperation among oil producers, let alone develop a system that would bring about monopoly-busting fair use of the nation's pipeline infrastructure.

THE TRRC AND THE LIMITATIONS OF STATE REGULATION

Pat Neff served as Texas governor from 1921 until 1925. In 1929, he was appointed chair of the TRRC, in what should have been a swan song for the end of a long political career.[44] One year later, in 1930, Houston millionaire Ross Sterling, railroad financier, real estate mogul, former president of Humble Oil, and chairman of the Texas Highway Commission, ran successfully for Texas governor; he was elected in part due to his time spent in the oil industry. Political leaders like Sterling and Neff were expected to maintain close ties to Texas oil producers. In particular, it was understood that they would work with independents to avoid any restrictive oversight that might encourage the expansion of oil multinationals in Texas.[45] Instead, both presided over some of the most contentious years in Texas regulatory politics and made deep-seated enemies among oil producers and in the legislature. But their failures set the stage for later successes and shaped the federal response to Texas oil waste.

Immediately after being sworn into office, Sterling and Neff were tasked with managing the East Texas crisis. In practice, this meant that they needed to ensure fair well spacing, regulate equal access to pipelines, and enforce production quotas amid a hostile and suspicious industry, all without clear enforcement mechanisms. This was an impossible task against mounting pressure. Under threat of federal intervention, Sterling pushed the TRRC to enforce a localized pro-rationing plan designed to raise prices. This would have dictated a monthly amount that each oil well in the East Texas field was allowed to produce based on estimated market demand. However, federal courts quickly ruled that pro-rationing was illegal price manipulation. When reports of gratuitous waste continued, Sterling resorted to martial law in 1931 as a desperate final straw. Production quotas were enforced by 1,200 National Guard troops for six months in East Texas. Such military control was protested in court by members of the Texas legislature and ultimately struck down by the US Supreme Court in 1932.[46] Efforts to use either the power of the governorship or the regulatory ability of the TRRC had been thwarted. With all their political capital spent, Sterling lost the

1932 Democratic gubernatorial primary and Neff was replaced as TRRC chair. Both were scapegoats to a legislature beholden to independents that detested their efforts, painting them as a conspiracy to control the East Texas Field on behalf of the largest Texas and national oil companies.[47]

However, before he left office, Ross Sterling established a coalition in 1932 to be led by Neff's successor at the TRRC, Ernest O. Thompson, to find a palatable regulatory solution to the problem.[48] Thompson was a fiery antimonopoly man who won the mayorship of Amarillo in the Texas Panhandle with a campaign to lower gas and electric utility prices. He played both sides against the middle to balance the competing interests of small producers and conservationists while increasing the size of the Texas oil transportation infrastructure.

Due to earlier problems with overproduction and low prices, the Texas legislature had added a vague statement supporting resource conservation to the state constitution in 1917.[49] However, a wild dispute remained in 1930 as to how this should be implemented. Some in the Texas legislature continued to argue that increased federal regulation of oil transportation networks—either to reduce physical and economic waste or to stabilize oil prices—provided an opportunity for major oil companies to strong-arm regulatory agencies and foster monopoly.[50] Using the specter of economic waste and the threat of federal regulation, Thompson justified expanding the powers of the TRRC as a natural compromise. He dramatically increased the TRRC's power over the next several years. The commission was given authority over any oil that was stored above ground in tank farms or in pipelines in an effort to limit oil stockpiling. That same year, the TRRC was given the power to hire the Texas Rangers to enforce well spacing laws.[51] Such changes produced further protest in the legislature, but such a middle road was more palatable to independents.

During these negotiations, it is certain that some in the industry pointed to the comparatively more orderly West Texas as a model of fair production and doubled down on old calls that better infrastructure, managed by independents, was the best way to contain excess oil.[52] Thompson, with his background in Amarillo natural gas, was also probably well aware of the success of voluntary pro-rationing in West Texas, Oklahoma, and Kansas during this period. In the Permian Basin, regional producers had negotiated among themselves in the 1920s to avoid market saturation, experimenting with a variety of cooperative methods that would become common in later decades.

Soon after the initial Permian Basin discoveries in 1923, some local producers who remembered ranching and farming in the economically volatile decades of the 1890s and 1910s became worried that the sudden production increases would destabilize oil prices. These oil companies and royalty owners in the Permian Basin worked together to regulate allowable oil extraction amounts. The large Yates Field was the site of much experimentation. The field was easier to organize because Ira Yates preferred to sell leases only on large tracts of land, meaning fewer producers and easier negotiations. He initially signed only sixteen oil leases, spread across 8,000 acres of his property.[53] Due to their size, these leases were more expensive and mostly were bought by relatively large companies, including Humble, Gulf, and Pure Oil, as well as Benedum-Trees, Transcontinental Oil, and the Mid Kansas Oil and Gas Company.[54]

Despite the potential for good spacing, producers in the Yates Field still initially struggled. In 1927, William S. Farish and the Humble Oil Company called a meeting in Fort Worth of all major leaseholders in the Yates Field to discuss overproduction. While these talks failed, a second attempt at voluntary regulation was more successful. Humble initially argued that everyone who used its pipelines should agree to a pro-ration system in which each company agreed to extract a set amount per day based upon proven oil reserves.[55] Foreshadowing the debates of the 1930s, some argued that this arrangement unfairly favored the largest producers, which had access to more land, and therefore more oil. Representatives from the small, independent Simms Oil Company proposed another idea, in which all proven fields were divided into one-hundred-acre "production units," with each unit given a production limit. Yates leaseholders agreed with this plan, and a state commission was established to monitor production and ensure fairness.[56]

The Simms plan did decrease the Yates production to one-fifth of its previous amount.[57] But this voluntary system had its limitations. Although it was loudly praised within the industry as a success, Yates represented only one field among many in the region.[58] Other fields, in particular the Hendrick Field, which was divided into more than five hundred very small, independent leases, only increased production during the late 1920s. The Yates Field efforts at controlled extraction were ultimately rendered moot as fears mounted that small, uncontrollable drillers in the Hendrick Field would extract all the region's oil before others could access it. Production increased once again throughout the region, again dropping both oil prices and well pressure. This led to another wave of calls for regulation and intervention by state officials.[59] This time, industry leaders such as W. B. Hamilton, of the Oil and Gas Bureau of the West Texas Chamber of Commerce, and state bureaucrats such as R. D. Ponter of the TRRC came together to push for regulation. In April 1928, the commission set allowable extraction in the Hendrick Field at 150,000 barrels per day, again one-fifth of its production capacity. As in 1927, these efforts would fall short of stabilizing oil prices, as California and Oklahoma production continued to increase during this period.[60]

Imperfect at best, such efforts worked as well as they did only due to the remote geography of West Texas. Limited oil transportation networks and the inability to get large quantities of West Texas crude to buyers helped to keep rampant speculation and overproduction in West Texas comparatively in check. Lack of infrastructure meant that if oil could not be sold immediately, it was very difficult to store aboveground.[61] Further, because oil leases in West Texas were controlled by a relatively small number of landholders such as John Scharbauer and Ira Yates, it was possible for leaseholders to negotiate between companies, keeping oil production predictable and relatively organized within a single field.[62]

In 1933, Sterling's replacement as governor, the populist Miriam Amanda ("Ma") Ferguson, began a second term. By 1935, Texas wildcat drilling had only increased sharply and, despite the TRRC's expanded powers, there was an urgent need for a truly comprehensive pro-rationing system. That year Ernest Thompson and other oil industry leaders proposed a new comprehensive oil conservation plan creating the Interstate Oil Compact Commission (IOCC), a voluntary coalition of oil-producing states that would collectively regulate interstate oil production in lieu of federal representatives.[63] Ferguson supported this plan. The IOCC received much local fanfare in the Texas press, as national oil markets did stabilize considerably after 1934.[64] The numbers flatlined enough during the second half of the decade that, in the end, the total supply of US crude oil decreased during the 1930s. However, such improvement did not represent unilateral success. Overall, the number of speculative wells dug in the Midcontinent region would still rise from 7,223 to 11,919 per year between 1931 and 1940.[65] This was due in part to the industry's financial constraints, in which contractual agreements prevented systemic nimbleness in the name of conservation.

In 1934, the *Abilene Report News* jubilantly announced the expansion of exploratory drilling in many Permian Basin fields.[66] This was not an indication of a renewed boom. The price of a barrel of oil remained down approximately 98 percent from pre-1929 levels. Decade-old leases were about to expire, and oil companies were reluctantly drilling to fulfill contract requirements despite still-low oil prices. Most of these were large oil companies that outsourced these jobs to independent drilling companies, cutting the costs of moving their own equipment to such an isolated area.[67] For example, local independent Ed Landreth in 1936 combined drilling contracts from twelve majors, including Gulf and Humble, to complete significant exploration in Gaines County.[68] As a result, several new fields were discovered in the Permian Basin during the late 1930s, including the large Goldsmith Field in 1935.[69] Such mixed results worsened the already deeply antagonistic relationship among Texas regulatory agencies, oil producers, and federal officials—a relationship made worse since 1932 by the election of President Franklin D. Roosevelt. New rumors circulated that full federal takeover of Texas oil was eminent.[70]

RESOURCE FAMINE AND WAR MOBILIZATION

This federal push for oil regulation was led by Harold Ickes, appointed as US secretary of the interior in 1934, just over a year into Roosevelt's first term. A Republican working in a Democratic cabinet, Ickes had a perspective on oil waste that was also tinged with a progressive ambivalence for industrialization and a moral imperative to manage natural resources efficiently.[71] As secretary of the interior, Ickes publicly disapproved of gratuitous wilderness destruction and saw oil conservation, not just price stabilization, as crucial to national security.[72] Such a perspective would pit him against Texas regulators, led by Thompson, who were preoccupied by a purely economic understanding of the waste problem.

Ickes very publicly called for the immediate nationalization of the industry, citing the ineffectiveness of voluntary cooperation and blaming TRRC collusion with oil companies for the renewed spike in drilling. However, his methods in practice were more moderate. Three weeks after being sworn into office, Ickes convened the governors from all oil states and recommended a complete moratorium on oil production until prices could be brought under control. Backed by Roosevelt, he echoed concurrent battles in the electricity industry as he called for oil conservation legislation putting government officials in charge of regulating oil as a public utility.[73] While many agreed that some kind of coordination was needed, the largest oil companies insisted that production quotas should instead be managed internally, led by their representatives and the IOCC.[74] Ickes believed that this was insufficient, and he responded by championing a flurry of bills before Congress designed to centrally regulate extraction rates and boost oil prices.[75]

In 1934, after these bills quickly failed, Ickes was placed in charge of Section 9 of the National Industrial Recovery Administration (NIRA), which authorized the federal government to regulate oil pipelines and oil transportation rates under the auspices of interstate commerce. The rule had teeth, authorizing the executive branch to take over any oil pipeline company or its subsidiary that was found in violation. This effectively controlled the oil supply through regulation of the freight transportation industry.

These dogged efforts made Ickes and Roosevelt bitter enemies in Texas.[76] However, some in the industry were more alarmed than others. Multinationals worried about government scrutiny but also wanted the predictability of stable prices. Some stated that working with federal officials was better than attempting to thwart them altogether. Case in point—in 1934, the previously staunchly anti-interventionist Amos L. Beaty, former president of the American Petroleum Institute (API), began pressuring oil executives to support government regulation.[77] Beaty was joined by key Texas leaders, including Texas's pragmatic, antimonopoly senator Tom Connally. In contrast, Texas independents, still vocally angered by the rapid and unpredictable price fluctuations that increased their financial risks, saw strict conservation regulation as benefiting only the large oil companies.[78]

The debate was interrupted in January 1935, as the US Supreme Court declared the sweeping NIRA unconstitutional. However, oil would not go unregulated for long. Only one month later, in February 1935, the Connally Hot Oil Act, sponsored by Connally, gave federal regulators the ability to penalize the extraction or transport of any amount of oil that exceeded state and federal quotas.[79] Connally, a supporter of farm relief packages for Texas ranchers and cotton producers in 1932 and 1933, described the bill as a boon for Texas oil producers, buffeted by Depression-era low prices. Roosevelt quickly selected Ickes and the Department of the Interior as administrators.[80]

Fearing further regulation, API president Axtell Byles delivered a petition before Congress in May 1935. Byles had been elected president of the API in turbulent 1933 and would serve in that position until his death in 1941. He was the former president of Tidewater Oil, a major East Coast gasoline provider and subsidiary of Standard Oil of New Jersey. Byles vehemently opposed any regulation placed on the industry designed to enforce what Ickes described as "slow, wise, and economical exhaustion."[81] Instead, he argued that oil was like any other commodity: "There is nothing in the inherent nature of petroleum, or in the conduct of the business, which requires or justifies the oil industry being declared a public utility any more than in the case of any other producer or manufacturer of a commodity of general use."[82] Such a statement represented an understanding of oil on purely economic terms, with an assumption that preservation of the industry and its many jobs were the most important goals.

While the API regularly weathered complaints of catering to oil multinationals, this stance was echoed by small producers. For example, on December 10, 1938, the *Abilene Reporter News* ran an article describing a meeting of the Mid-Continent Oil and Gas Association, in which members insisted, "Nothing is wrong with the oil business, we just have supply exceeding demand." Representatives called for locals to support lower oil industry taxes instead of further regulation.[83]

Such lengthy debates illustrated deep divisions between large and small oil companies. It also revealed Texas's nationalistic aversion to federal oversight during this period. Further, these shifting stances articulated differing understandings of risk and waste—broad concepts in a state of flux during the Depression. Namely, Ickes's perspective on oil was representative of exponential growth in federal attention to natural resource management. While oil remained a common flash point at the Department of the Interior, other alarming reports were coming in. Evidence of a global "timber famine" raised concerns about total deforestation and the collapse of key industries.[84] Catastrophic drought and locust swarms paralyzed agricultural production in the Great Plains, including much of Texas, and produced horrific dust storms that parched grassland and blocked out the sun. The long-held fear that industrialization would lead to environmental apocalypse seemed to be coming to fruition.

The government response to these problems was decades in the making. In the 1880s, University of Pennsylvania professor Peter Lesley and his assistant, John F. Caril, prophesied that the United States would run out of oil by 1935, sparking a national debate.[85] Ten years later, US Division of Forestry head Gifford Pinchot described a "conservation ethic" as badly needed to better manage the valuable and slow-to-regenerate natural resources in the United States. He called for centralized, scientific management. Such a stance allied wilderness advocates in the 1910s with federal officials such as US Geological Survey president George Otis Smith to support government-led preservation and resource management.[86] This included oil. By the late 1920s, American oil consumption had increased exponentially, and the specter of full depletion again reared its head. At this moment, the preservation of the domestic oil supply was described as a matter of existential—rather than simply economic—concern.

In response to these interlinked fears, federal actors turned to scientific development methods by the 1930s, hoping to better manipulate the natural world and make it respond productively to market forces. In short, the government would better allocate resources in the name of the collective good. Institutions from the National Park Service, to the Department of the Interior, to the US Department of Agriculture (USDA) all reassured Americans that scientific management, infrastructure, and state oversight would prevent environmental disaster and lead to general prosperity. Seemingly contradictory, this belief was in step with generations of American industrialists, land speculators, politicians, ministers, and popular writers who argued that wilderness existed to be controlled and improved by humans and undeveloped or incorrectly used land was simply wasted.[87] State agencies and old Progressive-era reformers formed uneasy alliances with conservationists and proponents of scientific management. A seeming symbol of national decline, resource waste was a concern for all these groups.[88]

Mid-1930s politicians discussing the US oil supply could not avoid such broad concerns about natural resources and the fate of the nation. Increasingly, such discussions were couched in expressing concern over oil's military importance. As secretary of the interior, Ickes oversaw the US Geological Survey and the US Bureau of Mines. His influence was felt in a 1934 report from the US Bureau of Mines that advocated for the expansion of oil-field unitization plans because "such a conservation program is essential, not alone because of the continued economic advantage of the Nation but also because of the necessity of maintaining an adequate supply immediately available for national defense."[89] Ickes, one year later, lumped environmental destruction with the imprudent use of natural resources, characterizing both as political and moral failings by past leaders: "It was unimaginable that the numberless acres comprising our national domain could ever be exhausted . . . the highest concept of statesmanship was to make it possible for the eager, aggressive pioneer to possess, to despoil; to move on, once more to possess, to despoil and then repeat the process indefinitely."[90] With this speech, given before the American Game Conference and broadcast on national radio, Ickes went on to call for the use of science and forethought in resource management.

Similar convictions were expressed by President Roosevelt in 1939: "Our energy resources are not inexhaustible, yet we are permitting waste in their use and production. In some instances, to achieve apparent economies today future generations will be forced to carry the burden of unnecessarily high costs and to substitute inferior fuels for particular purposes." He identified an array of interlinked factors: "National policies concerning these vital resources must recognize the availability of all of them; the location of each with respect to its markets; the costs of transporting them; the technological developments which will increase the efficiency of their production and use; and the relationships between the increased use of energy and the general economic development of the country."[91] For Ickes, Roosevelt, and others in the administration, concern for the environment was paired with a growing fear that the United States might simply run out of oil on the eve of world war.[92]

Assumptions that humans could fully predict, control, and optimize the natural world and a centralized, coordinated state was best equipped to manage this process sat at the heart of both federal and state efforts to curb speculation and wasteful extraction.[93] Famously, during the 1930s and 1940s, such belief manifested through the nationwide construction of large-scale infrastructure projects. The Civilian Conservation Corps employed thousands to build roads, dams, and recreational facilities in state and national parklands. Monumental dam and hydroelectric projects, epitomized by the Hoover Dam and Tennessee Valley Authority, electrified both the Appalachian poor and swaths of urban California. In Texas, the Lower Colorado River Authority (LCRA) halted annual flooding on the Colorado River in central Texas and provided mass electrification to the Texas Hill Country.[94] Federal conservation officers partnered with USDA Agricultural Extension System offices to promote and teach scientific land management practice, reducing erosion and soil decline on Panhandle cotton farms and on South Texas ranches.

In this tradition, beginning in the mid-1930s and lasting through World War II, different groups converged around the need to expand and better regulate the national oil transportation infrastructure, for both the good of the industry and the nation. Initially, while federal officials collaborated on legislative efforts to break the stranglehold that the majors held over the US pipeline network, locals simply clamored for more pipelines in West Texas.

In 1935, the US pipeline system was already sophisticated by global standards, stretching 250,000 miles, with 112,000 miles devoted to crude oil transportation. Another 3,500 miles of pipe moved refined gasoline, and another 150,000 miles transported natural gas.[95] Although this represented the rapid expansion of the American overland pipeline network, the majority of US crude oil and refined products still traveled slowly to the East Coast and then abroad via tanker ships navigated through the Gulf of Mexico and up the southern Atlantic coast. Even worse for Permian Basin producers, only a vanishingly small branch of this system reached the region. Bottlenecked by a lack of infrastructure, West Texas oil leaseholders and small producers perceived themselves to be besieged. They were under threat by large multinationals due to unfair oil transportation rates and thwarted by federal quotas on oil production. This was made worse in 1936 and 1937 after the discovery of the Foster Field, north of Fort Stockton.

Industry publications reported a new boom in the Permian Basin, but neither pipeline companies nor refineries would buy the oil.[96] Even after oil production rebounded after 1935, correspondence between oil driller Caven J. "Red" Davidson and his employees in the Permian Basin revealed that they were forced to shut down several wells after oil discovery in 1936 and 1937 because oil storage facilities and transport systems were not available to get the oil to buyers.[97] In 1938 and 1939, Humble and Gulf both continued exploration in the Permian Basin looking for high-grade crude, drilling in Crockett, Pecos, and Crane counties.[98] Later, extensive exploration near the city of Odessa, in Ector County, again raised the hope of a renewed boom. However, lack of pipeline infrastructure continued to limit these operations.[99]

Locals attempted to take the pipeline companies to court, with little success. In 1935, Gulf Oil, one of the Permian Basin's major leaseholders, came under federal investigation for monopolistic control over several pipelines.[100] In 1938, the West Texas Chamber of Commerce, a trade organization purporting to represent the interests of most communities in West Texas and the Texas Panhandle, made it a convention priority to secure lower freight rates for "producers, businesses, and consumers."[101] In 1939, the debate again heated up as representatives of the West Texas Chamber of Commerce publicly derided what they considered to be discriminatory rates for different sections of the country.[102]

Between 1931 and 1950, congressional bills to divorce pipelines from refineries and oil producing companies were faithfully introduced every year, with a single break during the 1948–1949 Congress.[103] Along with such symbolic help from representatives from the oil states, the Temporary National Economic Committee (TNEC) held lengthy debates on the issue from 1939 to 1941. During the hearings, William S. Farish, president of Standard Oil of New Jersey, publicly admitted that the majors owned or controlled 57.4 percent of crude oil gathering line mileage, 89 percent of crude trunk mileage, and a full 96.1 percent of all gasoline line mileage in the United States.[104] The committee ultimately suggested the divestment of oil pipelines from all major oil producers and refiners. However, the outbreak of war in Europe in 1939 severely complicated nascent efforts to curb industry monopolies.

War made the resource allocation problem much simpler. By 1940, the expansion of Texas oil production was central to the national economy and national security, and the construction and administration of domestic oil pipelines were sudden and immediate priorities for military leaders. Texas had the potential for a massive increase in oil production. The state produced 36.6 percent of all domestic oil, approximately half a billion barrels. One estimate stated that by 1940, oil employed around 250,000 people across all branches of the industry and the industry paid half of all state and local taxes. A full two-thirds of Texas counties contained oil and gas, and one-quarter of the state's total land area was leased for oil and gas exploration. Texas was the largest producer of natural gas and carbon black in the nation, and Texas refineries supplied 80 percent of US gasoline.[105] Despite such importance, a decline in the rate of pipeline construction during the Depression had made the state ill equipped to handle a sudden wartime need for more oil.

This problem came to a head in 1940, as a German maritime blockade prevented Texas oil tankers from reaching the East Coast and threatened a massive disruption in the domestic oil supply. To thwart the blockade, federal officials entered emergency talks with the largest US oil companies, hoping to coordinate the oil industry's infrastructure networks, money, and logistical personnel to prevent blackouts and a domestic fuel crisis. According to one celebratory account, this partnership resulted in a "transportation and distribution revolution," in which all branches of the industry collaborated to create a system that could accommodate immediate extractive expansion. Such expansion began as early as June 1941. Six months before the attack on Pearl Harbor that December, President Roosevelt formed what would become the Petroleum Industry War Council (PIWC), made up of the leaders of the nation's seventy-two largest oil companies. These companies controlled the largest and most technologically sophisticated oil transport and refining networks.

With Texas and Oklahoma the centers of American crude oil production and the majority of American industrial production to the north and east, the resulting Petroleum Administration for War (PAW) oversaw the expansion of the American pipeline network by approximately 7 percent, laying, relaying, or reversing 17,684 miles of pipe stretching across the Midwest and rural South.[106] This expansion required the creation of new trunk lines, as well as the expansion of a spidery network of feeder lines serving these larger trunk lines. Two trunk lines, known as the "Big Inch" and "Big Little Inch," became the public relations showpieces of this expansion project, billed as demonstrating the American oil industry's efficiency and technical sophistication.[107] A new system of temporary gathering lines—designed to gather oil from isolated or underproducing districts into consolidating storage tanks—was also built to link previously unprofitably remote fields to the East Coast.

West Texas was not at the center of this building effort, and according to historical accounts, this severely limited the region's potential for wartime expansion. However, Texas oil companies did receive federal contracts to build pipelines in the region. For example, the PAW requested the construction of a pipeline that reached from Jal, New Mexico, to Midland, Texas, and then on to Cushing, Oklahoma. Work on the pipeline was a joint project between Shell Oil, Sinclair, the Texas Company, and the Empire Pipeline Company.[108] In 1941, the federal government contracted Magnolia Petroleum Company, by then a subsidiary of Standard Oil, to build an eight-inch line from Mallet Station in Cochran and Hockley counties to

Seminole, Texas. The next year, Magnolia built a twelve-inch line from Corsicana to Midland, Texas.[109] Magnolia laid more pipe in 1944, foreshadowing numerous postwar projects and setting the stage for a later boom in the region. Such lines connected the Permian Basin with tanker ships in Houston, gas producers in New Mexico, and East Coast refinery networks.[110] Many of these quickly constructed lines, including the famous Big Inch, were prone to leakage if not failure, and required reconstruction or abandonment after the war. Wartime expediency changed priorities; it did not remove the industry's long-standing risks.

Whatever his personal opinions on the environmental impact of oil pipelines or the efforts to reduce monopoly in the industry, Ickes was also a pragmatist. He understood that quickly expanding oil infrastructure required close cooperation with the same oil companies that he had lambasted in 1934. Although the US Office of Price Administration froze oil prices at 1941 numbers, members cooperated, to much fanfare. However, this was not simple patriotism. In the name of increased efficiency, the PAW offered PIWC members prime government contracts to immediately expand the US oil transport network.[111] Ickes relied heavily on his deputy director, Ralph Davies, vice president of Standard Oil of California, to direct logistics. In postwar reports, histories, and assessments, virtually all military and government officials agreed that these coordinated, centralized construction resulted in increased efficiency and drastically reduced oil waste due to technical or logistical failure.[112]

The numbers illustrate the size of the effort. Of the estimated seven billion barrels of oil consumed by American forces over the course of the war, six billion came from US oil suppliers. Most of that shipped from Texas. According to the PAW, oil demand during the five years of war consumed the equivalent of one-fifth of all oil produced in the United States since 1859. By 1943, every county in Texas was engaged in oil exploration and leasing. Of 254 counties, 168 produced oil and 82 engaged in processing and refining.[113] By the end of the war, American crude oil production had increased by 27 percent and US refinery output had increased by 30 percent.[114] By 1945, US refineries were producing thirty-five million gallons of gasoline every day for military use alone.

On the ground, however, the positive impact of these efforts was not so universal. While the needs of wartime oil production benefited the Texas economy as a whole, the isolated Permian Basin remained at the edge of such development. The region was plagued by labor shortages as previously out-of-work oil workers were drafted or left for defense jobs. For those still drilling, the shortage of valuable machinery or materials slowed efforts. Perhaps most important, the Permian's sour crude was not desirable for being refined into aviation gasoline. According to Olien, "Between 1941 and 1942 the number of wells completed in the Permian Basin dropped by almost 50 percent."[115] If production had increased, pipelines would not have been able to keep up. In particular, locals reported with frustration that the Wasson and Slaughter fields, though isolated, could have produced much more during this period.

Daisy Miller Bradford died in August 1934, three years before the start of World War II, after a failed appendicitis surgery. While she did become wealthy as a result of oil being discovered on her land, the results of her faithful efforts might have surprised her. Bradford took a localized risk with clear economic goals. Its far-reaching results challenged easy understandings of the best way to address environmental risk and the role of government in the economy. She did not live to see the fraught battles over pipeline construction and control that rocked the Texas legislature in 1935. Nor did she witness the repeal of the NIRA and the fierce opposition to the Connally Hot Oil Act. If she had, she might have been surprised that, by the end of World War II, regulators, politicians, independents, and multinationals had formed a wary alliance. However, for Texas legislators, Depression-era calls to reduce resource waste and increase industry efficiency were inextricable from efforts to control Texas oil wealth. Many tensions remained, between East and West Texas oil producers, between big and small oil companies, and between state and federal regulators.

Each of these groups understood the construction of oil infrastructure in different ways. Texas leaders and small producers saw more infrastructure as an industry-proven way to address the waste problem, allowing them to move otherwise unsellable oil to market and allowing oil-producing regions to reach their full economic potential, outside the sway of monopolistic multinationals. During the same period, federal officials took a more existential stance on the waste question, viewing an ability to avoid full depletion of the nation's natural resources as imperative for long-term national security and social health.

The outbreak of war forced federal officials to put aside these broader concerns, aligning them with the largest American oil companies to usher in a long-desired expansion to oil transportation infrastructures. This is not to say, however, that questions about oil's environmental risk simply disappeared. After the war, continued efforts to manage waste, avoid full depletion, and reap economic rewards from extraction inextricably bound Permian Basin oil communities to a growing national and international oil system.

Chapter Four

WATER RUNS OUT IN THE "TALL CITY"

In 1947, Fred Hogan, mayor of the rising Permian Basin city of Midland, acquired an extensive tract of land for the city. Located to the north and east of downtown, he modestly named it "Hogan Park" and developed the space as a large golf and recreational venue.[1] The perceived need for a new municipal golf course was indicative of the city's—and the region's—rising aspirations. However, Hogan's real concern was the water rights beneath the land. Midland was the largest city in the Permian Basin and already oil's local financial hub. The city had experienced swift growth during World War II and benefited from the growing industry's need for office space in the region. It was also running out of water.

One year earlier, in 1946, representatives from Midland had joined those of four other Permian Basin cities. They hired engineers and put together a plan to construct a dam and reservoir on the Colorado River to supply the city. Hogan, however, was not taking any chances with the city's future resources. He simultaneously worked to secure groundwater for Midland and its already booming suburbs. As local leaders debated their options, the Permian Basin's water problem was subject to statewide commentary. To the chagrin of regional boosters, such a lack of water was described as a barrier to further industrial expansion. An ominous 1947 article in the *Austin Statesman* predicted that "a drought of unusual duration could result in water rationing, damage to crops, discontinuance of industries and even a change of population."[2] One year later, Hogan's distrust in swift dam construction was proven right. In 1948, members of the Texas Water Conservation Association noted that the dam proposal had stalled, blaming lack of federal funding.[3] Debates about the project continued. Efforts to balance the water needs of a growing oil industry against the needs of an expanding population dogged the development of Midland and other urban centers in the Permian Basin for the next decade.

As this story indicates, postwar oil workers, public officials, and politicians in the Permian Basin followed a tradition set by railroad speculators, ranchers, and early wildcatters, and remained bound by very physical environmental constraints. Like their predecessors they would simultaneously seek economic security within abstract, speculative financial systems. Such trust was built from oil expansion. In 1953, eight years after the end of World War II, President Dwight Eisenhower's administration lifted sales restrictions on gasoline and rubber, and Americans bought cars in record numbers. Although average oil prices hovered around only $2.51 per barrel for most of the 1950s, the demand for gasoline, synthetic rubber, and new plastics increased.[4] Such demand fueled new exploratory drilling abroad, as well as new domestic exploration in California, Oklahoma, and the Texas Permian Basin. In this context, oil's rising middle class, riding high on a wave of oil money and excited by the prospect of cheap loans, real estate speculation, and industry longevity, fueled the swift expansion of a new suburban Midland and Odessa, even as local leaders scrambled to address limited supplies of both local oil and local water. The resulting growth of new suburbs and water-intensive oil well management systems was billed as a marker of community stability and longevity in the local press. However, such growth only put further pressure on scarce resources. Exemplified by regional efforts to manage the water supply, oil producers and municipal leaders again and again hedged against the reality of full resource depletion by employing new technologies, producing yet other environmental hazards that defied the ability of either financial or technical mechanisms to fix.

GROWING POPULATION, GROWING PRESSURES

While not the focus of federal oil infrastructure efforts, World War II was an economic catalyst for the Permian Basin. In particular, the importance of Midland and its sister city, Odessa, to Texas oil production ballooned at midcentury. Both were connected financially to Texas's largest cities through banks, speculative investment, and an untold amount of drilling contracts. They were also physically linked by an already-extensive pipeline network that reached Houston refineries, Chicago distribution hubs, and Pennsylvania chemical plants. Both cities would soon become stops on Interstate 20, which would begin construction in 1957. Despite such busy development, both remained geographically isolated, located on flat, desert terrain approximately halfway on the four-hundred-mile journey from El Paso to Lubbock. Crucially for their longevity, the cities sat just beyond the far western watershed of the Colorado River and had relied for decades on limited local groundwater for both human consumption and oil production.

Most of this shallow groundwater was alkaline and high in toxic sulfur and other minerals, and by the 1950s, this water was often contaminated with crude oil. In the 1920s and 1930s, local water had been a source of both humor and frustration for regional oil speculators.[5] Permian Basin water was notoriously unpalatable for drinking and hazardous for drilling. Oral histories described, with a tone of resignation, water that could be lit on fire, cloudy and discolored water, and water that even livestock initially refused to drink.[6] For example, James Wheat, of Loving County, Texas, remembered that new farmhands were advised not to drink the water, and livestock required weeks to become acclimated to drinking it.[7] According to Wheat, the mineral-heavy groundwater damaged boilers and machinery alike: "Car engines, radiators; anything you used it in will give you trouble. You can boil it in the damn teakettle and it will stop it up. You boil some in a pan and you will get a quarter inch of white corrosion and scale."[8]

This was a serious problem regionwide. Oil drilling and processing required millions of gallons of water. Water powered the steam engines that ran early drills. Water was needed to put out fires. Workers and pack animals on isolated drilling rigs required water for drinking and bathing. As a result, the history of early speculation was riddled with efforts to build pipeline systems that could pump potable water to drilling locations, new oil towns, and to a small-but-growing network of local refineries.[9] While steam engines and horses became increasingly obsolete by the 1930s, water use only increased as most operations turned to rotary drills that required a constant flow of specially mixed drilling mud to lubricate drill bits and move debris out of drill holes.

Water also defined the history of early boomtowns, and Midland was no exception. A centrally located oil logistics, transportation, and finance center, the city's population had doubled between 1920 and 1930, and again between 1930 and 1940, despite the hardships of the Great Depression. Midland civic leaders had long worked to secure reliable water for the city. The earliest permanent city reservoir was built in the early 1920s on east Wall Street, in southeast Midland. New reservoirs at Cole Park, farther east of the city limits, were drilled in the late 1920s.[10] However, these were not enough to sustain Midland. The city drilled five new water wells, which ran dry by 1930, only two years after the start of the local boom.

By the late 1930s, the population of nearby Odessa had quadrupled.[11] Oil was already central to the economy and, according to one Odessa city directory, the city housed fifty-seven oil-well supply companies, ten well-servicing companies, ten truck lines, twenty-three well-drilling contractors, and twenty-one trucking contractors in 1938. One oil-well supply company can be seen in figure 4.1. Another twenty-eight trailer camps

FIGURE 4.1. 1942 image of an oil well supply company building in Odessa, Texas. Photo courtesy of the Library of Congress Prints and Photographs Division.

and twenty-nine oil camps were located in surrounding Ector County.[12] In the early 1940s, this required more well drilling at what came to be called Rosedale Wells and another fifteen water wells at Wadley Well Field in far-northeast Midland. Such development meant that Odessa and Midland were no longer simply waypoints or boomtowns. They instead contained the diversified business networks of established cities, with tract housing, shopping centers, and cultural amenities.[13]

All of this required water. According to one period report, "The individual living in a typical Texas city needs an average of about 100 gallons of water daily."[14] Case in point—annual water usage in Odessa increased from 206,600,000 gallons in 1938 to 1,403,950,000 gallons twelve years later. Citizens in Odessa were asked to ration water during the summer, and complete city well depletion was announced in the local papers.[15]

Despite municipal efforts to find more water, the problem only got worse after the war. Fred Hogan was an oil speculator and real estate developer made famous for his contributions to the downtown Midland skyline in the 1920s. He retained local celebrity and, in 1942, he was elected president of the venerable Midland Country Club, established in 1924.[16] An avid regional booster, Hogan traveled often to Houston and Dallas to secure investors for Midland ventures. He served as the mayor of Midland from 1946 to 1947—just in time to lead the city through the first of many postwar water crises.

In the late 1940s, both Midland and Odessa still subsisted almost completely on well water. Hogan Park was the showpiece in Hogan's plan to augment the city's unreliable wells. However, the water problems were cumulative. As the water table lowered due to the extensive use, the minerals and salt common to the region seeped in, contaminating the water that was left. A similar problem occurred in local rivers. According to one 1947 report, "Salt pollution is particularly bad on the upper reaches of the Colorado and the Pecos [rivers]."[17] As a result, attempts to rely on local groundwater were only a stopgap. The city kept growing, and the oil industry kept needing more and more water. This problem was complex and cumulative. Hogan expanded the local bureaucracy. He set up a city manager system, in part to coordinate water logistics as local officials appealed to the legislature for dam-building funds.[18]

Because there was no surface water near the city that could be dammed, Odessa officials turned to the Colorado River, three hundred miles to the east in Borden County. Beginning in 1946, they proposed a plan to dam the Colorado River north of the town of Colorado City, as well as to construct a reservoir that would supply water to a network of key Permian Basin oil cities, including Midland, through a series of pipelines. According to the 1946 application, the dam was to be 2,400 feet long. It would impound 110,000 acre-feet of water and create a lake surface of 4,400 acres.[19]

This was a massive industrial undertaking. But it was par for the course in a region that had seen an influx of oil rigs, tanks farms, and the McCamey Pit. In 1946, a coalition of five Permian Basin cities (Colorado City, Big Spring, Snyder, Odessa, and Midland) officially submitted a plan to the Texas Board of Water Engineers for water rights on the upper Colorado River. The efforts were spearheaded by Julien J. B. Thomas, the chief engineer for the Big Spring Texas Electric Service Company, the utilities provider for Big Spring, along with D. A. Bandeen, manager of the West Texas Chamber of Commerce, and M. C. Ulmer of Midland, president of the group that would come to be called the Colorado River Municipal Water Association (CRMWA).[20] Thomas was a former engineer for Texas Power and Light Company (TP and L), a Dallas-based electricity monopoly that merged with the Texas Electric Service Company in 1945. TP and L had experience with several central Texas dam projects during the Depression and hoped that the dam could produce hydroelectricity.

As they waited for approval, drought parched Texas in 1947 and exacerbated widespread concern about resource scarcity. Massive urban migration to cities such as Dallas, Houston, San Angelo, and Corpus Christi stressed municipal water systems across the state. The water supplies of these cities had been stabilized by successive dam projects in the 1910s and 1920s in North and Central Texas and was further augmented during the Depression through the creation of Lake Texoma, Morris Sheppard Reservoir, and the many Lower Colorado River Authority (LCRA) dams on the Colorado River.[21] However, the rapid increase in urban populations postwar was coupled with the rise of irrigated farming, which according to one critic meant that "dry-land farms have become lush orchards and truck farms."[22]

Some began discussing creative alternatives. In 1947, one commentator in the *Austin Statesman* ominously announced, "Sewage May Be One Answer to State's Water Shortage," and described efforts in Midland and other West Texas cities to use water from a sewage treatment plant to irrigate "feed crops and cotton." In a rare display of environmental concern, Dr. George W. Cox of the Texas State Health Office cited the pollution, not just the depletion, of surface water as a particular problem: "Texas this year had the worst drought in more than a decade in which the rationing of water in numerous towns brought home . . . the alarming fact that Texas does not have an adequate water supply. With a shortage of water, the situation has been made more critical in recent years by the dumping of sewage into clear streams, polluting those sources of water beyond human use."[23] Cox proposed that any "new industries coming to the state, each requiring huge quantities of water," use sewage instead of potential drinking water. He argued that "the future of Texas's economy lies in the proper utilization of every drop of its unpolluted surface water supply."[24] However, before serious effort was put into reclamation, the drought was busted in the spring of 1947 with torrential flooding. In May, even arid Odessa received five inches of rain. The *Austin Statesman* reported, with a palpable sigh of relief, that "Homer Morre, a small boats salesman[,] took friends on cruises through the [Odessa] commercial area."[25] Midland received two inches of rain in May and another quarter inch of rain in October.[26]

Of course, one rainy season did not solve the problems posed by a growing population and scarce resources. The push for dam construction continued. The legislature and federal officials were reluctant to fund the project. Thomas, Ulmer, and the CRMWA sought the support of Texas governor Beuford Jester, member of the TRRC and a former oil industry lawyer. Jester was no stranger to the water needs of oil production, and he signed legislation for a bond issue in 1949. In turn, the formation of the Colorado River Municipal Water District (CRMWD) was approved by the legislature that same year and construction began. Nevertheless, both Midland and Odessa again faced extreme water shortages in 1950. As one commentator in the *Odessa American* put it in 1950, "A city cannot grow beyond its water supply."[27] Few were interested in such warnings.

Conversations about both urban growth and water supply continued in the Texas legislature into the early 1950s. Perhaps unsurprisingly, subsequent efforts to build water infrastructure were stymied by budgetary concerns and regional infighting. However, even less expensive water conservation or coordination efforts were further complicated by Texas's historically anemic approach to regulation, which was singularly focused on protecting private property rights. The Texas Board of Water Engineers, the first statewide organization to manage water, was a Progressive-era, agrarian holdover founded in 1913 to negotiate surface water rights among Texas farmers. Throughout the 1910s and 1920s, the Board of Water Engineers promoted coordination among landowners and helped to form a variety of conservation and reclamation districts.[28] Like the TRRC, the Board of Water Engineers was most concerned with protecting small landowners from resource monopoly. And, also like the TRRC, it was ill equipped to help manage a large-scale water supply crisis.

Signaling the beginning of a new, more intensive regulatory era, the legislature in 1945 tasked the Texas Department of Health with enforcing drinking water standards for all public water supplies. In 1948, an eighty-person advisory council met in Austin to fully revise the Texas Water Code, dividing jurisdiction between ground and surface water. Representatives from all major cities were in attendance, including lawyer William L. Kerr of Midland. Although the representatives described the old water code as a "dinosaur," they were unable to develop a satisfactory new plan.[29] Ultimately, a 1949 Texas Supreme Court ruling mandated that all Texas groundwater would be regulated in a system very similar to oil—surface owners could do what they would with the groundwater beneath their land, regardless of the consequences for adjacent properties.[30]

Surface water would be subject to an array of municipal and legal agreements. In 1953, the Texas legislature created the Texas Water Pollution Control Advisory Council as part of the health department. This was Texas's first state-level organization to address pollution, but it maintained a light touch. Water quality control remained largely up to individuals and municipalities through the 1950s. In 1957, the legislature formed the Texas Water Development Board to forecast water-supply needs and fund water-supply and conservation projects.[31] Crucially, its largest task during the 1950s was mediating disputes among communities and finding ways to increase the water supply for municipalities.[32]

Oil producers, then, underwent little state scrutiny when securing their water needs. This was convenient for Permian Basin industrial expansion. However, this also put further local pressure on the Permian Basin's limited groundwater after the discovery of the massive, interconnected Spraberry-Dean oil fields in 1950.

The discovery had been predicted during the war. As early as 1944, a multitude of Permian Basin oil scouts, drillers, landmen, and geologists agreed that the Spraberry contained significant oil deposits.[33] However, the oil was trapped in tightly packed, subsurface sand. This made drilling slow and, paralleling the 1920s and 1930s, too expensive to extract.[34] In 1948, Magnolia, Humble, the small, independent Tex-Harvey Oil Company, and others made new oil discoveries in West Texas and far eastern New Mexico, confirming the extent of the Spraberry Field.[35] While these initial wells did not produce much oil, Humble Oil, the Republic Natural Gas Company, and an array of small producers hit large oil deposits in Midland, Reagan, and Upton counties in 1950 and 1951, confirming that the Spraberry and adjacent Dean fields encompassed a connected series of oil deposits stretching southeast from Andrews County, on the New Mexico border, to the northern edge of Crockett County, south of San Angelo.[36] However, the majority of the field's oil was located less than twenty miles northeast of the Midland city limits.[37]

Oil in the Spraberry-Dean Field was deep underground, with an average well depth ranging from 5,100 to 8,300 feet—a startling 1,000 feet deeper than the average US oil well at the time.[38] This affected its development in a variety of ways. While the massive size of the Spraberry-Dean produced exclamations of untold riches in the local press, ongoing production challenges meant that the discovery had a more modest profit margin for individual leaseholders. Due to its depth, drilling costs in the Spraberry-Dean were high, on average $125,000 per well and twice the national average.[39] Therefore, with oil prices low throughout the decade, only larger independents and major oil companies could realistically afford to drill in the Spraberry. Historians have documented how the problem of rising costs hit the entire industry during this period, leaving small operations struggling.[40] This encouraged industry consolidation as larger independents and majors used new technologies such as gas injection and well flooding. It also spurred the development of new, more specialized oil detection methods.

Workers in these larger, more technical operations lived in Midland and Odessa and depended on the cities' limited water resources. In 1940, the Midland population was only 9,352, so the city was not yet a truly urban hub. However, boosters proudly announced in 1949, one year before the nearby Spraberry discovery, that the population had jumped to 27,700, "due largely to oil company expansion."[41] As this swiftly growing population put further pressure on local water, the CRMWD announced in 1951 that, despite a lengthy back-and-forth over funding between Texas representatives and

Congress, they had instead fully funded the dam project through the sale of $11.8 million in bonds.[42] The construction company J. W. Moorman and Son began work swiftly in March. This could not happen soon enough, and cities in the region continued to search for alternative water sources. In 1951, Midland joined other Permian Basin cities in building experimental desalination plants to purify brackish local groundwater.[43] Odessa and Big Spring were still experiencing water shortages and rationing in 1952. That year, the CRMWD constructed thirteen new water wells and built pipelines snaking south from Martin County to ailing Permian Basin communities. The CRMWD dam project was finally completed in July 1952, and filling began. The new Colorado River Dam created Lake J. B. Thomas on the estate of the Conrad Ranch.[44] Local officials proudly announced that it had been completed without either federal assistance or state tax dollars.

However, instead of relieving pressure from either oil operators or city residents, the new dam and pipelines system only facilitated increased water usage. The combined populations of both Midland and Odessa had exploded between 1950 and 1960, increasing approximately 172 percent over a ten-year period.[45] Midland alone saw the most growth, with the population increasing 300 percent over the same period.[46] While Midland was increasingly a single-industry city, such development presented speculative real estate opportunities for oilmen with money to invest. However, almost immediately, the combined pressures of increased water usage and oil production reignited the water problem. Similar to efforts in the 1930s, attempts at financial risk reduction produce a spiraling cycle of ever-growing resource use. Many turned to financial mechanisms to shield themselves from risk, as oil's environmental risks remained high and a dependence on natural resources continued to undergird the regional economy. Such risk-reducing development would have been impossible without the construction of new dams and water wells throughout the region, which were constructed with the investment help of oil producers, who in turn needed to increase oil production to pay their debts. This system was perhaps exemplified by Midland's self-imposed nickname, "Oil's Wall Street."[47]

Significantly, oil and real estate speculator and Midland mayor Fred Hogan rode Midland's wave from oil boomtown to established city. Born in the mining town of Butte, Montana, Hogan searched for oil in California and New Mexico before arriving in the Permian Basin in 1924. With his wealthy and well-connected father, former Anaconda Mine employee and

Montana state senator Thomas Hogan, Fred became a regional promoter and land speculator. In 1928, the duo financed the twelve-story, brick Art Deco Hogan Building (later renamed the Petroleum Building) in downtown Midland. The Hogan Building immediately surpassed several long-term-rental hotels as Midland's tallest structure. Hogan planned to lease office space to arriving oil companies, but his timing was not ideal. West Texas land speculation was a losing proposition during the Depression. Although the Hogan Building sat vacant through the early 1930s, office leases boomed again after World War II.

Such cycles of boom and bust did not end for land speculators in the postwar era. However, there were key differences. Local property developers still relied on regional banks but also often sought national or international investors. While they continued to accept the industry's financial volatility and used diversified investment to hedge against price fluctuations, speculative profits were to be made by 1950 on rents on housing and large-scale commercial construction rather than through secondary lot sales and wholesale town sites. During this heady era of expansion, Permian Basin civic leaders behaved as if environmental limits—including both water scarcity and oil depletion—could be optimized out of existence through dams, pipelines, and other infrastructures.

In such a context, the city's wave of new multiblock office complexes were both necessary to shelter a growing white-collar workforce and status symbols that projected confidence in the industry's longevity. Midland's downtown was a monument to oil wealth, and it only expanded over the course of the next decade. In 1947, the same year that city officials presented the dam project to the Texas legislature, local news reports excitedly reported that J. W. Bateson of Dallas had signed a $556,800 contract to build a new ten-story office building in Midland, "one of the biggest office buildings between Fort Worth and El Paso." Contracted by real estate investor Bert Cole Jr., he named it the "Midland Tower" after construction ended in 1948. These reports opined that he leased the spaces out immediately to become the "oil company headquarters for five major oil companies."[48] It was soon joined by the First National Bank Building, built in 1952, and the Petroleum Life Building.

While breathless, the local press coverage did mark a real and dramatic change to the previously dusty town. By 1950, approximately 250 oil companies leased offices in Midland, and these numbers only grew.[49] In 1955,

Midland housed approximately 370 oil production and shipping companies, and the cluster of massive steel and marble structures in downtown was home to the majority of the city's seventy-eight geologists, as well as the region's largest oil companies.[50] Of West Texas cities in the 1950s, only Lubbock and Abilene also supported a single building above fifteen stories.[51] By the late 1950s, even though the city's population remained below 60,000, Midland housed eight skyscrapers and over two million square feet of office space.[52] These numbers continued to increase into the next decade.

Such massive construction allowed real estate speculators to build local empires, with power similar to the largest oil leaseholders. For example, local rancher Jack B. Wilkinson branched out into commercial construction in the late 1950s to build three of the tallest buildings in Midland, including the six-story Wilkinson Foster Building and the fourteen-story V & J Tower. Wilkinson's namesake, the Wilco Building, was designed by the prolific Abilene architect Dan Boone and was completed in 1958. At twenty-two floors, it was the tallest building in West Texas until 1970. By 1960, Wilkinson owned—and leased out—one-third of all office space in the city.

Wilkinson did not see this construction boom as excessive, saying, "Pretty soon Midland was the headquarters of the Independent oil man in Texas. During the fifties almost every square foot of space was rented, so we built more offices. People said we were over-building, but that wasn't the case. Almost every building made money for its investors. It was hard to go wrong in Midland."[53] For a time, Wilkinson was proved correct. A decade later, the number of oil companies in Midland doubled again, reaching over 650 in 1964.[54]

Surrounded by new parking lots and the wide cars of new oil money, such construction intentionally demonstrated the oil industry's importance to Midland and, by extension, Midland's importance to the regional economy. It was the industry hub in which important business deals were made, extraction quotas were negotiated, and oil scientists, engineers, and surveyors delivered their reports. Midland's large, vertically oriented downtown skyline indicated industry permanence and prosperity, and city leaders cultivated the city's connections to oil's commodity marketers and logistical industries. City boosters smoothed the way for new arrivals with a wave of municipal advertising.

Illustrating the city's dominance and the region's characteristically flat, treeless terrain, according to the Texas State Historical Association,

Midland's city center could be seen for "thirty miles in any direction."[55] As early as 1947 and throughout the 1950s, at least one Midland baseball team was named the Skyscrapers.[56] The July/August 1965 issue of *TP Voice*, the company magazine of the Texas and Pacific Oil Company, described Midland as the "Capital of the Permian Basin" and boasted that it housed the "tallest building between Fort Worth and Los Angeles." The Midland Chamber of Commerce, oil companies, and the regional press often used this anecdote in promotional materials, calling Midland the "tall city" to demonstrate its growing sophistication and regional importance.[57]

SUBURBAN SECURITY

For the industry's geologists, engineers, surveyors, lawyers, and other workers, the rise of suburban developments in Midland and neighboring Odessa represented an economic stability that had never existed in the region before. Similarly, for the developers of these new neighborhoods, environmental risks like resource scarcity could seemingly be optimized out of existence. Such stability belied the reality of a finite oil supply and historically unpredictable global commodity prices. It also flew in the face of ongoing region-wide water shortages, perhaps ominously signified by the image of a Midland home with a kitchen garden precariously maintained by a private windmill system in figure 4.2. Against such a backdrop, the families and individuals buying new homes were participating in a new but swiftly growing form of American risk reduction, in which the home itself became a source of investment income. While such risk management did not free homebuyers from the realities of environmental risk, it did provide a potential stepping stone to diversified wealth.

During the 1950s, oil workers experienced broad changes in the structure of American business. During this period, the white-collar workforce ballooned and large corporations assumed a greater role in American political, social, and economic life. Walking back concessions made by federal authorities to industrial unions in the 1930s, these corporations, exemplified by the largest American oil companies, employed more and more people in white-collar office jobs. To attract credentialed employees, Texaco, Standard Oil of California, Standard Oil of New Jersey, and others took over an array of services analogous to the federal social safety net put in place during the Depression. They heavily advertised lavish benefits that

FIGURE 4.2. 1939 Russell Lee photograph of a house in Midland, Texas. The residents used an individual windmill and private well to furnish water for the yard, garden, and flowers. Photo courtesy of the Library of Congress Prints and Photographs Division.

included paid vacation time, health insurance, home mortgage discounts, and life insurance coverage. Such packages were explicit union busters that drowned out the old outcry of monopoly with the seeming stability of cradle-to-grave employment.[58] Such corporate paternalism inspired employee loyalty. It also reinforced a growing national focus on very long-term planning and dovetailed with the postwar rise of the American middle-class use of financial mechanisms to avoid risk.

The property insurance and hazard insurance industries expanded rapidly during this era. With the rise of postwar suburbia, the single-family home was marketed as an important financial investment that provided security and respectability for growing nuclear families. According to builders, the insurance industry, and the federal agencies that subsidized many postwar mortgages, this key investment had to be protected from losing its value. As a result, the expanding ranks of the American middle class used the predictability of annual or quarterly insurance payments to shield themselves from seemingly unpredictable environmental dangers such as fire or flood. Crucially, compensation in the event of such disasters was a monetary payment, and like the Progressive-era actuaries who put a numeric value on workers' health, home insurance companies assigned predictive values to families' most intimate possessions. Other mechanisms, including homeowners' associations, national zoning laws, property insurance, and mortgage systems, were together designed to reduce the financial risk of owning property. Mortgages were easy to get, and federal loans helped ease cash-poor people into relationships with banks. In a process that would become explicit later in the century, such mechanisms tacitly encouraged Americans to understand their homes as long-term investments—as sources of future liquidity that needed to be maintained and protected to hold equity in advance of their eventual sale.[59]

As home risk assessment and household safety campaigns were promoted during this period by organizations from the Federal Civil Defense Administration to the State Farm Insurance Agency, systemic public health problems such as water pollution and broad-scale economic dangers like oil depletion sat uneasily within narratives of industrially optimized risk reduction and an individualized system of asset accumulation. What should be done if the extractive processes that provided the economic incentive for suburban expansion hurt the value of the homes that people were encouraged to buy as investments? How could individuals be expected to both accept their vulnerability in a locally volatile resource economy and benefit from a national trend toward stable, single-family investment? In practice, it is doubtful that many people explicitly asked themselves such questions. However, things were clearly changing, and oil with it.

After World War II, the United States entered a national housing crisis. Developers built swaths of tract housing to rapidly boost the supply of single-family homes. Texas was no exception. In the late 1940s, it experienced a building boom, addressing a statewide housing shortage. For example, in one week in February 1947, Texas builders constructed 574 homes that cost less than $7,000 apeice.[60] As in the 1920s, many new homebuyers were migrating to the oil fields to take advantage of the industry's high wages and guaranteed employment. This time, however, many of the lucrative oil jobs were white collar, as national oil companies sent representatives and management personnel to staff their newly expanded offices in Midland office towers. They were joined by a wave of returning GIs, many of them single men from other parts of Texas and the United States, either contracted by large oil companies or independently looking for work in the oil fields. These workers were paid even better than the already high industry average.[61]

Statistics illustrate this change. Permian Basin wages remained well above the state average during the 1950s, and as extraction and processing efforts expanded, regional employment consistently hit 95 percent.[62] In 1949, the median Midland family income was $4,200, higher than the national average, and would only increase during the next decade. According to a 1957 interview with the manager of the Texas Employment Commission, more than half of Midland's workforce was employed either directly in oil or in adjacent industries, and 35 percent of Odessa's labor force was engaged directly in oil production.[63] By 1959, median family income had risen to $7,100, significantly higher than any other city in Texas, including neighboring Odessa.[64] Even after oil extraction slowed again in the mid-1960s, new people continued to be attracted by the oil industry's high wages, which, averaged at $6,279 per year in 1965, was over $2,000 higher than the state average.[65] While the median income in Odessa rose more slowly between 1950 and 1960, Midland had the highest average per-household consumer income in the state by 1965, at over $8,000.[66] These wages, and oil employees' ability to pay mortgages on new homes, depended on the stability and longevity of oil production. Oil money transformed formerly itinerant oil workers into propertied homeowners—long-term investors worried about asset appreciation. As in the 1930s, drilling could not stop. Therefore, the water could not run out.

According to one blustering 1949 article in the *Austin Statesman*, "Oil has probably caused more spectacular growth among Texas cities than any other force." The author cites the spectacular postwar growth in Snyder and Colorado City, oil boomtowns.[67] Midland oil workers used their new affluence to achieve the postwar American suburban dream. And cheap land, postwar innovations in prefabricated housing, and regional speculation in single-family-home construction meant that many middle-income oil workers were quickly able to afford their own single-family homes.

Midland's city center was built on a nineteenth-century grid pattern, creating a square footprint bisected by what would become Interstate 20. And in the immediate aftermath of the 1950 Spraberry discovery, the city could not avoid logistical chaos, which was strikingly similar to previous booms.

In the tradition of the haphazard shelters constructed at 1920s drill sites or the temporary boarding houses of 1930s McCamey, freshly arrived oil workers in Odessa, Midland, and other oil towns lived in rented trailers, campers, and hotels. The Midland city government attempted to regulate growth, developing the "Midland City Plan, 1950," which emphasized the city's "charm and individuality" and focused specifically on the quick expansion of single-family, residential subdivisions for the swelling population.[68]

Such a focus reflected both rising worker expectations and new technologies. Rather than temporary lodging, workers desired and expected private homes with space for their families. Further, expanded regional roads and the postwar ubiquity of car ownership made it possible for oil drillers and well service personnel to live in town with their families and commute to drilling sites instead of living in worker apartments, trailer parks, or company-funded work camps. Even further, for workers, the choice to buy homes reflected an assumption that the industry would survive in the region long enough for the single-family home to become a risk-reducing financial asset.

Indicative of these trends, postwar suburban development was developer led and reshaped the city map. In the late 1940s and early 1950s, contractors built hundreds of small, two-bedroom houses just west of downtown. These homes sold for $8,000 to $12,000—priced strategically at what an average oil-field worker could afford, but about $1,000 more expensive than the Texas average for an entry-level home.[69] Developers made a tidy profit. Builders broke ground on the Permian Estates neighborhood during this period, a neighborhood with homes ranging in size from 700 to around 1,600 square feet. These early- and mid-1950s ranch-style homes were built with either wood siding or brick veneer, and they sat on curved, suburban streets surrounding a park named for local sheep rancher and early Midland businessman Zachary Taylor Brown. The houses induced basic amenities like interior wood paneling, fireplaces, and front porches. Such home construction was lucrative, and local developers were excited to cash in. Case in point—before Jack B. Wilkinson began speculating in Midland skyscrapers, he invested in residential construction in the early 1950s.

Wealthier, white-collar industry employees such as engineers, geologists, and surveyors also bought new homes in Midland during this period. During the mid-1950s, many of these wealthier families built custom homes on the city's northwest side. Reflecting midcentury trends, Midland housing developments including Wilshire Park, Urbandale, and Club Estates were filled with winding, parklike streets by the end of the decade, with homes that boasted amenities such as two-car garages, air conditioning, wall-to-wall carpeting, draperies, and yard fencing.[70] A 1955 and 1956 dip in oil prices led to a slowdown in Midland population growth. However, residential speculation remained good business. Local contractors continued to build new homes, especially larger three-bedroom homes on the city's northwest side. With the population stagnant in the late 1950s, residential prices dropped later in the decade. However, with residents looking to cash in on their initial investments, this only led to a renewed wave of home buying. Many middle-income families took the opportunity to upgrade into even larger homes. A trend in home upgrades peaked in 1959 as the US Census reported that a full 43 percent of Midland's population moved into new accommodations.[71]

However, only some residents had access to such mobility. Like most midcentury Texas cities, Midland housing development was governed by de facto segregation, which limited the economic and physical mobility of nonwhite residents, who in 1960 made up approximately 10 percent of the local population.[72] The city's Black and Hispanic residents lived in a secluded neighborhood called "The Flats," south of the railroad tracks. City directories from the period illustrate a growing Hispanic community of several hundred people.[73] However, schools were segregated, and until 1946, these Hispanic residents were barred from attending school past the eighth grade.[74]

Segregation also limited economic mobility. In an oral history interview, one former resident remembered her father and uncle working as laborers in the oil fields near Odessa: "I am not going to say that [Hispanic] opportunities have been as great to move up as they have for others. For the most part, [Hispanics] are going to be involved in the labor-type jobs."[75] In 1959, the median income for African American families was $3,489, about half that of a white Midland family.[76] These residents were employed as semiskilled machine operators, laborers, or service workers, or they worked in private homes. While some probably worked oil jobs, a full 60 percent of Midland's Black population worked in personal service, while another 22 percent worked in the wholesale and retail trades.[77] Perennially low wages were reflected in neighborhood housing. A 1962 Princeton study described very poor conditions in most Flats homes, which contrasted

FIGURE 4.3. In 1939 Russell Lee photographed the economic disparity between Midland's affluent downtown in the distance and the city's segregated Hispanic neighborhood in the foreground. Photo courtesy of the Library of Congress Prints and Photographs Division.

starkly with the suburban, white neighborhoods to the north. The Flats was made up of "two-and three-room shacks, frequently lacking some or all standard plumbing facilities." As can be seen in figure 4.3, roads were not paved, and water quality was an ongoing public health problem.[78]

However, the housing boom of the late 1950s and early 1960s also affected Flats residents. As the postwar boom slowed and the Midland population flatlined, Midland realtors became desperate to unload their excess inventory. As wealthy whites moved into larger homes farther west, older, smaller homes nearer the city center were left available. Some were abandoned altogether. Most of the vacancies were concentrated in some of the oldest residential areas, on the eastern side of town just north of the Flats. In 1959, one report estimated that approximately 1,100 of these smaller homes simply sat empty. Over the next decade, boom turned into bust, and nonwhite families moved into these homes, expanding the existing Black neighborhood.[79] For many Flats residents, this movement north was a strategic step up. However, this history of segregation reveals clear cracks in Midland oil boosters' facade of universal affluence. By the late 1950s, the continued municipal search for water would reveal other breaks in the narrative.

Changes to the Midland landscape were mirrored across other new suburban enclaves in the US South and West, as lax regulation and access to cheap natural resources attracted a growing number of industries.[80] In Midland, homebuilders largely disregarded the limits of the local environment when designing new neighborhoods and homes, installing water-intensive lawns, pools, and golf courses in a region famed for its arid climate. And, in a story similar to the growing pains of other Southwest extractive cities such as Phoenix or El Paso, water would continue to be a pivot point that strained the ability of local leaders to ignore, finance, or optimize all environmental risks.[81] Compounding the problem in Texas, there was little local or state coordination or planning for how best to address municipal water issues, aside from continued well creation. State and local water agencies had little enforcement power, and local political leaders were reluctant to implement water quotas or to fine either businesses or individuals for overconsumption.

The sole state agency tasked with addressing water issues, the Texas Board of Water Engineers, offered little practical advice, but it did point out in a 1952 report that urban development put new strain on the Permian Basin's scarcest resource.[82] Still, city officials seemed determined to prove such protestations wrong. Midland's high-rise construction and ballooning water storage facilities grew in tandem. For example, the First National Bank of Midland completed construction on a new three-story bank building in 1953, just as the city opened the McMillen Water Well Field, which could pump up to 4.5 million gallons of water per day. That same year, the *New York Times* announced in 1953 that the city of Midland was selling over three million dollars' worth of water revenue bonds for further water and sewer improvement.[83]

Seemingly successful in their bid for funding, over the next decade, Midland built two five-million-gallon, in-ground storage tanks and a one-million-gallon elevated storage tower at the McMillen site and constructed yet another one-million-gallon tower, centrally located on Shell and Midland drives. Just three years later, in 1956, the city announced the discovery of a vast water field north of Midland, in Marlin County on University Fund Lands. Representatives from the city estimated that "the area is capable of producing an average of 20 million gallons of water a day."[84] However, this was seemingly insufficient because the *Wall Street Journal* advertised in 1957 that Midland city voters had approved yet another plan to market bonds worth $3.9 million in water system revenue to further expand their water infrastructure.[85] The city began drilling the Paul Davis Well Field in the late 1950s, which included another two 2.5-million-gallon ground storage tanks and a new pump system.[86]

In tandem with such furious expansion, the First National Bank completed yet another high-rise addition in 1959. The latest building's sleek, modernist facade stood proudly above Midland's largest, water-intensive golf-course suburbs and seemingly represented a new level of constructed permanence for an industry and regional economy historically plagued by boom-and-bust uncertainty.[87] One 1959 article excitedly noted the quickly growing populations in both Midland and Odessa. However, some evidence of the water problem infiltrated even the most ardent boosters. The otherwise excited author ended by noting, "Although water is a problem . . . the cities feel they can take care of future needs."[88] Belying such excitement, the new McMillen Well Field would last less than a decade and was fully depleted by the mid-1960s.[89]

As this history indicates, the transformation of West Texas towns like Midland from itinerant and makeshift work camps to sprawling suburban metropolises was a self-conscious projection of affluence that belied the region's environmental limitations. Helping residents ignore these constraints were local developers who channeled growing taxes into amenities and infrastructure that the Midland Chamber of Commerce promoted heavily. The Midland Memorial Hospital and public recreational area Hogan Park opened to much fanfare in 1950. Between 1950 and 1960, the well-funded Midland School District built sixteen new schools to more than double the district's capacity.[90] The Midland Chamber of Commerce and industry boosters linked such suburban construction to the city's growing gentility and sophistication. They heavily publicized the construction of "respectable" community amenities. For example, the local press proudly announced the founding of the Midland Symphony Orchestra in 1953, and in 1956, Midland County constructed a two-story city library. The Midland Community Theater built a new playhouse in 1958, advertising heavily in the local paper.[91] Other city development was heavily publicized as demonstrating Midland's measured, ordered growth and increasing good taste. Between 1955 and 1960, the number of churches listed in the Midland city directory increased from fifty-seven to eighty-two.[92]

WELL INJECTION AND RESOURCE DEPLETION

In the short term, oil production clearly provided many locals with individual wealth and community growth. The local industry was vital to the national economy, and despite protestations of looming resource depletion, the Permian Basin continued to deliver. During the 1950s, the Permian Basin became the most important domestic oil producer in the United States. By 1955, the region led the world in total feet of speculative drilling per year.[93] In 1958, over 40 percent of all Texas oil came from the Permian Basin.[94] That same year, the region ranked second in total American oil production and third in the world.[95] And it was very clear to municipal leaders that Midland's high employment, influx of investment wealth, and steady flow of residential construction depended on a stable oil industry. Similarly, oil companies that invested in Midland pipelines, storage depots, and office space knew that such development represented sunk cost risks.

In the longer term, to avoid the total collapse of the local economy, oil companies needed to guarantee that they could make oil depletion predictable. Since the 1910s, under financial pressures to reduce waste and guarantee long-term production, oil companies had turned to water-intensive technological solutions to keep oil wells pumping. In the 1950s, they used a combination of new unitization regulations and organizational agreements to expand water flooding and well injection operations, guaranteeing the supply of one resource by putting yet more pressure on another.

A settled well that was nearing the end of its life was colloquially called a "stripper well" because the goal was to strip the last drop of oil from it. By the mid-1950s, most active Permian Basin wells were stripper wells. As these oil wells were depleted, well pipes became flooded with salt brine water that had leached into oil deposits from nearby salt domes.[96] For most of the twentieth century, the solution to this problem was to pump the invading saltwater out of the ground and let it run unobstructed through the surrounding desert, covering miles of desert vegetation with a thick, frostlike crust. As plant life died and was blown away, the lack of ground cover left an eerie, bleached moonscape that was unsuitable for either commercial ranching or human habitation. This was a particular problem in the Hendricks Field. As early as 1929, only 6 of its 565 wells were producing without gushing saltwater.[97] Such wells were high cost and produced low profits. This gave them, individually, a low priority for most oil companies. However, unitization of these stripper wells increased the effectiveness of secondary recovery systems, especially well injection, that reduced the presence of invading saltwater and increased profits.

A legal definition for "unitization" is "the consolidation of mineral or leasehold interests covering all or part of a common source of supply."[98] In lay terms, that meant the designation of a single company as the operating manager for an entire deposit of oil, regardless of surface property lines or previous mineral lease agreements. This designated company directed all extraction and maintenance efforts in a field with all parties collectively agreeing to a percentage of the total profits. Proponents argued that unitization allowed well managers to better maintain well pressure across an entire oil deposit, extending the life of the field as a whole. Scholars have shown that such agreements encouraged period trends toward industry consolidation.[99] After the chaos of the 1930s, however, a growing number of engineers and landmen argued that surface property boundaries were meaningless underground, as fluid mechanics guaranteed that drilling in one part of an oil deposit had negative impacts on drilling efforts in another part.[100] For these groups, unitization was the best option to slow depletion by ensuring even well spacing and a fair division of profits. Such a pragmatic understanding of natural resource management was built from decades of research.

The best way to preserve subsurface well pressure was a question that had puzzled oil engineers and scientists for decades. In 1913, geologists understood that well spacing was critical to maintaining well pressure and drillers used pumps to create suction.[101] One of the earliest methods, first attempted in 1915, was a process ominously called "blowing" a well with compressed air. Former Oklahoma driller James Delaplain explained that he quickly discontinued blowing wells in 1924 at the Seminole Field: "Then they found pretty soon that [blowing a well] was kind of dangerous so they changed to gas, and they recycled the gas then and we produced some natural gasoline that way with the compression and pooling of the gas as we recycled it." Blowing wells fell out of favor nationally by 1927, due in part to its potential for explosion.[102] However, it was clear that some kind of material was needed to maintain suction and drive oil up well pipes.

In a 1927 pamphlet written for the American Petroleum Institute (API), Hugh S. Taylor of Princeton University described the principles of well pressure and confirmed theories that injecting water into a well would boost the amount of oil captured.[103] That same year, the US Bureau of Mines and the API conducted an exhaustive survey of natural gas in oil wells across the country. In a 1929 report, the bureau concluded that management of subsurface natural gas deposits played a key role in maintaining well pressure and again confirmed that water or air injected at high pressure could be used as an alternative if needed.[104]

Although its origins date to the overproduction debates of the late 1920s, unitization paired with well flooding became increasingly popular in the postwar era. Oklahoma put in place the first mandatory unitization law in 1945, and as early as 1947, some in Texas called for a similar system, citing massive oil waste in West Texas. For example, Houston petroleum engineer William J. Murray investigated the Yates Field and reportedly found leaks in an estimated twenty wells on University Lands, saying that "30 million barrels of oil have already been lost."[105] Murray attempted to gain support for a University of Texas study to demonstrate the need for fieldwide conservation plans. However, ever concerned about the waning power of small oil companies, the Texas legislature did not legalize unitization until 1949.

Despite initial ambivalence, the Permian Basin immediately led the state in voluntary unitization agreements.[106] Between 1949 and 1952, eight unitization agreements were submitted by large oil companies in the Permian Basin, including Gulf, Atlantic Oil, Stanolind, and Cities Services. All were approved by the TRRC.[107] A 1952 annual report from the Wichita, Kansas–based Vickers Petroleum, described using both water and gas injection in combination to direct subsurface oil to desired extraction points.[108] Vickers advertised both water and gas as incredibly cheap, easily accessible resources. According to Vickers, the natural gas used in well injection was simply the recycled by-product of oil extraction, and water was infinitely renewable. Echoing this perspective, the TRRC in 1953 combined many of the small fields in the Spraberry-Dean into a single large entity called the Spraberry Trend. This unitized entity became the largest single-producing unit in the Spraberry-Dean Field, covering approximately 500,000 acres in Midland, Glasscock, Reagan, and Upton counties. Coordinated water flooding began quickly in Midland County amid ongoing fears about municipal water scarcity.

Such a singularly focused bid for industry stability reflected both Depression-era national pundits and postwar Texas water regulators who addressed supply-side, environmental risks as failures of resource management and technical problems that needed to be fixed. In this vein, American postwar energy policy continued to promote the centralized coordination of oil assets and infrastructure construction. Significantly, a federal attempt to seize control of Texas's offshore oil in the name of national security riled Texas politicians for the duration of the 1950s. Even as Texas legislators virulently opposed this effort, in an era of skyrocketing consumer demand, the TRRC enforced new production quotas that kept 1950s extraction levels well below maximum potential.[109] The TRRC restricted the number of days that oil producers could run wells and set a limit on the maximum daily rate of production for each well. However, the patchwork of lease agreements, land rights, and subcontractor contracts that made up the Texas oil economy made enforcing such quotas challenging at best. While often at odds, both federal and state regulators supported voluntary unitization as both more efficient and as a way to provide extractive stability within a nominally free market.

As a result, despite the language of resource conservation, unitization was not environmental stewardship. Well injection, the precursor to hydraulic fracturing, was a technological fix that created new problems even as it fixed others. The focus on subsurface geology required a lack of attention to the surface impact of drilling. For example, if wells in the Spraberry Trend began to underperform, operators drilled numerous well holes at strategic locations within the oil field. They then used high-pressure hoses to flood the subsurface oil reservoir with millions of gallons of salt brine, drilling mud, or natural gas at extremely high pressure. This boosted overall well pressure and extended oil production.[110] While better than using potable water, well injection using brine combined with drilling mud or chemicals only compounded the exposure of adjacent environments to toxic substances and put growing pressure on local groundwater and on the new reservoirs built by the CRMWD. It was also logistically complicated, requiring not just the transport of drilling equipment to isolated locations, but also the acquisition of water rights and then the transportation of millions of gallons of water and other fluids. This was very expensive, and therefore its growing popularity represented a clear sign of the industry's precarious position.

Despite the logistical difficulties, the promise of financial stability led many oil companies and rights holders, along with TRRC regulators, to approach water flooding as the obvious next step in what they described as the life cycle of Permian Basin oil wells. This put local oil producers, often residents of Midland and other water-scarce Permian Basin cities, into desperate competition for water with ranchers, local farmers, and their own local governments.[111]

In a pivotal example that illustrated the conflicted and at-times contradictory desires of industry and local officials, the Scurry Area Canyon Reef Oil Company, manager of the unitized, well injection-fueled Canyon Reef Oil Field, became the largest customer for the CRMWD 's Lake Thomas water. Well-injection operations began in the Canyon Reef Field in 1951, one year before the much touted reservoir was completed, and the operation used approximately 3.7 billion gallons of water per year.[112] A Texas Historical Marker, erected at the Reef Field in 1967, proudly explained that "the programs showed by 1955 that free American enterprise can work out voluntarily the most modern and efficient conservation procedures."[113] In an organizational history, the CRMWD proudly noted that the oil company paid very well for the water from Lake Thomas, pointing out that the partnerships allowed the CRMWD to discharge its bond issues years early.[114]

Similarly, in 1958, the Welch Field Engineering Committee, an organization that managed the Welch Field in Gaines and Dawson counties, south and east of Denver City, commissioned a report on the cost and effectiveness of water flooding. The report concluded that the fields should be unitized and water flooding should be applied to increase production significantly. Tellingly, the report noted that field managers would need to procure several million gallons of water to support the water-flooding program. It cautioned that the field had direct access to only a few shallow wells and would need to compete for water rights with local agriculturalists.[115] During the same period, numerous Permian Basin leaseholders commissioned local driller Caven J. "Red" Davidson and other drilling contractors to estimate the cost of water flooding on their holdings. Such estimates only became more popular in the early 1960s as speculative drilling slowed. For example, in 1962, Davidson and a committee of engineers gave similar recommendations to leaseholders in Crane County.[116] Pressure on local water was further augmented during this period by the growing water needs of small local refineries and, in the mid-1950s, by the construction of the Odessa Petrochemical Complex in Odessa, which consumed millions of gallons of water daily.

Indicating that unitization and well flooding were perceived as indicators of long-term stability, large national and international investors lined up to buy mineral rights in the unitized Spraberry-Dean Field throughout this period. Case in point—in 1952, the New Continental Oil Company of Canada purchased 2,880 acres and thirty-five producing wells in Midland and Glasscock counties for approximately $6 million.[117] Similarly, the Chase Manhattan Trust in 1957 bought mineral interests on 291 sections of ranch land (186,240 acres) straddling Ector and Midland counties. The land already had forty-three completed oil wells.[118]

The stark dichotomy between the economic success of unitization and well-flooding operations and the growing pressure on the region's water supply indicates the unavoidable tensions within municipal and state authorities' responses to oil industry risks during the 1950s. State leaders were slow to acknowledge that there was a need to regulate not just oil production in the name of profit preservation, but also the growing water needs of oil in the semiarid and drought-prone state. In the Permian Basin, three decades of largely unregulated oil production, followed by the increasing popularity of water flooding as a tactic, further depleted an already limited water supply. This was coupled with dramatic population growth, meaning that oil threatened the same suburban expansion that was supposed to provide a financial safety net for the industry's growing middle class.

Midland's oil economy both produced prosperity and trapped residents in a cycle of ever-intensifying resource use that sat uneasily against growing, national risk reduction systems based on consumer regulation, corporate paternalism, and the spread of large-scale banking at midcentury. In this context, the risks posed by water depletion, environmental contamination, and fundamental dependence on the acquisition of more and more oil could not be identified as deterrents to industry expansion. As a result, Permian Basin oil communities could not escape the limitations of this extractive industry, in which the risks and rewards posed by oil were addressed in economic terms even as community survival depended on addressing very physical and local environmental constraints.

Chapter Five

AN OILMAN IS NOT A UNION MAN

In 1963, the same year that the US Congress passed the first Clean Air Act, the Oil Chemical and Atomic Workers Union (OCAW) sent representatives to West Texas on a fact-finding mission. Hoping to expand union participation in the region, they made contact with workers at the Cosden Refinery in Big Spring, Texas, on the northeastern edge of the Permian Basin. The refinery can be seen in figure 5.1. The two-decade-old facility had recently been bought by American Petrofina, a subsidiary of the Belgian multinational.[1] Cosden Corporation produced gasoline, asphalt, plastics, and other petrochemicals, including polystyrene used in disposable food packaging. The company held multiple lucrative petrochemical patents.[2] Since 1956, Petrofina had been expanding its American holdings, buying the Panhandle Oil Company, headquartered to the east of the Permian Basin in Wichita Falls, and gasoline service stations throughout the region. In 1963, this moment of transition seemed like an opportunity for the OCAW. Union field notes from the trip listed eight members of the International Union of Operating Engineers (IUOE), Local 826, working at the plant; however the plant probably employed around one hundred people.[3] Representatives met with Alfred Goodson, a Big Spring resident since childhood and a longtime operator at the Cosden Refinery. He was the political force behind the IUOE in West Texas and had served as vice president of the American Federation of Labor in Texas for ten years.[4] Despite

FIGURE 5.1. Undated image of the Cosden Refinery. A sign standing in the foreground reads "Cosden Higher Octane Gasoline." Photo courtesy of the Petroleum Museum, Lee Jones Jr. Collection.

Goodson's vigorous leadership, his home union was anemic at best. Goodson signed an OCAW union card, but the OCAW abandoned the attempt without recording an official vote. This unsuccessful effort was par for the course in the Permian Basin.

In the early 1960s, rising global competition produced renewed waves of oil industry mergers, and the oil industry's largest union sought to take advantage of the era's growing uncertainty. However, it remained hard to rally West Texas workers. This was in part because Permian Basin wages remained well above other Texas oil-producing regions during this period.[5] The OCAW turned to new tactics. In the 1960s, public awareness about the dangers of industrial production was growing. Rachel Carson's famous *Silent Spring* alerted Americans to air pollution in 1962, and one year later, federal officials, spurred by activism from the United Steelworkers and other unions, began working under the new Clean Air Act to document industrial air and water pollution across the nation. In this context, OCAW organizers quickly realized that health and safety was an area where they could most help their constituents. During the mid-1960s, American refinery and chemical plant workers built alliances with federal agencies and worked to pass new legislation to ameliorate both workplace danger and threats to long-term community health.[6] By the end of the decade, such worker concern reinforced a national political movement that argued that industrial communities should be shielded from the environmental and public health risks produced by those industries. This partnership culminated in the formation of the Occupational Safety and Health Administration (OSHA) and the Environmental Protection Agency (EPA) in 1970. Over the same period, such changes were deeply opposed by both large and small oil companies, which brought accusations of paternalistic federal oversight and unreasonable regulation that only aided industry consolidation.

Such competing priorities were starkly apparent in West Texas, where oil companies followed established patterns. Early in the decade, they attempted to ease financial risks and appease state and federal calls to reduce natural resource waste by building new refineries and chemical plants, more pipelines, and natural gas fields in the Permian Basin. However, industry efforts to employ financial mechanisms and technological fixes to address resource waste and contamination concerns also produced further environmental consequences. Oil processors also brought a new-to-the-region class of permanent industrial workers to run their operations. As a new influx of stationary industrial workers encountered the transient drilling economy, the OCAW and other unions faced strong opposition in the region.

REFINING THE DESERT

Refining and petrochemical production grew in the Permian Basin as a node within a growing national oil-processing network. This was decades in the making. The city of Houston, with its famed Ship Channel on the Gulf of Mexico, had been Texas's largest refining hub since the 1910s, and Houston led the way in the rapid expansion of Texas oil processing during the 1940s and 1950s. According to the US Bureau of Mines, Texas refineries processed only 54.2 percent of Texas crude oil in 1933. By 1941, this number had increased to 85.9 percent. During this same period, the total amount of refined petroleum products produced in Texas doubled.[7] In 1941, the United States had approximately four hundred refineries nationwide, and the Texas Gulf Coast was already one of the largest refining centers in the country. Wartime infrastructure projects further expanded operations. By the 1950s, however, Texas oil producers faced new pressures, increasingly competing with multinationals and Middle East producers. As a result, the growth of local refining and petrochemical production was a strategic move, not simple speculation. Texas oil producers were looking to diversify and cut costs. As a result, new investment followed exploratory drilling operations to the remote Permian Basin.

Refining in the Permian Basin had gotten off to a slow start. In the 1920s, protracted attempts at local refining ended in failure, in part due to the region's lack of water. Humble closed its McCamey refinery in 1932. Oral history accounts differ as to exactly why.[8] Some said that the refinery burned down. Some said that it was destroyed in a catastrophic explosion. Others believed that it was either a casualty of the Great Depression's low oil prices or the cost of shipping to Gulf ports was just too high.[9] All are plausible; however, price was probably paramount. The biggest problem for West Texas refiners had never been demand, but rather the region's low-quality oil and the limitations of early refining technology.

Into the early 1930s, small West Texas refineries used a mid-nineteenth-century refining process called "straight run" distillation to produce gasoline. Colloquially called "teakettle" refineries, these small operations were similar in shape and design to the small, home-operated stills used to make Prohibition-era whiskey and were prone to leakage, malfunction, and explosion. However, straight run distillation was technically simple and the equipment was inexpensive. It utilized only a series of large metal tanks and the fuel to boil crude oil at high temperatures.[10] Pipelines moved crude oil from a tank farm into a series of pipes set within a tall, cylindrical fractionation tower called the "primary distillation unit." There, crude oil was heated to approximately 600°F, often using residual gas from previous refining runs. As it was heated, different chemical components in crude oil boiled at different temperatures. Gasoline, the lightest hydrocarbon, quickly transformed from a liquid to a gas and rose to the top of the tower. It was then removed, processed for impurities, and blended with other chemicals for consumer use. Similar processes produced fuel oil, kerosene, and other chemicals.[11] However, straight run distillation was inefficient, burning off a high percentage of usable hydrocarbons in the distillation process. Further, it took comparatively longer for these early refineries to burn off residual impurities in Permian Basin oil, which was mostly "sour crude" and notoriously high in sulfur. This created greater air and water pollution near refineries. It also dramatically increased the amount of oil waste in an already inefficient distillation process. For this reason, the per-barrel price of Permian Basin crude oil had always lagged other regions and disincentivized local gasoline production.

Later, the popularity of more complex refining techniques, in particular William Burton's thermal cracking process, made the Permian Basin's lower-quality crude easier to process and therefore more valuable. Thermal cracking was a secondary process completed after straight run distillation, which extracted a higher percentage of gasoline and other materials from crude oil. To complete thermal cracking, oil distillates were heated several more times after the first straight run. These subsequent heating runs got much hotter, reaching approximately 1,000°F or more. As more and more chemicals were siphoned off during each run, vaporized hydrocarbons passed through a series of towers to further break down more of the hydrocarbons, producing more gasoline and other chemicals per barrel of crude oil.[12] These processes were improved during World War II as industry-military partnerships revolutionized oil refining. All told, government and industry together spent over $1 billion on refinery expansion, equipment upgrades, and research.[13] Later, oil companies competed to obtain exclusive rights to the more efficient cracking processes developed during wartime. For example, Socony-Vacuum developed "magic bead" catalysts used in cracking, while other companies perfected new innovations in thermal cracking and obtained exclusive control over a water-intensive, fluid catalytic cracking process developed during the war.[14]

By the late 1940s, as workers like Alfred Goodson took jobs as the Cosden refinery in Big Spring, numerous new refineries were springing up in the Permian Basin, fed by the increased demand for petroleum. Industry leaders hoped that Texas's newly expanded pipeline network, as well as the region's more reliable supply of water, would better control the flow of oil.[15] Such construction was led by majors and large independents. Magnolia Oil, Phillips Petroleum, and Humble expanded their operations.[16] By 1944, Phillips operated a refinery in Cactus and Continental Oil maintained refineries in Denver City and Wichita Falls. Seven years later, in 1952, the Sid Richardson Carbon Company opened a gas plant in Kermit, joining Magnolia's refining and gas production facilities throughout the region. By 1953, the Lone Star Gas Company had constructed a natural gas plant in Shamrock and the American Potash Company opened in Dumas.[17]

Work at these refineries was different from rig work, and operators encountered different hazards. Air quality was a particular concern. While refining had undergone dramatic technical improvements over the previous decades, the job still required constant human observation and assessment, which increased cumulative worker exposure to invisible toxins. For example, employee handbooks and insurance manuals reveal standard operating practices at Mobil Oil and the General Petroleum Company during this period. Individual workers were assigned a specific zone or set of tasks each work shift. Skilled and semiskilled technicians with titles such as "operator" or "process operator" made up most of the workforce.[18] These workers spent most of their time monitoring and servicing complex chemical distillation machinery. Daily, they measured chemical reactions, monitored and recorded temperature gauges, operated heavy machinery, and maintained, repaired, or replaced equipment.[19]

According to employee manuals, refinery and petrochemical plants were supposed to provide workers with breathing and fire protection when in "close proximity" to chemical fumes, distillation equipment, and raw materials.[20] However, official emphasis on protective equipment differed depending on the company, and while safety manuals and guidelines had existed for decades, enforcement was spotty at best. According to worker testimony filed with the OCAW during the 1960s, inadequate individual or atmospheric protective equipment at Texas refineries was known to produce an array of immediate health hazards for workers.[21] Crude oil and natural gas were corrosive materials that damaged human skin, and constant exposure resulted in surface burns. Without consistent use of fire-protective suits, burns from superheated liquids, overheated pipes, or pressurized steam release were common.[22] More concerning was employee contact with large quantities of hot-to-molten raw liquids and noxious gases, alternately heated or cooled through the manipulation of hand-crank steam valves or by adding various catalysts to create specific chemical combinations.[23] Methane, sulfur, and other gases released by opening storage tanks were highly toxic, and could cause loss of consciousness and death after only short-term exposure.[24]

Leaks and spills were known problems that exacerbated dangers to workers. Crude oil was sorted at West Texas refineries into tank farms according to oil grade, a designation defined by the level of gasoline content and chemical impurities present in crude oil. During storage, crude oil of any grade corroded pipes and containers quickly, making leak detection an ongoing battle, as different hydrocarbon mixtures were combined during the fractionation process to produce an optimal chemical balance. During fractionation, not only did towers leak vaporized sulfur, methane, benzine, and other chemicals into the atmosphere, but scheduled off-gassing and burn-offs that were required to maintain optimal temperature and pressure also produced more pollution. These released chemicals followed prevailing wind patterns, affecting the air quality for workers but also blanketing nearby communities.[25]

REPLACING RISK WITH RISK

The rise of refining in the Permian Basin coincided with the postwar emergence of a local petrochemical industry. It represented an effort to capitalize off resource waste, as new advancements in petrochemical production created markets for the region's excess natural gas.[26] However, as with refining, petrochemical production put further pressure on the region's limited water resources and led to significant, systemic pollution.[27] Efforts to reduce waste resulted in further resource intensification and the creation of new hazards.

Permian Basin petrochemical production was led by Odessa, Midland's sister city, centrally located within the Permian Basin's large oil and natural gas reserves. In the early 1950s, the shift to petrochemical production was a strategic choice made by the Odessa Chamber of Commerce and Mayor Jesse Owens, a local member of the Texas Railroad Commission (TRRC). In 1952, Owens tapped local oil prospector and banker William D. Noel to lead a multitiered effort to facilitate petrochemical development in the city, specifically fueled by local natural gas.[28] The stage had been set in 1946 when Noel and three longtime business associates, E. G. Rodman, M. H. McWhirter of Monahans, and J. B. Tubb of Crane County, formed the Odessa Natural Gasoline Company. All had made their early fortunes in Permian Basin oil exploration and were looking for diversified investment.[29] Odessa Natural Gas made a profit processing waste gas produced during drilling, and the company began courting investors to expand the facility. Citing the small regional population and distance from large industrial centers, the Houston-based lawyer Paul Kayser, president of El Paso Natural Gas (EPNG), then a regional pipeline company headquartered to the south in El Paso, agreed to fund the construction of an initial butadiene and styrene plant in Odessa—but only if the chamber could demonstrate a regional market for at least 75 percent of the products produced.[30] Butadiene and styrene were important in the production of other synthetics, and Noel and his committee were confident that industry would breed further industry. They convinced the Akron, Ohio–based General Tire and Rubber Company to build a new plant in Odessa, immediately becoming the main buyer of EPNG petrochemicals. In 1953, EPNG spun off a subsidiary, El Paso Natural Gas Products Inc., and began construction plans for the plant.[31]

Two years later, in 1955, this subsidiary began excavating the foundation for the Odessa Petrochemical Complex, five miles south of central Odessa on undeveloped, unincorporated ranchland.[32] In figure 5.2, the plant location can be seen as a grey box protruding from the city's southern edge. The land was cheap and relatively isolated, with an average price of $25 per acre. Noel was elected president of El Paso Natural Gas Products, locally known as El Paso Products. Upon its completion, the facility made El Paso Products one of the largest single employers in Odessa, a city of approximately 80,000 people.[33] A large industrial corridor quickly grew up around the plant, and the massive industrial facility became the crowning jewel in EPNG's regional natural gas empire. Billing it as the "largest inland petrochemical plant in the world," Noel, Kaiser, and the Odessa Chamber banked heavily on constant growth in local demand for petrochemicals and plastics. In the short term, they would be proven correct. The project made Noel millions.[34]

While personally lucrative to Odessa city officials, such parallel diversification was not a unique idea among oil producers. The petrochemical industry was undergoing massive expansion in the 1950s, and investment in growth was a common risk reducer. An offshoot of the refining industry, the growth of American synthetics was fueled by an abundant supply of cheap domestic oil and the legacy of established government-industry partnerships. Key early petrochemical research was completed at Sun Oil's Marcus Hook, Pennsylvania, lab, where researchers had developed early synthetic rubber and produced heavy-duty plastics from crude oil during the Depression.[35] Later, during World War II, the federal government jumpstarted further research, asking major oil companies to find synthetic solutions to massive shortages in gasoline, natural rubber, and 1,000-octane aviation gasoline. Patent laws were suspended.[36] Immediately after the war,

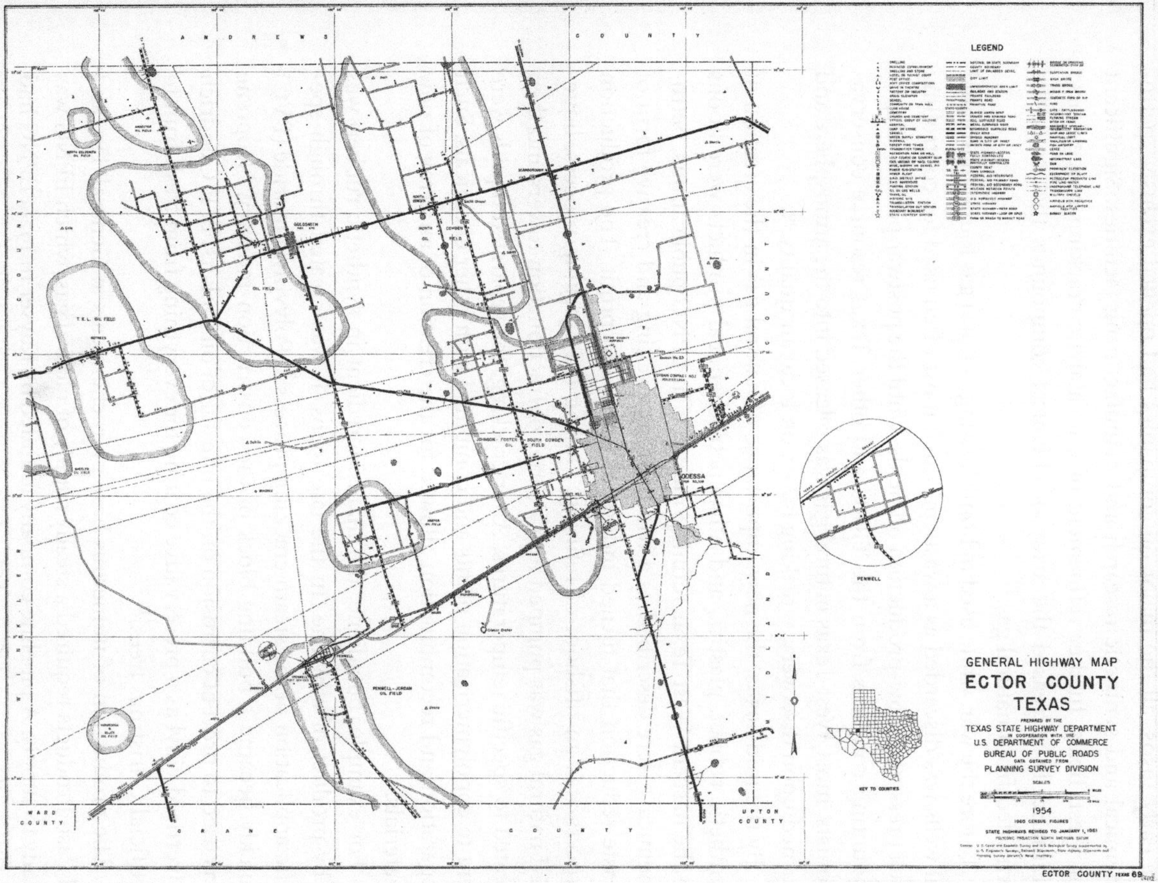

FIGURE 5.2. 1961 Texas Department of Transportation highway map of Odessa, Texas. The Odessa city footprint appears in gray on the right side. Roads connect surrounding oil fields with the city. Interstate 20 and the Texas and Pacific Railroad bisect the city. Image courtesy of the Texas State Library and Archives Commission Archives & Information Services Division.

the majors scrambled to expand synthetics research laboratories, and by the early 1950s, all the major oil companies had opened exclusive petrochemical and synthetic research and manufacturing facilities. Significant for West Texas, further refinement of the catalytic cracking process also dramatically increased the array of chemical compounds that could be extracted from natural gas.[37]

Before the war, while used in home heating, natural gas found in isolated oil wells was discarded as a waste product, most often used for controlling well pressure in low-production oil fields. Until the postwar period, despite mounting concerns from the TRRC and other Texas resource conservationists, most West Texas natural gas was released into the atmosphere and burned upon discovery, wreaking havoc on local air quality.[38]

By the mid-1950s, the new importance of natural gas in the creation of synthetic rubber, plastics, and other petrochemical products were boons to the nascent West Texas refining industry. In EPNG publications, petrochemicals were described as a windfall—an exciting and creative form of waste reduction that turned industrial waste into profit. The production process was an offshoot of refining. During the cracking process, liquefied natural gas was pumped into a series of fractionation towers and then heated to specific temperatures. After cracking, the separated liquids were sent to copolymerization plants and combined with other chemicals. Such separation and recombination allowed for the creation of an array of new materials.

For example, butadiene, the main ingredient in synthetic rubber, was a by-product of ethylene. In the late 1940s, it was created through specific application of the steam cracking process.[39] Polyvinyl chloride (PVC) quickly became a building block of the construction industry. Neoprene was used to prevent corrosion on the interior of oil tankers. B. F. Goodrich advertised vinyl as a preservative coating for everything from fresh fruit to artificial Christmas trees.[40]

The production of numerous base petrochemicals at General Tire and El Paso Products required a steady supply of natural gas, which EPNG was ready to supply. A pipeline company founded by Kayser in 1928, EPNG had traditionally profited from West Texas's geographic isolation and lack of alternative transportation infrastructure. EPNG's first big contract was the construction of a pipeline system for the city of El Paso that would transport natural gas from wells in Jal, New Mexico, to heat homes and businesses in

El Paso's growing industrial centers.[41] The company had expanded during the 1930s and 1940s to become the main natural gas distributor in Texas. After World War II and the rise of natural gas in industrial production, EPNG pipelines were more important than ever before. The company formed a natural gas production and distribution monopoly that dominated the Southwest and northern Mexico for much of the century.[42]

Like other larger oil companies, EPNG used expansion and diversification to hedge against risk. In the 1950s, the EPNG subsidiary facility in Odessa was just one of EPNG's several oil refineries and petrochemical facilities throughout Texas. With these facilities, EPNG had perfected the art of trapping and reusing residual gas—natural gas found during oil exploration—for industrial production.[43] EPNG's movement into consumer products production was built on an assumption that the market for petrochemicals would remain relatively stable through an uncertain era for crude oil profits. EPNG would be proven correct.

Odessa's Petrochemical Complex expanded rapidly throughout the 1960s, following a trajectory set by similar extractive zones throughout the United States. It rode on the continued wave of Permian Basin oil expansion. In 1962, the massive Ellenburger natural gas field was discovered and became a seemingly infinite source for local refiners and chemical producers.[44] By 1965, Andrews, Ector, and Reagan counties led the state in total exploratory feet drilled.[45] As new wells were set up for natural gas capture, William Noel oversaw plant expansions. El Paso Products absorbed the Brooklyn-based Beaunit Company in 1967, as well as the plant's first inhabitant, Odessa Natural Gasoline, in 1968.[46]

By 1968, the Odessa Petrochemical Complex housed six companies, including Noel's own El Paso Products, Rexall Chemical Company, Shell Oil, Big Three Industrial Gas and Equipment, and a Morton Salt brine purification plant. The General Tire and Rubber Company expanded its operations, adding a manufacturing plant to its chemical operations. By 1970, the Odessa Petrochemical Complex encompassed ten separate production facilities on two separate campuses, was spread over 640 acres, and was valued at over $300 million.[47] Conflicting reports from this period record anywhere from 800 to 1,400 people employed at the plant.[48] Plant expansion provided a new type of industry importance for Odessa and Permian Basin oil and gas. It was a source of profit and a financial risk reducer for the Odessa Chamber of Commerce. It also was a significant environmental and public health hazard for both workers and other people in the surrounding community.

Reports in the 1970s and 1980s by environmental regulators, including Texas regulators and the EPA, documented an array of environmental problems at the plant.[49] While records from the 1960s are absent, many plant operators continued to use the same equipment for decades. Further, oral history accounts and court records state that many of these impacts had been ongoing in some form since the plant's construction. Documented problems extended well beyond the gates of the plant, including air pollution, uncovered and decaying solid waste storage, crude oil and other chemicals that leached into groundwater below the plant, and high levels of chemicals in the nearby stream, Monahans Draw.[50] Plant leadership prided itself on its waste reduction. It heavily publicized a plan to reuse and treat its wastewater, setting up an agreement to repurpose city wastewater for use at the plant.[51] However, this was quickly offset by the plant's record of significant air pollution. Steam pressure releases during the cracking process produced particularly toxic results. Also, nightly incineration of waste rubber and other solids created sudden spikes in air pollution.

Many plant workers lived within earshot of the vast complex; however, even workers living farther north were subject to similar at-home exposure. A 1980 EPA investigation into the toxicity of styrene and ethylbenzene found that both were easily vaporized and traveled airborne very long distances.[52] Benzene in particular was significantly toxic. OCAW health investigator Glen Paulson explained, "Acute benzene poisoning is fatal anesthesia, and chronic poisoning is primarily injury to the bone marrow."[53] In an oral history interview, Neil Carman, a scientist who led a 1990s-era Texas Air Control Board investigation into waste emissions at Odessa's General Tire and Rubber, stated, "Sometimes the whole city of Odessa would smell of styrene, it smells like airplane glue."[54] Period epidemiological studies linked styrene and ethylbenzene exposure to nervous system and reproductive disorders among chemical plant workers.[55]

Other hazards were the result of incorrect waste storage. For example, water used by General Tire and Rubber during the polymerization process was expelled into concrete tailing ponds that leaked chemicals into the soil and groundwater. Further, these wastewater evaporation ponds concealed solid industrial waste at bottom. This waste chemically reacted with added liquid waste to leach toxic hydrogen sulfide into the air. In an oral history interview, former Odessa NAACP president Gene Collins explained that the problem would get worse whenever General Tire and Rubber performed maintenance on the waste ponds. Carman said, "And whenever they would do that, the whole south side of the city would be just gassed." He went on to say that "it was so bad it was actually making people sick."[56] For residents, pollution was unavoidable.

While it is unclear how city officials interpreted these environmental problems in the mid-1960s, it is obvious that locals were well aware of unpleasant odors coming from the plant.[57] During the 1950s and 1960s, developers built larger suburban housing tracts extending north and east of town, away from the Petrochemical Complex. As the plant expanded over the next two decades, the city's growing population of racially white industry foremen, machinists, and independent oil drillers, white-collar plant managers, engineers, and sales managers migrated north. While also partially the result of pushback against school integration and white flight, housing prices dropped dramatically in the older, smaller homes in central Odessa, closest to the plant. Over the next three decades, lower-income, Hispanic, and Black families moved into central-south Odessa. These families would experience the most exposure to the plant's toxic emissions.

Neil Carman explained, "And the worst thing, there was an elementary school, Hays Magnet Elementary School right across Interstate 20 from this plant and . . . a couple of teachers had been there since the 50s, and they said it—it was a nightmare. It was very hard for them to teach there and the people in the neighborhood said it had stunk forever." He went on to say, "And yet, unless people complained, we couldn't do anything about it. But the people on the south side were mostly poor, blacks, Latinos, and a few poor white people."[58] In an oral history interview, former South Side resident Delma Abalos remembered the neighborhood's poverty and lack of infrastructure investment: "When I lived on the south side, we did not have sidewalks. . . . When it rained, we would get out there and play because the water was high enough we could splash in it. There were no streets and there were no ditches for the water to go."[59] City officials did not allocate money to improve the toxic neighborhoods nearest the plant.

Even as pollution grew, refining and chemical production quickly became central to the Odessa economy, and as with oil drilling, local leaders were not interested in entertaining criticism of the industry. Half a century later, Joann Littleton, former Odessa City Council representative for the South Side, explained the city leadership's perspective in an oral history interview: "If we close down Dynagen [General Tire and Rubber], Odessa is going to be a ghost town."[60] Gene Collins expressed a similar local sentiment: "Out here in west Texas [is] where anything that smells funny is the smell of money. I don't care if it's H2S. That's money."[61]

Reflecting this perspective, and undoubtedly also influenced by the starkly segregated nature of Odessa at the time and shaped by the broader political and social power of oil in the city, the vast majority of Odessa refinery and petrochemical workers remained hesitant to show public support for the OCAW's shift to health and safety. As a result, the Permian Basin remained an outlier within a growing national movement for federal health and safety oversight in the American energy industries.

AMERICAN OIL UNIONS STRIKE OVER QUALITY-OF-LIFE ISSUES

The OCAW's shift to health and safety was a reaction to dramatic changes in the labor movement and in American refining and chemical work. According to labor historians, between the activism of the Progressive era and the late 1960s, the United States made only limited headway in improving industrial health and safety. Over the same period, the number of workers in oil and gas refining had increased dramatically, according to one account, peaking in the mid-1950s at around 200,000 people.[62] However, this peak was followed by swift decline. According to a National Petroleum Council report from 1967, the number of American refinery workers shrunk to approximately 123,000 only a decade later. Similar trends were reflected in the chemical industries.[63] This was not due to a slowdown in oil markets. Instead, layoffs were indicative of swift technical advancement in the industry that reduced the need for human intervention into oil processing. For example, by 1969, while Texas supplied around 40 percent of all American petrochemicals, the total number of plants in the state had dropped by half.[64] As a result, OCAW health and safety efforts in the 1960s represented a strategic attempt to build new alliances with federal officials, even as the threat of automation and antiunion legislation buffeted OCAW and other unions.[65]

Refinery automation was the result of technical advancement and industry optimization efforts, but the form and function of this process were inevitably affected by widespread unionization at refineries in Texas and throughout the United States during the same period. The union that would become the OCAW began in 1918 as the Oil Field, Gas Well, and Refinery Workers of America.[66] In 1937, five years after Frank Pickrell discovered oil in the Permian Basin, the union changed its name to the Oil Workers International Union (OWIU). By the end of the war in 1945, almost all Texas and Louisiana Gulf Coast refineries were unionized, either with the OWIU or one of several other small unions.[67] Immediately after the war, a refinery strike wave swept through Texas and spread nationally.[68] Workers were angry about wages, which had stagnated during the war. For instance, a strike broke out in 1945 at the General Tire and Rubber Plant in Waco, Texas.[69] That same year, Texas members of the OWIU struck, calling for higher wages. Similar wage disputes erupted in Mobil Oil refineries, mostly concentrated in the Midwest.

Texas officials, working to cultivate a postwar reputation as a haven for industry, responded quickly to quash such renewed labor activism in the state. In 1947, Texas political leaders from the governor to local city councils partnered with the Texas Manufacturers' Association and regional chambers of commerce to successfully lobby for new regulatory restriction on unions. They also vocally supported the Taft-Hartley Act, which restricted union bargaining power. During this period, Permian Basin newspaper opinion pages were rife with passionate, pro-industry letters and antiunion diatribes supporting unchecked oil industry growth. A private ad placed in the *Odessa American* by local oil contractor T. E. C. Bunch on July 18, 1948, was representative. He reported that there was absolutely no conflict between West Texas labor and industry: "I believe the relations that now exist here in Odessa between contractors and organized labor are healthy and that no conflict exists or is anticipated between local contractors and local unions, and that ours is the American way of settling any differences that might arise." Bunch went on to assure readers that the oil, chemical, and refining industries had "a common purpose in our democracy–better living for all of us."[70] Such perspective linked the state's refining and petrochemical industries to national quality of life concerns, leaving little room for worker grievances.

Despite pushback, the OWIU spent the next several years working to leverage wartime industrial importance into higher wages. In 1952, the same year that Midland began construction on its extensive new water wells and one year before construction began on the Odessa Petrochemical

Complex, the OIWU and other affiliated unions launched a nationwide strike to secure wage increases at refineries and chemical plants across the United States. However, although several small, affiliated unions did negotiate pay raises, the strike did not produce industrywide wage gains for refinery workers.[71] This did not dissuade the OIWU. Over the next two decades, the union organized membership drives and strikes in Texas's largest refining hubs in Houston, Texas City, and Port Arthur, with refinery and chemical workers continuing to dispute layoffs, increasing hours, shrinking benefits, and stagnant pay.

With failure in 1952 a sign of strong resistance, the OWIU sought to consolidate its power. In 1955, two years after the failed industrywide strike and at the peak of American refinery employment, the United Gas Coke and Chemical Workers of America, an offshoot of the United Mine Workers, merged with the OWIU to become the OCAW.[72] In 1956, one year after the merger, the OCAW represented approximately 210,000 workers across the oil and chemical industries.[73] The OCAW grew with the industry in the 1950s. In 1958, it represented over forty Texas local branches with 31,895 workers—the most in the union.[74] Perhaps as a result of such gains, the OCAW would be met with vocal hostility in the Permian Basin.

Looking uneasily to the north and west as the OCAW's presence in refining and petrochemical plants expanded, Permian Basin elites were quick to denounce union recruiters in the mid-1950s. Tellingly, in the wake of the 1952 industrywide strikes, West Texas newspapers such as the *Odessa American* avoided mentioning unions altogether. Other strikes were described as a "threat" and often paired with discussion of the importance of the oil industry to national defense.[75] Later, an exemplary 1957 Odessa op-ed described union representatives in apocalyptic terms, telling residents that "they are here" and warning readers about union organizers' standoffish and anticommunity behavior: "They will be standing or sometimes sitting in little groups." The full-page essay ended by invoking unions as a threat to the economic cohesion of the community, cautioning readers that "unions can't possibly create wealth, except for their leaders."[76] It is clear that both local newspaper editors and Permian Basin business leaders saw local unionization as both a real possibility and a real threat.

Such virulent opposition was belied by the fact that union drives at West Texas refineries and petrochemical plants yielded few results in the 1950s. In 1951, OCAW predecessors focused significant resources on the Potash

Company of America in Dumas, north of the Permian Basin. Approximately thirty workers signed union cards, however these numbers did not herald a union surge in the region. The OCAW arrived in Odessa later in the decade. In 1959, organizers contacted workers at the Odessa Petrochemical Complex and three production operators at the General Tire and Rubber Company signed union cards. Little information exists about these workers, Charles Jackson, Billy J. Eves, and C. R. Moony. Their names in census records do not match the addresses listed. It is possible that they did not stay in their homes long or that the information is incorrect. It is unclear if they were particularly concerned about worker health and safety. However, one can assume that they were probably subjected to high levels of air pollution on the job and regularly smelled the "airplane glue" stench of styrene production. They recorded nothing to indicate if they were worried about automation, but it is likely that they experienced new workplace practice that eroded worker autonomy and job site control during this period.

Refinery automation dramatically expanded in the 1950s, as new technologies such as remote controls and new sensors decreased the manual workload for operators. For example, by the mid-1960s, Odessa Petrochemical Complex boosters advertised that the facility had replaced manual tests to measure chemical combinations and human monitors at equipment gauges with sensors and early computers.[77] While these innovations increased measurement accuracy and efficiency, they also reduced the number of workers needed to maintain the plant.[78] According to one history, "Technical innovation in petrochemicals in particular creat[ed] ghost towns of plants, empty of all but a few workers."[79] With such context, we can assume that Jackson, Eves, and Moony's employer, General Tire and Rubber, watched the union drive closely. The Odessa plant was just one of many General Tire facilities throughout the United States, including a larger, heavily unionized plant to the east in Waco.[80] With just three cards among hundreds of employees at the Odessa facility, the OCAW did not record a vote.

Despite such failures, the OCAW followed a careful strategy. A union drive, like a strike, was a gamble. While done in the hope of shielding against current and future workplace hazards and problems, publicly voting to join a union represented an initial, potentially catastrophic risk for individual workers. In West Texas, for instance, workers risked the very real potential of retaliation or loss of their jobs. Increasingly, in the postwar period, refinery workers did not see such risks paying off and union numbers began to stagnate. In 1962, the OCAW attempted to push back against this trend by demonstrating union importance to the industry. That year, in the union strongholds along the Gulf, OCAW members at Shell's Texas refineries and chemical plants staged a wall-to-wall general strike.[81] Beyond OCAW concerns about national membership totals, these workers were responding to a wave of cost-cutting layoffs throughout the 1950s. OCAW leadership attempted to leverage the attention garnered by the strike into union expansion.

The OCAW's aborted 1963 membership drive at the Cosden Refinery in Big Spring took place during this push. Similarly, that same year, the union headed back to Odessa to run a full membership drive at the Rexall Plant at the Odessa Petrochemical Complex, which had just opened in 1962. Rexall was a large petrochemical producer based out of Los Angeles that, like El Paso Corporation, had expanded rapidly in the early 1960s to construct plants throughout the Southwest and Midwest.[82] Rexall's Odessa plant focused on polyethylene production, supplied by ethylene from the adjacent El Paso Petrochemical Plant.[83] Despite consolidated efforts, only eight Rexall workers signed union cards.[84] The renewed push had ended in failure. Along with the failure at the Cosden Refinery, the OCAW held a failed plant election at Rexall and of eighty-two workers who voted, fifty-seven chose not to join the union. The simultaneous wall-to-wall Shell strike was coordinated and bitter. It also ended in failure, requiring major union concessions.

Taken together, these failures were a grim indication of decline. The power that the OCAW and other industrial unions had enjoyed during and immediately after World War II was gone. They were also indicative of major changes in the industry. According to one estimate, by the 1960s half of all workers in the chemical industries were white collar, largely because most of the other employees had been laid off.[85] White-collar workers such as engineers, sales representatives, and management staff had a long history of union opposition. For the operators, laborers, and machinists who remained, a national decline in organized labor's social and political status during this period made unionizing less appealing.

Oil was part of a larger trend. By the 1960s, unions were increasingly blamed for the loss of American jobs due to outsourcing and offshoring across the nation, and overall membership was at the beginning of a long decline. Old narratives of worker solidarity competed badly with the mid-century American Dream of individualized property ownership and wealth accumulation through personal investment and independent employment. Simultaneously, unions were increasingly at a disadvantage against popular accusations of grift, mismanagement, and communist ties.[86] In response to such obstacles, the OCAW would seek to change the tide through a national appeal to worker health and safety in the late 1960s. From its inception in 1955, the union claimed that its mission was "improving living conditions for all workers in the oil and chemical industries." By 1968, this meant partnering with federal officials to develop exposure standards and programs for regulation and industry oversight.[87]

THE RETURN OF HEALTH AND SAFETY

The OCAW returned to Rexall again in 1964, with similar results. Union representatives held a vote, and of 109 workers, 73 voted against the union.[88] The union had more success outside the Odessa Petrochemical Complex, with workers signing dozens of union cards at Foote Well Services and Plastic Applicators Incorporated in 1966, and at the T. E. Mercer Trucking Company the next year.[89] Still, the OCAW returned once again to Rexall in 1967 and 1968, passing out flyers to employees. Rexall employees had contacted the union after a dispute over limited employee vacation time, set at just three weeks annually after ten years of service. This escalated in 1969 as the OCAW formally accused Rexall of using its vacation policy to thwart unionization. The union won its case before the National Labor Relations Board but once again, it did not win a majority.[90]

With these efforts ongoing, OCAW strategy shifted in the late 1960s from an emphasis on financial risks—in the form of wages and employee benefits—to environmental risks and worker health. In 1969, union president A. F. Grospiron told a union convention, "It seems to me that the labor union's responsibilities go far beyond the plant gate. The union must be concerned with the total environment of its members and of other people, too."[91] It was a significant and ongoing policy change that was in part a response to the union's failure to produce wage gains. OCAW leaders felt renewed pressure to demonstrate their worth to members. Hoping to reverse creeping decline, they argued that worker "quality of life" also encompassed worker health and federal regulatory agencies should be allies in this fight.[92] This new strategy required a reframing of risk that was unpalatable to some members. In particular, it required workers to cede hard-fought control over aspects of daily workplace practices to regulators. Such a shift was already taking place in national policy circles, which eased the way.

The OCAW's new campaign aligned with both rising standards for safety and community health across the nation and Americans' increased daily experience with state regulators. In the 1960s, heightened expectations for leisure time, domestic hobbies, and consumer abundance sat uneasily with the prospect of on-the-job maiming or long-term, debilitating injury. Workers were also homeowners, citizens, and capitalist consumers and interacted with an array of new federal agencies in these capacities.[93] This consuming public, of which Texas oil and chemical workers were part, already expected regulators to minimize health and safety risks in the home and their communities. New federal agencies focused on consumer safety were already warning against all kinds of household dangers, from leaded paint, to coal-fired furnaces, to seatbelt-less automobiles.[94] Some hazards bridged the imaginary gap between producing and consuming communities. For example, new agencies picked up on the conditions in uranium mines and their impact on the health of community members, especially children.[95]

Other American industrial communities were not exempt from such trends. For example, in Detroit, Philadelphia, and Long Beach, California, the growing dichotomy between expected cleanliness and safety in the home and workplace contrasted with the reality of bad air, respiratory problems, irritated eyes, corroded and blackened buildings, and mysterious illnesses.[96] While particular popular attention was given to the development and expansion of municipal waste management and water purification services in the popular press, urban air quality was also a source of public concern and debate.[97] Consensus was building among officials that comprehensive, federal environmental legislation was necessary.

In this context, OCAW Health and Safety Office director Anthony Mazzocchi worked to bring union health and safety efforts into the public eye. In 1967, Mazzocchi decided not to create an internal OCAW health and safety board, arguing that it would "absorb the issue before the workers could express what their problems are."[98] Instead he decided to push for federal enforcement. This would require significant regulatory changes, as the OCAW was responding to a piecemeal system that governed American industrial health and safety in the mid-1960s.

Some basic pollution remediation did exist at American refineries during this period. For example, by the 1950s, some companies standardized waste dumping practices and timed off-gassing or burn-offs to take place at times when most people were indoors.[99] However, this simply moved obvious pollution out of sight. Later, American industrial health and safety was regulated through a 1960 amendment to the 1936 Walsh-Healey Act, which set minimum safety standards for any company that received at least $10,000 in federal funding. Significantly, the act covered only employers that secured large federal contracts.[100] Lack of enforcement further hampered any meaningful protections. State and federal regulators mostly worked in cooperation with large industrial employers to expand their operations. For example, although Texas passed a state Injection Well Act in 1961, which regulated waste dumping into groundwater sources, it exempted the oil industry. Similarly, the Texas Air Control Board was founded in 1965 in response to the federal Clean Air Act. However, while the board employed inspectors at field offices in Odessa and other major industrial centers, it relied largely on refineries and chemical companies to self-report their levels of air contamination, with little enforcement mechanisms prior to 1973.[101] Day-to-day exposure guidelines continued to be developed through internal industry review and workplace consensus.[102]

For Mazzocchi and other OCAW leaders, it was clear by the late 1960s that this internal system increasingly was not functioning, in part due to lack of information. Workers were faced with a growing array of new dangers. Especially in the chemical and nuclear industries, hazards were often impossible to detect with the human senses, and monitoring required sophisticated equipment. For example, hydrogen sulfide was odorless and colorless but had a dramatic impact on public health, even in small doses. As Anthony Mazzocchi put it, "The mad rush of science has propelled us into a strange and uncharted environment. . . . We grope in the dark and we can light only a few candles."[103] Such invisible risks were both similar to and different from the oil fields, where the dangers of chemical reactions also existed but were overshadowed by more immediate dangers like fire, explosions, or injury caused by heavy machinery. Further, unlike most drilling rigs, refineries and chemical plants were long-term, large-scale facilities located near or inside urban centers. Even with automation, hundreds of workers were on site during a single shift. And since workers often lived in the same town or city as these plants, they could not escape the resulting problems of widespread air and water contamination. For example, at the Odessa Petrochemical Complex, both the Texas Air Control Board and Texas's system of local Water Control Boards began monitoring groundwater and air emissions in the 1950s. Almost immediately, inspectors found measurable amounts of benzine and other chemicals leaking into local groundwater. Complaints about airborne emissions from the plant were common.[104] However, state officials did not have the enforcement authority to require cleanup. Further complicating matters, oral histories indicate that Texas monitoring and testing standards at refineries and chemical plants were often arbitrary and did not correspond to safety. Remediation of known problems happened slowly at best.

Within the OCAW, Mazzocci had widespread support. According to historian Robert Gordon, "No workers were more concerned about workplace and environmental pollution than the members of OCAW."[105] However, the battle for federal oversight was uphill. During the second half of the 1960s, President Lyndon Johnson's administration passed key environmental legislation and proposed multiple bills for environmental oversight and national health and safety legislation, with hopes to amend the Walsh-Healey Act.[106] This was initially unsuccessful, as the US Chamber of Commerce and other business leaders rebelled at Labor Department oversight over health and safety. The push continued. In 1968, after the election of President Richard Nixon, the OCAW worked with the United Steelworkers and the AFL-CIO to renew public pressure.[107]

The OCAW extended its campaign into environmental safety beyond the workplace, launching a mailing campaign to raise awareness about the hazards posed by gas pipelines beneath urban and residential homes.[108] Later that year, in 1969, Mazzocchi and Paulson compiled a dossier of worker testimonials for use in a hearing before the congressional Labor and Education Committee. They toured North American OCAW locals, holding conferences in New Jersey, Kansas City, Atlanta, Houston, and other industrial centers collecting testimonies about health and safety issues at refineries and petrochemical plants. On the tour, Mazzocchi and Paulson enlisted local public health experts to explain the consequences of chemical exposure to oil workers. According to Mazzocchi, "The value of this document is that in its vivid portrayal of the environmental problems of the workplace, it dramatizes the need for corrective steps on a massive scale."[109] Put another way, he wanted workers to understand environmental risk as unacceptable and worker health as potentially improved through federal regulation.

Mazzocchi was particularly concerned about the undocumented long-term effects of refinery work. However, he was not reactionary, saying, "Hydrocarbons are not as bad as many things because they are not chemically reactive. The thing that they can do is kind of dissolve the fats in the skin or in the tissue of the lungs, and this is not good. But they don't go in immediately and react and mess things up. As to whether there would be a synergistic interaction, to this there is no answer."[110] Long-term health effects among workers, such as asthma, emphysema, and cancer, were reported but not yet formally studied. The most significant health problems were often cumulative rather than immediately dangerous, and assessing the impact of exposure over the lifespan of an individual or a community was a complex and expensive prospect.

Because few formal studies existed, Mazzocchi used powerful witness testimony to illustrate long-term health hazards. In town hall after town hall, oil workers described cancers, nervous system disorders, involuntary sterilizations due to chemical exposure, poisonings, and a variety of catastrophic accidents in vivid terms.[111] For example, Harold Smith of Local 8–447 in New Jersey narrated, "I had an uncle. He also worked in a chemical plant. He died of cancer, this cancer in the throat. He had a tube in his throat and it was a result of working in this chemical plant. . . . a certain chemical that he inhaled got in his throat and his throat was a mess and he died. I mean, I don't like the expression—he died like a dog."[112] Similar tales came from Mazzocchi's visit to Texas. Morris Aken, director of OCAWU District 4, described workplace hazards on the Gulf: "We had two or three people killed in the Mount Pleasant Refinery of American Petrochemical; there are no real safety precautions there. Then recently, we had an accident at the American Oil Refinery in Texas City, where some people were killed, including one young ambulance driver who . . . was trying to save some people."[113] OCAW members also expressed concern about the lack of regulatory standardization. Several called for the union to enforce external safety testing and monitoring services at oil refineries.[114] More than a decade later, the statements collected by Mazzocchi and Paulson would be backed up by epidemiological research that found an array of elevated cancer risks, especially stomach cancer and leukemia, among retired workers at Texas oil refineries.[115]

In using these stories to push for a federal response, Mazzocchi and OCAW leaders specifically embraced a position that state regulators, uniquely qualified to assess the long-term health and safety risks for workers in refining and chemical production, were needed as impartial intermediaries. They advocated for more third-party plant inspections, more specific regulations for workplace health and safety, and later the creation of "right-to-know" laws for communities located near industrial production.[116] Such campaigns articulated a belief that employers were directly responsible for worker health and safety, and workers and communities had a right to information about how these industries operated. They argued that government should enforce these rights. Such an OCAW position required a sea change in heavy industry workplace culture, in which federal regulators, long understood as intruders, were instead invited to be intermediaries not only to prevent workplace accidents, but also to avoid long-term health consequences in surrounding communities.[117]

In this way, the late 1960s represented a high point for attempts to manage risk at the federal level. Efforts by the OCAW and other unions led directly to new, federal workplace safety laws. In 1969, for example, the Coal Mine Safety and Health Act was spurred by grass-roots activism among West Virginia coal miners. President Nixon presented a revised health and safety bill to Congress that same year. Negotiations continued into 1970, and when it finally passed, OSHA was created.[118]

During these congressional negotiations, OCAW leaders and federal regulators collectively expressed an assumption that public health and environmental protection were crucial to a functioning democratic society. Through a similar impetus, the founding of the EPA was based on an assumption that a certain level of environmental health was required for economic progress. The EPA began to standardize chemical monitoring and exposure testing at chemical plants and refineries. Despite such gains, historian Charles Noble articulates the truly tenuous nature of such beliefs: "The 1960s were years of social protest . . . including a struggle against oppressive working conditions. This discontent did not lead to a movement by rank and file workers or the unions for the reform of the workplace. But it played a pivotal role in sparking and legitimating the efforts of a small group of Washington-centered health and safety activists who translated that discontent into a movement for federal regulation of occupational safety and health."[119] Both Mazzocci's campaign and the arrival of new federal regulations to protect workers were not publicly welcomed by Permian Basin oil workers.

Surviving OCAW records offer little detail about specific union efforts in the Permian Basin and do not speculate as to why opposition was so fierce. The local press is also silent. The completeness of such silence, with union elections not even receiving negative coverage in the staunchly antiunion local press, suggests at least some apprehension that granting attention to dissent would instigate local worker agitation.[120] The OCAW's lack of success in West Texas is comparatively remarkable. In 1969, there were only 180 union-represented refinery workers in all of West Texas and eastern New Mexico. In contrast, there were approximately 20,000 OCAW members in Texas.[121] While this dichotomy should partially be attributed to the comparatively smaller size of the Permian Basin refining and chemical industries, that does not fully explain it.

In 1965, Odessa's ten petrochemical plants and approximately 1,000 employees represented the third-largest concentration of petrochemical producers in the state, only lagging Houston's industrial centers.[122] Region-wide, refinery employment made up a significant percentage of the industry. In 1966, the El Paso Natural Gas Company maintained thirty-seven refineries in twenty-five towns throughout the region. According to the OCAW, industrial Odessa housed thirteen plants, most of which were part of the Petrochemical Complex located south of the city. In contrast, Midland, a center for oil administration, had only four. Other new refineries popped up both in towns and directly next to oil fields in some of the region's most isolated areas.[123] Phillips Petroleum operated nineteen gasoline plants in towns strung across the desert. Pan American Petroleum operated fourteen gas plants, and the Cabot Corporation owned seven gas products plants.[124] Amoco operated twelve plants. Smaller towns to the north of the Permian Basin, such as Big Spring, Borger, and Pampa, all contained four or more plants. These ranged from a Sid Richardson Carbon Company plant in Big Spring to Phillips Petroleum's Copolymer Plant in Borger. Other plants in smaller towns throughout the region produced fertilizers, sulfur products, and fiberglass, as well as gasoline, salt, and natural gas.[125] In this context, it is not clear if this consistent reluctance was due to egregious management opposition, coercion, or intimidation. Union records demonstrate that

OCAW leadership was reluctant to invest significant time and personnel in attempting to unionize West Texas, sending organizers only intermittently and alone or in pairs. They also preserved minimal records.

Whatever the OCAW's logistical reasons, the spatial, racial, and cultural makeup of West Texas in the 1960s probably didn't help. The Permian Basin had never been either an industrial or a union stronghold. Throughout the 1920s and 1930s, local ranchers and large landholders used intimidation and sometimes violence to avoid coordination among small farmers, sharecroppers, and agricultural workers. Later, state institutions such as the Border Patrol, the Texas Rangers, and unsympathetic Texas courts made it doubly dangerous for Hispanic or Black farm workers to unite with white wage laborers.[126] As a result, while oil-field workers successfully unionized in other, less isolated areas of the West and Midcontinent, this did not happen in West Texas. Many Permian Basin refinery and chemical workers had family, friends, and past work experience in the oil fields. By 1965, the region's economy had been dominated for sixty years by this system of contract-based, informal labor. In contrast, refining and petrochemical production were new industries to a region without an independent manufacturing tradition or workplace identity.

The region's cultural and social boundaries of risk assessment had been forged over the preceding forty years of oil production. In the 1960s, Permian Basin economic and social hierarchies remained intertwined with speculative cattle ranching and monocrop agriculture, economies in which hierarchies were built from land ownership, not wage labor. Further, even in 1969, West Texas remained primarily an oil-producing, not oil-processing center. This meant that the cultural and economic trends of the extractive economy were entrenched and hard to disrupt. Boom-and-bust fluctuations in profit and employment status were met with speculation and land-use diversification, not collective action. Jobs were contingent and temporary, and workplace risk remained largely personal, best managed by individuals.

Case in point—when asked to describe local unionization efforts in a 1970 oral history interview, former cowboy and oil-field worker William Wolfe recited an apparent response to Permian Basin union organizers from memory: "Let me tell you something mister . . . you are standing on my land. Now if you've decided you want to create something like they do in the big towns and hit somebody in the head, you better have those people, whoever you are going to send out, to take out plenty of insurance because they will all get killed around here. It's a wide-open country." In response to this story, the anonymous oral historian asked Wolfe, "Wouldn't you say, from the very beginning, that the oil business was a business of individuals and was not a collective enterprise? Every man stood on his own feet?" Wolfe agreed.[127] Regional narratives that unions were a product of the big city and did not fit in with West Texas culture were common refrains. Wolfe went on to report that unionization efforts in oil fields near McCamey were unsuccessful, but he admitted that workers at the town's Humble refinery did strike on occasion.

For Wolfe and probably many other oil workers in the region, environmental risks were to be expected, and worker grievances would not be fixed by joining a union. The oil industry's many dangers were short term, conflagrations that were suddenly visible and quickly dispersed. Large-scale industrial plants, refineries, and chemical facilities added to oil's environmental strain. However, for locals like Wolfe, any push to use the regulatory structures of the federal government to ameliorate oil's environmental and industrial risks butted against the region's industrial culture. While smog, outgassing, and water pollution were problems felt throughout oil cities, some neighborhoods experienced them more than others. In a trend repeated throughout industrial communities in the South and West of the United States, any push for health and safety reform in West Texas ran up against both the pervasive culture and economic logic of extractive production and were stymied by local racial and ethnic divides in the region's urban centers and towns. If the meaning of personal security and physical safety was carefully limited to apply only to economic safety, community leaders and oil company managers could continue to use oil industry expansion as an answer to all future community risks.

Chapter Six

THE BUCKLE OF THE SUN BELT

On December 13, 1974, an article appeared in the *Austin American-Statesman* discussing the era's "energy crisis" and resulting boom in Permian Basin oil production. Multiple local oil industry leaders were interviewed. All were excited by suddenly high oil prices. At over $10 a barrel, prices were more than double their 1970 average. However, the interviewees also expressed anger at the possible end to key tax breaks for domestic oil producers. Ed Thompson, executive vice president of the Permian Basin Petroleum Association, lamented, "If we could just get the government out of everybody's business, we could probably WIN real quick."[1] Harry Clark, vice president of economic development for the First National Bank of Midland, agreed, assuring readers that oilmen in the Permian Basin were "keeping a watchful eye on the federal government."[2] Such hand-wringing over taxes was a long-standing industry lament that united West Texas independents and Houston executives. It was indicative of continued industry frustration over federal regulation and ongoing resource-sovereignty battles between Texas politicians and Washington. It also reflected a sense of pride that Permian Basin oil producers had responded to help supply the nation with needed energy. Such importance would garner West Texas oilmen powerful allies later in the decade, as another sudden pause in oil imports amplified local industry calls for the removal of domestic drilling restrictions. During this crucial period, oil's perennial outcry of government overreach dovetailed with a national movement for deregulation and the dismantling of newly created federal risk-reducing structures.[3]

Supporters of what became known as deregulation could point to the contrast between Texas and other industrial and extractive centers during the 1970s. While the industrial Midwest and East languished in stagflationary decline, Texas spent the mid-1970s luxuriating in an oil-driven boom. Oil-lubricated Texas banks, including the Permian Basin's First National Bank of Midland, and financed a concurrent boom in residential construction. The expansion of the oil services industries boosted Texas's presence in the high-tech and computing industries. During this period, the dusty and isolated Permian Basin continued to be the center of Texas oil production and was the home of a new generation of Texas oil millionaires who made very visible displays of their wealth. Stories of garages filled with multiple Cadillacs, private jets, and Texas-sized oil estates were relayed by a wave of national reporters who descended upon the region.[4] They found, for example, the established local oil speculator Aaron Giebel of MGF Oil, who built multiple 9,000-square-foot mansions.[5] Similarly, the natural gas wildcatter Clayton Williams reportedly built a ballroom-sized office and filled it with trophies from his numerous exotic animal hunts. There was also the wealthy oil driller John Lee Cox, who became regionally famous as the "Spraberry King" due to his many discoveries during the late 1970s. Along with a residence in Midland, Cox owned a 70,000-acre ranch in West Texas.[6] These men were joined by blue-collar oil-field workers who enjoyed very high employment and wages relative to the rest of the nation. Popular media ran numerous exposés on oil workers who exhausted their ample earnings on new cars, easy sex, and other luxuries.[7]

Far from being cowed by such reports, Texas legislators argued that the renewed oil boom demonstrated the state's economic and geological superiority. Even as Texas Oil Chemical and Atomic Workers Union (OCAW) members struck at Shell refineries in 1973 and instigated a national boycott of Shell Oil to protest the industry's environmental damage, the legislature touted Texas as the heart of a rising "Sun Belt," which would be the catalyst for American economic and social revitalization.[8] According to boosters, city planners, and state officials, the booming oil metropolis of Houston was indicative of the success of Texas's oil-dominated economy.

While the Permian Basin had few truly urban areas, the sizable oil communities in Midland, Odessa, and surrounding towns were also representative of the era's shifting trends. A political bellwether for the breakup of the twentieth-century Democratic coalition, Midland's and Odessa's voting records indicated a dramatic shift toward pro-business, small-government Republicans by the late 1940s. Case in point—even as the rest of Texas remained solidly Democratic, Midland residents had not voted for a Democratic presidential candidate since the re-election of Harry Truman in 1948. Republicans made inroads in the Permian Basin through supporting key oil policies, exemplified by Dwight Eisenhower's landmark 1952 presidential win in Texas after he promised to award the state control over Continental Shelf oil.[9] In 1964, Ector and Midland counties were two of only sixteen Texas counties (out of a total 254) to vote for the conservative Republican Barry Goldwater instead of the Texas Democrat Lyndon Johnson in the 1964 presidential election.[10] And by the early 1970s, Sun Belt politicians on either side of the aisle promised that reduced government bloat and business-friendly tax policies would prevent the spread of labor unrest and racial strife that marked Midwest and East Coast industrial centers throughout the 1960s.[11] Such promises were palatable to many white Permian Basin residents worried about both oil prices and school integration.[12]

As the appropriateness of numerous national-level regulatory agencies were called into question by the energy crisis and growing political backlash, West Texas oil companies, employees, and civic leaders did not stray from their old strategies. As was the case in the 1930s, in the mid-1970s, locals had decades of experience increasing efficiency and reducing waste through optimized logistics and new technologies. However, the Permian Basin's tolerance for environmental risk in the name of oil affluence would continue to be tested.[13] As domestic production scaled up after 1973, so did pollution. In West Texas oil towns and cities, both workers and residents experienced more air poisoned by natural gas flares and more water contaminated by salt brine and well-injection chemicals. This included smaller towns like Denver City, as well as Midland and Odessa, which in the 1970s still navigated shrinking water supplies and the ever-growing resource needs of well-flooding and refining operations. Locals applied the tools of the oil industry to these and other problems. Still, despite the industry's seeming perpetual expansion, Permian Basin oil production remained a risky business, balanced on a knife edge that depended on high oil prices and continued, predictable production in the regions' aging oil fields. Neither was guaranteed.

A NEW KIND OF BOOM

In October 1973, the Arab members of the Organization of Petroleum Exporting Countries (OPEC) embargoed oil shipments to the United States in protest for American involvement in the Yom Kippur War. This rocked the global oil market and American energy consumers. Early that year, American net oil imports sat at approximately three million barrels of oil per day, mostly from OPEC countries.[14] This number cratered after the embargo, and domestic production could not pick up the slack. Consumer panic produced long lines at the gas pump. That winter, high heating costs brought fears about the end of American post–World War II dominance and revived widespread popular antipathy for oil producers.[15]

American oil majors bore the weight of this domestic anger. Even before foreign oil had stopped flowing, oil prices had begun to rise in 1970 as depletion made domestic wells less productive. As prices spiked in 1971 accusations of inefficiency, bad management, and conspiracy emerged.[16] Allen Murray of Texas-based Mobil Oil testified before the US Congress in the summer of 1973, four months before the embargo. In statements not dissimilar from Texas's response to the 1930s crisis, Murray bemoaned the bad press: "Almost daily it seems, some new charge is reported, to the effect that the 'energy crisis' is merely an invention of the oil companies. The companies have somehow 'created' a fuel shortage, we hear, to raise prices or to drive independent marketers out of business."[17] Such accusations of market manipulation were echoed in Texas one year later, after a concurrent 1973 natural gas shortage was met with Texas Railroad Commission (TRRC) pro-rationing.[18] However, in a marked departure from past controversies, the most vocal calls were not for federal intervention to rein in big oil. Instead, independents in Texas and other oil-producing states pushed loudly for the end of extraction allowances designed to preserve the domestic oil supply. Responding both to the industry's expanded political importance and independents' protestations of financial precarity, oil's trade organizations and lobbyists spent the decade pushing hard for deregulation as a way to boost profits, ultimately winning key battles.[19]

The oil shortage meant that, for once, the interests of domestic producers aligned with those of federal officials. Beginning in 1973, national fears of foreign dependence resulted in a decade-long effort to roll back regulatory barriers on US oil production. President Richard Nixon ended oil import quotas put in place after World War II and called for the construction of new domestic oil stockpiles. His administration also pushed laws encouraging domestic drilling. In August 1973, Phase Four of the Economic Stabilization Act removed federal price caps on domestic oil.[20] Later that year, the Emergency Petroleum Allocation Act (EPAA) allowed the price of newly extracted oil to rise as high as $10.82 a barrel by December 1973, while the price of the existing aboveground oil supply was kept artificially lower.[21] In 1976, the Energy Conservation and Production Act further loosened price caps on domestic oil, allowing certain categories of crude to reach over $14 per barrel.[22] While not yet full economic deregulation, these laws were signs of things to come; they signaled that the creation of industry-constraining agencies like the Environmental Protection Agency (EPA) and Occupational Safety and Health Administration (OSHA) would not be repeated.

In public addresses throughout this period, Nixon called on Permian producers, and others, to rally in the face of national emergency.[23] The industry response sparked a wave of technical innovation, extending the life of aging Permian Basin oil fields. While unitization and water flooding had been controversial in the late 1960s, the spike in oil prices after 1973 made both incredibly profitable. Worry about the cost of deep drilling was put aside as exploratory operations multiplied. Permian Basin drilling crews expanded operations in the Delaware and Midland basins and traveled to new fields in the Anadarko Basin of western Oklahoma and in the Texas Panhandle. Significantly, there were more than 3,000 oil companies operating in the Permian Basin in 1973, and workers flocked to increasingly technical West Texas oil jobs in drilling, oil processing, and petrochemical production.[24] Comparisons between the 1966 and 1973 Permian Basin oil directories demonstrate that an expanded network of refineries and petrochemical plants propped up the economies in many of the region's old oil towns, including Crane, Kermit, Andrews, and Denver City, all with populations of between 1,000 and 5,000 people. With even small-town refineries and gasoline plants employing thirty-five people on average, they were looked on as major employers.[25] Labor shortages in the region meant that both drilling and processing work rapidly diversified. Popular magazines and the OCAW *Union News* reported women taking rig jobs, and OCAW field notes demonstrated a significant uptick in Hispanic hires at Permian Basin refineries, transport companies, and chemical plants.[26]

Workers were also needed in the numerous oil-field services companies that conducted a variety of oil-detection and well-flooding tasks. They also completed early hydraulic fracturing operations in the region. An increasing number of these oil workers had college degrees in engineering and geology. This was indicative of big changes. Mody Boatright described oil's scientific shift in the late twentieth century (specifically the 1970s) as follows: "An orderly development has replaced the periodic chaos that formerly occurred." For him, much of this stability was the result of new discovery technologies: "This orderly production has been made possible by the development of instruments for securing the data necessary to determine the best procedures for obtaining the maximum recovery in any field."[27] He was describing the industrywide pursuit of more oil data, with oil detection companies pioneering the analysis of magnetic fields, seismic vibrations, radioactivity, and other properties of rock and sand to predict the presence and amount of subsurface oil.[28]

Such innovation was a long time coming. Since the late 1940s, major oil companies had invested heavily in geophysical research and development, either forming their own laboratories or rewarding independent patent holders for new discoveries.[29] Along with the famous Geophysical Services Incorporated (GSI), founded by Texas oil-field services pioneers Everette Degolyer, Eugene McDermott, and John Karcher, other geophysical and oil technology companies sprang up in Tulsa, Houston, Dallas, and Midland during the 1950s and 1960s.[30] In 1955, the Midland city directory recorded seventy-four independent geologists and five geophysicists, including a branch office for GSI.[31] By 1973, while GSI had been subsumed by internal company mergers, the oil services giant Halliburton had dramatically expanded operations in the Permian Basin, and Schlumberger had opened a regional office.[32]

In the postwar era, geophysicists working for these and other companies perfected an array of technologies, such as the magnetometer and the seismograph, for industry use. These technologies offered new ways to record and map subsurface geology and predict the location and size of oil deposits without the need to drill an expensive hole.[33] By the 1960s, geologists had definitively mapped the Spraberry Trend and other large oil deposits in the Permian Basin.[34] In the renewed boom of the 1970s, such technologies were paired with more advanced well-flooding technologies in which oil-field services companies pushed a variety of materials into aging oil wells to boost pressure and increase yields. They used alternating combinations of hydrocarbon gases, polymers, and surfactants to increase the viscosity of either oil or water, applying all of them strategically depending on the needs of the specific drill site.[35] Beginning in 1972, flooding wells with carbon dioxide was pioneered commercially in the Permian Basin's Sacroc Field in Scurry County.[36] Federal funds expanded research into flooding wells with an array of chemicals and different mixed-water solutions. As former Atlantic Richfield (ARCO) employee W. Hoxie Smith put it, "All the majors would send their new hires here [Midland]." He added, "This is the lab for the oil and gas industry."[37] Other testing was conducted throughout Texas and in Oklahoma. This work transformed oil extraction and the Permian Bain.

The career of the Odessa driller Caven J. "Red" Davidson illustrates the environmental impact of such new technologies. Davidson owned and operated the Davidson Drilling Company with his brother, H. W. Davidson, out of Odessa between 1925 and the early 1970s. Davidson not only employed new predictive technologies as they emerged, but later in his career, he moved into experimental well flooding and early fracking.[38] He began drilling in the mid-1920s, an era in which key information like the approximate well depth, the amount of water used, and the consistency and probable geological composition of the mud being ejected from the well hole was hard won. His handwritten daily records described constant machinery breakdowns due to unforeseen geological changes that dogged his drilling efforts.[39] In the 1950s, Red Davidson's logs became more detailed and the drilling process more sophisticated. Most entries included notes on the type of well injection and surveying systems used, details about the condition of the well pipe, and notes about drill bits and other machinery. Later reports from the late 1960s appeared in computer printouts and were conducted to support unitization, well-flooding, and fracking operations. These also included statements from seismograph contractors, chemists, and geologists, as well as detailed well-spacing maps and reports detailing the types of unitization agreements employed in a field.[40]

In correspondence, Red Davidson himself made clear that even with the reduction in quotas and the incentives brought by high prices, the amount of oil that the Permian Basin could produce using traditional oil drilling methods had already peaked.[41] However, while some Permian Basin drillers moved on to new fields, he instead branched out into so-called enhanced recovery techniques that helped to extract more oil from established wells. While instigated by only the largest oil companies, Davidson and his team were paid well for their services as contractors, building infrastructure for these new systems. Fracking and well flooding were still in-development technologies.

After Red Davidson quit the business, continued experimentation meant that in the late 1970s, Amoco, a subsidiary of Standard Oil, pioneered Massive Hydraulic Fracturing (MHF), which dramatically increased the effectiveness of enhanced recovery in old wells. MHF also used much more water than the older water-flooding and fracturing methods developed in the 1950s. These older methods used approximately 400 pounds of sand and around 750 gallons of fluid for each well. By the end of the 1970s, a single MHF well required around 500,000 gallons of fluid mixed with one million pounds of sand and ceramic beads, all of which was injected and then became unrecoverable from the well hole after the flooding process.[42]

As these numbers imply, the new boom was extremely expensive and resource intensive, and it relied heavily on an array of new data. However, these new techniques produced results. Well injection and hydraulic fracturing helped to push total regional production to a peak of two million barrels per day in 1973.[43] In 1974 alone, wildcat drilling operations increased by over 21 percent in the region, aided by new subsurface imaging technologies. One year later, in 1975, total well completion in the Permian Basin rose again, by 31 percent.[44] And while these numbers dipped a bit over the next several years, such increasingly ordered, technologically-dependent extraction was the oil industry's clear-cut bid to ensure industry longevity and minimize financial risk. For employees at American majors and independents who lived and worked in the area, the massive influx of knowledge about the subsurface world brought by new oil technologies was an industry revolution. It also might have been coupled with conversations about the industry's impact on the region's limited water resources.

Well flooding and early fracking further deteriorated regional water. New lakes of toxic salt brine water emerged, and existing streams were further contaminated. According to a 1970 study of twenty-seven playa lakes and streams in West Texas, twenty-four were already unsafe for human consumption. All exceeded the recommended sulfate concentration.[45] Such contamination only got worse after 1973. For example, Whalen Lake and Shafter Lake near the small oil town of Andrews, to the west of Odessa, were small, salty playa lakes. Oil production made the water in these lakes deadly for birds and other wildlife. Urban water was also affected.

In an oral history interview in 2001, longtime Midland resident Midge Erskine described a multidecade battle with local authorities over well flooding and improper waste dumping. She discussed how this began in the 1970s, as state officials interpreted a lack of organized public outcry as tacit acceptance of contamination: "The water commission comes out and says, oh your water is safe and you know it isn't . . . so then they end up saying you've got all these dead snakes down in there, that's what turned your water green and they did nothing about it."[46] Similar stories emerged in the early 1980s among oil workers and their families living in trailer parks east and south of Midland. Reports that tap water had turned yellow or green and smelled or tasted bad remained the topic of local consternation, if not organized protest.[47]

Countering such ominous signs was the era's energy crisis, which prompted local oil producers to turn to experimental technologies, hoping to delay resource depletion and expand the oil economy. More jobs, expanding suburban sprawl, and renewed financial opportunities discouraged discussion about still-unsolved problems with local water contamination and general environmental decline. This dichotomy came to a head in 1975. Two years after the OPEC embargo, and one year before local US bicentennial celebrations would laud oil as the region's national destiny, efforts to quickly ramp up production resulted in globally publicized tragedy.[48] The resulting investigation brought uncomfortable attention to the oil's environmental impact on one small Permian Basin town and, for a time, called into question the growing push for deregulation and a greater acceptance of environmental risk.

THE H2S DISASTER

In theory, everyone knew the risks. The entire Permian Basin was crisscrossed by pipelines and marked by steadily bobbing pump jacks. Gas flares lit up the night sky and tainted the air with the rotten-egg smell of sulfur.

Like most West Texas oil fields, the wells near Denver City were decades old, established along with the town during the previous boom of the late 1940s. In the mid-1970s, drillers were back in Denver City, many hired to install and maintain experimental well-injection systems designed to extract the last oil from these old wells. With housing at a premium, it was not unusual for oil infrastructure such as drilling rigs, pump jacks, storage tank farms, and pipelines to be located very close to occupied homes, many of which were inhabited by oil industry employees and their families. It was only a matter of time before something went wrong.

Late on the night of Saturday, February 1, 1975, a valve failed on an experimental well-injection pipeline operated by ARCO. The pipeline was located just 150 yards from a small farmhouse owned by J. C. and Glenda Patton, located on the outskirts of town. On the night of February 1, the Pattons were hosting guests including Lee Amerson and his wife, Alma, of Portales, New Mexico, and J. R. May and his wife, Edith, from Arlington, near Dallas. Also visiting was fourteen-year-old Clara Peevy, a neighbor and close friend of the Pattons' seventeen-year-old daughter, Delores. When a powerful rotten-egg stench woke Glenda around five o'clock Sunday morning, she knew that the smell came from the pipeline. Glenda first called local police and then her pastor before her family attempted to flee the spreading gas. Glenda, J. C., Delores, and their guests fled the house in pajamas, crowding into the two cars parked in the driveway. Tragically, both vehicles were already filled with a mixture of carbon dioxide and hydrogen sulfide (H_2S). Everyone was incapacitated before being able to move either vehicle. Despite Glenda's many phone calls, help ultimately arrived too late. Later that morning, James Tucker of the Texas Highway Patrol arrived with members of the Denver City volunteer fire department. Donning oxygen tanks and breathing equipment, they found the remains of the entire Patton family, along with their relatives and friends.

Tucker and the other first responders had been delayed by the discovery of another victim inside a crashed pickup truck blocking the road leading to the Patton house. Nineteen-year-old Steve Sparger worked for ARCO on the night shift, monitoring pipelines. Sparger was on his way to the Patton house to address the leak when he was caught in the gas cloud. Based on the position of his truck, investigators theorized he had smelled the gas and attempted to reverse the vehicle out of the cloud. However, his truck had gotten stuck in a drainage ditch lining the road. Sparger was overcome by the gas before he was able to turn around.

When Denver City firemen arrived at the Patton house, they initially began a frantic search and rescue attempt, fearing one of the Pattons' grandchildren was still inside the home. When the child was discovered elsewhere, they attempted to stop the leak. However, the pipe was covered in a thick layer of frost, built up from the leaking carbon dioxide. Firefighters had to call for an additional truck of hot water to melt the ice before they could shut down the pipeline.

Once the pipeline was off, the discussion began. In a single night, one hydrogen-sulfide leak had killed nine people and an unknown number of dogs, cats, horses, cattle, and other animals. ARCO's pipeline-monitoring efforts and safety response systems had spectacularly failed to prevent tragedy, instead actually leading to another death. The tragedy rocked the small community of five thousand people and sparked a national inquiry into safety and risk management in oil production. In this case, a confluence of bad weather, technical failure, bad timing, and human error had deadly consequences. But questions remained. If ARCO was following all federally imposed regulations designed to preserve air and water safety, who or what was to blame? Was further oversight the best way to prevent future tragedy?

During an internal investigation, ARCO determined that a pressure release valve had spontaneously failed during the night, releasing the deadly gas. Carter Barcus, a Dallas-based public relations official for ARCO, informed the local press that the valve leak had been too small to trigger internal safety sensors, which would have automatically shut off the gas.[49] The earliest hours of February 2, 1975, were drizzly and cold, which was unusual in arid and warm West Texas. This trapped heat low to the ground, creating a fog that blanketed the town and halted Denver City's near-constant wind, which would have dissipated the gas cloud. When also asked to comment on possible causes of the accident, T. J. Crutchfield, division superintendent for El Paso Natural Gas (EPNG) in Midland, avoided mentioning the valve itself. Instead, he theorized that the damp and cold weather helped tie the gas to the ground and prevented it from dissipating. Pat Heckman, the supervisor of EPNG's Wasson Plant in Denver City, where ARCO purchased its injection gas, readily agreed that the lack of wind that morning helped make the situation worse.[50]

Local press and residents publicly echoed the assessment of industry representatives, also framing the tragedy as an unfortunate and unpreventable accident. Two days after the leak, Robert Borden of the *Odessa American* emphasized that the victims' deaths were quick and painless.[51] When asked by the local press about efforts to prevent future technical failures, Yoakum County Judge O. H. Holder explained, "There's no bitterness toward any oil company or anything like that . . . because they expect accidents like that to happen and they do happen."[52] Holder seemed satisfied by the investigation: "I think your oil companies will probably come up with something. I think they'll learn a lesson. As for the county, they've done as much as any county could do." He said later, "We can't say that it's not going to happen in Denver City or in Odessa. We have wells like this in the town of Denver City. It's one of the hazards you have."[53] Clara Peevy's mother did not publicly blame the company for the death of her daughter either, saying only, "I just don't know why such things have to happen."[54]

In the following weeks, state and national press descended on the isolated community. One such headline is depicted in figure 6.1. Locals quickly expressed exhaustion at the attention and a lack of interest in stirring up public controversy. Gene Snyder of the *Denver City Press* lamented that journalists from the nearby city of Lubbock "kept [the story] alive, and we were trying to forget." *Texas Monthly* interviews with Permian Basin residents indicated a similar reluctance to publicly blame ARCO for the accident. One unnamed woman explained, "My husband used to work for the oil company and we've still got relatives who do." She added, "They've been good to us and, well, that's our livelihood. But at the same time, we sure do hate to think of what happened to those folks in Denver City."[55] Such statements reflected loyalty to the industry that dominated the regional economy, and once again articulated an assumption that oil's systemic risks were simply beyond anyone's ability to predict or control.

Economic dependence was a real concern. If ARCO or other producers were forced to shut down their well-flooding operations, many in the area would lose their jobs. Further, such seeming apathy also represented a real local familiarity with the industry's environmental problems, which had been ongoing for decades. As in other Permian Basin oil towns, sensory evidence of oil production was inescapable in Denver City. The rotten-egg smell of leaking gas was a long-standing sign of danger known to workers and other residents. Stories of sulfur gas blowing off of gushers and across

"Man must be left free to discriminate and to exercise his freedom of choice. This freedom is a virtue and not a vice. And Freedom of choice sows the seeds of peace rather than conflict."—F. A. Harper

THE ODESSA AMERICAN

A FREEDOM NEWSPAPER

PERMIAN EDITION
Price 15 Cents

Vol. 50—No. 34 Odessa, Texas, Monday, February 3, 1975 28 Pages—2 Sections

Denver City Gas Leak Kills Nine

By BOB HORN
American Staff Writer

DENVER CITY — Nine persons tried frantically to outrun death and almost made it, but leaking gas from an oil well wafted through the fog and killed them.

Tom Merrill, who saw death coming, gathered his wife and two young sons and escaped.

Eight of the dead were found outside a house, about 50 yards from the Merrill home and 100 yards from the leaking wellhead.

Some of them dressed in bed clothes, they tried to flee through the rain to safety about 5 a.m. Sunday. Five were found in one car, two in a pickup truck and the eighth had fallen under the truck.

"The house showed all the way through desperate efforts were made to leave," one witness said. "Chairs were overturned and beds rumpled."

The ninth victim, an oilfield worker sent to investigate the leak, was found dead in his pickup truck.

The dead were identified as J.C. Patton, 46, his wife, Glenda, 36, their daughter, DeeDee, 17; Clara Peevey, 14, DeeDee's friend; Alma Lee Amerson, 52, his wife, Edith, 40, of Portales, N.M.; J.R. May, 57, his 56-year-old wife, and Eugene Sparger, 19, the oilfield worker.

Mrs. May was the mother of Mrs. Patton and Mrs. Amerson.

Cas Windham, area supervisor for Atlantic Richfield, which owns the well about 3 miles from Denver City in the Texas Panhandle, said the hydrogen sulfide and carbon dioxide fumes leaked from an experimental injection well in which Atlantic Richfield was using gas instead of water to recover more oil.

What began as a small family reunion for the Patton family Saturday afternoon, ended abruptly about 5:15 a.m. Sunday as eight persons tried to escape and slumped dead in a car and pickup.

Steve Eugne Sparger, 19, a night rider of Atlantic Richfield was also found dead in the pickup he was driving to the area to scout out some pipeline trouble. Sparger apparently slumped over dead at the wheel of his pickup as he drove down the road about four miles north of here and the vehicle ran into the muddy bar ditch before coming to a halt.

The Merrill family, living about 50 yards from the Patton home, narrowly escaped death when Mrs. Merrill was awakened by the smell of the gas. She awakened her husband who quickly loaded the family in their automobile.

* * *

Merrill's first thought were to help his neighbor, but as he turned onto the paved road in front of his modest country home his wife fell unconscious in the floorboard of the car and he raced to get her to the Denver City hospital, stopping along the way to turn in the alarm to the Denver City Volunteer Fire Department.

Yoakum County Justice of the Peace D. H. (Hoyt) Starling pronounced the nine victims dead at the scene due to gas poisoning. He did not order any autopsies.

Funeral arrangments for the nine victims were pending at the Singleton Funeral Home in Denver City.

The nine victims died after carbon dioxide gas, mixed with hydrogen sulfide gas, began escaping from an injection well about 100 yards from the Patton home shortly before 5 a.m. Sunday.

The well is operated by Atlantic Richfield and is one of four wells in a secondary recovery project. E. H. Barnett, an ARCO official blamed the gas leakage on a cracked nipple atop one of the well fittings.

After the carbon dioxide gas started escaping from the well fitting it formed heavy layers of ice over the entire well and a hot water truck had to be called in to melt the ice before the gas could be shut off about 9 a.m. Sunday.

After the deadly gases had cleared from the area about 9 a.m. Sunday, volunteer firemen, law enforcement officials, and oil company personel were able to get to the Patton home where they found eight of the victims outside the home in a car and pickup where they died trying to escape.

Dave Davis, a Denver City volunteer fireman and one of the first on the scene, said five of the victims were in a car, two others in a pickup and Patton was lying on the ground behind the pickup.

Mr. and Mrs. May were in the pickup. Dolores Patton was slumped behind the wheel of the car. In the car with her were her mother, Miss Peevy, and Mr. and Mrs. Amerson.

"The car was still running when we got there," Davis related. "It was in reverse and had backed in a circle, coming to a halt when it hit some parts of a tractor."

Merrill said that his wife woke him shortly after 5 a.m. when she smelled gas.

"I got up and put on my clothes and opened the door when it hit me," he recalled Sunday morning as he stood shivering in a cold rain outside his home. "I called Patton to wake them and he apparently went outside his house because Mrs. Patton called me back and said that he could just barely get back inside and

See DENVER, Page 3-A

* * *

More News On Tragedy

A pictorial report on the tragedy which took nine lives Sunday near Denver City may be found on Page 6A.

Additional stories about a couple who miraculously escaped may be found on Page 1B, along with stories about how the tragedy stunned the town.

An additional photo and information about funeral arrangements for the victims may be found on Page 2A.

* * *

(Staff Photo By Bob Horn)

GAS SPEWS FROM WELL NEAR DENVER CITY DEATH SCENE
...Eight Persons Died Outside J. C. Patton Home

Record For Peacetime---

Ford Asks Big Budget Deficit

WASHINGTON (AP) — President Ford formally asked Congress today to vote a record peacetime budget deficit of $52 billion for fiscal 1976 and signed a "plain truth" economic report that painted the gloomiest picture yet of the nation's ailing fiscal health.

In presenting the $349.4 billion budget, Ford forecast rising unemployment and an even more rapid increase in the cost of living.

He proposed remedies to recession, inflation and energy shortages, saying "they require American to turn in a new direction."

Ford again asked Congress for prompt action and said: "From all Americans we must ask for perseverance and a willingness to tolerate some painful measures necessary to retain good economic health."

In a noontime ceremony, Ford signed the annual economic report of the President, scheduled for release on Tuesday. He said projections in the report show "that we will have turned the economy in a new and more favorable direction well before the end of this year."

He mentioned several of the projections, saying total production between mid-1975 and the end of 1976 should increase by a

Related Stories, Page 4B

five per cent annual rate, adding some 2 million workers to the nation's payroll "so that unemployment — though still high — will be going down."

"We estimate a rate of inflation between December of 1974 and December of 1975 of a little more than 8 per cent," Ford said as he signed the economic report.

"While these projected figures present no rosy picture, they forecast the real improvement we expect in the coming months . . . ," Ford said.

"You will find no attempt to evade the plain truth here. The figures used are honest and conservative, — and we hope to do better than the forecast."

Earlier, as he put his signature to the budget in the Oval Office, Ford replied to sharply critical initial reaction from Congress by saying:

"These are not normal times and the measures I propose — to give the economy a boost with tax rebates and reductions, and to provide greatly expanded assistance to the unemployed — are responsible for some of the deficit. Lagging receipts from tax revenues contribute to most of the remainder of this deficit."

The President warned Congress that the deficit "will be even larger" if it fails to go along "with reductions totaling $17 billion which I have requested."

And he warned: "If we are to achieve long range economic stability in this country, free from ever-rising inflation, we must put into effect permanent reductions in program expenditures."

Ford said government expenditures "are controllable if the Congress and the President join together to hold down excessive spending."

Because of the size of the deficit, Ford said he was prepared "to go far beyond custom and good manners in pledging my utmost cooperation" with the Congress to help stimulate the economy and reduce the rate of federal spending.

In the initial Congressional reaction, Rep. Al Ullman, D-Ore., chairman of the Ways and Means Committee, said it was "highly doubtful" that Congress would approve all of the $17 billion in budget cuts proposed by the President.

Ullman said Ford has proposed trimming social programs by $6 billion, and that Congress won't approve cuts in such areas as Social Security increases and food stamps.

Congress may decide to make its own cuts, Ullman said, but they were likely to be in areas such as defense.

Ford was expected to seek an $11 billion hike in defense spending, but Ullman

See FORD, Page 8A

Evacuation Terms To End Occupation

GRESHAM, Wis. (AP) — The conclusion of the Menominee Warrior Society's seizure of an unused mansion hinged today on terms for evacuating the militant demonstrators.

An agreement for the Menominee tribe to acquire the property from the owners, a Roman Catholic order, was hailed as a victory for Indians nationwide.

But until the details can be worked out, an estimated 40 demonstrators remain in the 64 room mansion and the National Guard has tightened its 625 man security force around the rural property.

Robert Bryan, legal adviser to the demonstrators, told the American Indian Movement (AIM) the demonstrators want assurances of protection from angry whites, who have threatened reprisals for the takeover.

Bryan said further talks were underway in the mansion about evacuation details; he did not elaborate.

The Guard promised military protection for the Indians, who have occupied the estate for more than a month. Under the

tually empty since 1968, adjoins Menominee land.

The Alexians announced the agreement Sunday. They said they had met the deed demand and asked church groups help the tribe finance a "fair" but unspecified payment. The Alexians originally had asked $750,000 for house and land.

Dennis Banks, AIM executive director and a veteran of the 71-day 1973 takeover of Wounded Knee, S.D., called the deed settlement "one victory in the longest war."

Inside Today's
ODESSA AMERICAN

SUGAR PRICES — Lower Sugar Prices Helped Cut The Family Grocery Bill In The First Month of 1975. (Page 7A)

CAR SALES — United Auto Workers President Leonard Woodcock Says Car Sales Will Be Back To 1973 Levels Before The End

FIGURE 6.1. The media quickly descended on Denver City, and images of the Pattons' home appeared in newspapers across Texas, as in this front-page story from the *Odessa American*. Image courtesy of the *Odessa American*.

oil camps and incapacitating, blinding, or killing workers were common.[56] In oral histories taken in the 1950s, workers vividly remembered dropping their tools and running if they smelled sulfur and recounted Depression-era efforts to develop makeshift sulfur gas-warning systems out of linked strings of bells and steam whistles.[57] While well management had dramatically improved by the 1970s, drilling accidents, pipeline leaks, and H2S remained known risks. In 1967, for example, two workers were asphyxiated one mile north of Denver City while repairing a machine that gathered and disposed of salt brine water used in well injection operations.[58] Later, six oil-field workers repairing an improperly welded crude oil pipeline were killed by sulfur gas in December 1974 near Abilene, east of Denver City.[59]

In October of that same year, two workers were killed while cleaning equipment near Snyder.[60] Still, the region's low-grade oil, expensive to refine and particularly toxic, was extremely lucrative in 1975 in the context of the global energy crisis. The local popular press regularly reminded residents that oil had always produced "the smell of money" in the Permian Basin.

Oil's economic importance could not have been far from the minds of the numerous locals who publicly expressed a belief that sensory familiarity and the ad hoc systems developed to manage oil's environmental risk were adequate safeguards. In an interview with the *Odessa American*, W. C. Faulkner, an Odessa businessman and former oil-field worker, argued that "the situation just isn't that dangerous and a man just doesn't get gassed too often because you learn to respect it."[61] Faulkner reminded readers that he "has worked in the oil fields most of his life and came to this part of the country in the early 1930s. . . . Everyone in the oil fields has worked around the sour gas, or hydrogen sulfide, all [our lives] without any problems."[62]

Such a perspective seemingly cut across class lines. The Pattons' neighbor, Tom Merrill, spoke with the press several times. He emphasized that his personal familiarity with industry dangers actually saved his family. Merrill worked for Shell Oil, and in 1975, he owned a home only fifty yards from the Pattons. Like Glenda Patton, Merrill smelled the telltale rotten-egg smell early Sunday morning. He reported to the local press, "I recognized the odor and knew what we were up against." He reportedly spoke to the Pattons on the phone about the danger before he and his wife and two sons fled to the hospital in Denver City. According to Merrill, once he got in the car, his wife immediately passed out. Essie Merrill was admitted for H2S poisoning but ultimately recovered.[63] They left behind a cat and dog that were killed by the gas.

In a marked contrast to such perspectives, national and international news organizations used the tragedy to call for a broad federal inquiry into oil pipeline safety. Blame spread globally and was quickly assigned to ARCO in publications from the *Wall Street Journal*, to the *Los Angeles Times*, to the *Jerusalem Post*. Well injection was a particular target of the criticism.[64] Despite the fact that H2S was a well-known hazard in the region, the press described it as a newly discovered "epidemic" in Texas oil fields, the result of new technologies developed by irresponsible and incompetent oil companies. Such publicity reframed decades-old industry practices as unacceptable risks, implicitly making a sharp distinction between oil producers and the communities in which they operated. Oil companies were not a part of these communities, but an environmental burden placed upon them in the name of profit. And according to the national press, locals should not be held personally responsible for managing such risks imposed on them by such outsiders. For many local workers, while they probably felt genuine sadness at the deaths of the Pattons and their guests and were concerned about future accidents, such fully oppositional narratives probably did not match their personal experiences. For local oil producers, such attention also raised the unwanted and expensive specter of further federal intervention into daily operations.

THE CAMPAIGN AGAINST REGULATION

On February 3, 1975, one day after the Denver City tragedy, OSHA and the soon-to-be independent National Transportation Safety Board (NTSB) sent investigators to Denver City. They did not receive a warm welcome. OSHA sent Noah "Mike" Shopenn south to Denver City from Lubbock, in the Texas Panhandle. Shopenn was a longtime resident of West Texas and an industrial hygienist and health physicist for OSHA and the US Department of Labor.[65] His fellow investigator, Henry Shepherd, boarded a flight from Washington, DC, as the acting director of the new NTSB Pipeline Safety Division. The NTSB was set to become operationally independent later that year and Denver City was part of Shepherd's national investigation into pipeline accidents. As the NTSB's new director, he was probably eager to present his resulting summary report to Congress.

Although their investigation was nominally on behalf of the victims and the local community, Shopenn and Shepherd found their efforts immediately rebuffed. Upon his arrival, Shepherd discovered that local officials had already closed the case, which had been opened only the day before. Undeterred, Shepherd ordered autopsies on the victims. However, he was informed that they already had been embalmed. Embalming drains the body of blood, making it impossible to test for blood oxygen levels or the presence of toxic chemicals. Denver City Justice of the Peace Hoyt Starling had quickly decided to close the case and release the bodies. This decision was picked up by the *Lubbock Avalanche-Journal*, which informed readers that Starling had previously spent twenty-seven years working for ARCO. He explained that he had declined to order autopsies simply because the deaths were so obviously due to gas poisoning.[66] Shepherd rebutted this contention, pointing out that the goal was to determine exactly which gas killed the nine people—carbon dioxide or H_2S. Starling reassured Shepherd that he had consulted a Dallas pathologist and, on that advice, ordered several of the dead animals in the area frozen for analysis.[67]

Despite the back-and-forth posturing, lab results from the dead animals confirmed that there was no mystery. The injection well contained 95 percent carbon dioxide, 4.5 percent H_2S, and 1 percent miscellaneous gases, and 4.5 percent was more than enough to kill. When confronted by the press, ARCO representatives readily admitted that their well-injection systems normally contained H_2S. ARCO's public relations officer, Carter Barcus, lamented, "Of course, the community is familiar with the oil industry and these hazards. It doesn't make it any easier to take though."[68] As his statement implied, H_2S was endemic to the region, and locals should have been aware of the danger. Also implicit was the understanding that if locals wanted to boost production in almost-depleted fields, they were depending on risky operations like ARCO's experimental pipeline.

Amid the backdrop of the energy crisis and national calls for more domestic oil production, it was unclear how both optimized industry expansion and greater attention to health and safety could be implemented together. ARCO was a venerable oil company and had already invested much in the experimental injection system. It was founded in 1915 as Rio Grande Oil Company, based in El Paso, and supplied fuel to US army battalions fighting the Mexican revolutionary Pancho Villa.[69] Two decades later, in 1936, Rio Grande Oil was subsumed in a merger with several other oil companies to become part of the California-based Richfield Oil. In 1964, Richfield opened a large research and development laboratory in Plano, Texas, which specialized in geophysics and oil exploration.[70] Just two years later, in 1966, Richfield merged yet again, this time with the Sinclair Oil Corporation of New York and the Atlantic Refining Company, based in Philadelphia and at one time part of the Standard Oil Trust. After the merger, the new oil major, Atlantic Richfield (ARCO), was based out of Los Angeles with its oil and gas division headquartered in downtown Dallas.

ARCO rose to prominence in 1968 as one of the initial discoverers of the vast Prudhoe Bay oil field in Alaska.[71] In the middle of a national debate over the environmental impact of drilling in pristine Alaskan wilderness, the oil crisis had boosted ARCO's West Texas operations. The company constructed an extensive extraction and transport infrastructure specifically to facilitate carbon dioxide injection.[72] The operation represented not only sunk costs, but also efforts to optimize new technologies and reduce resource waste—goals that had long aligned with federal resource management agencies. The investigation by Shopenn and his team were indicative of a new trend, the expansion of federal health and safety oversight, which had mushroomed in the early 1970s.

One year earlier, on March 27, 1974, an anticorruption push had prompted legislation to separate the NTSB from the US Department of Transportation. The newly independent NTSB assumed jurisdiction over all fatal pipeline accidents in the United States—a daunting task. In 1974, the NTSB's new Office of Pipeline Safety only had two employees, Barry Sweedler and Acting Chief of Pipeline Safety Henry Shepherd, who led the investigation into the Denver City tragedy. Sweedler and Shepherd were together given the herculean task of administering new safety regulations on the nation's entire interstate pipeline system, 13,534 miles of which had been constructed in 1970 alone.[73]

Despite such limitations, Congress expected results, as pipeline accidents and fatalities had become more common, in part due to the uptick in domestic production after the 1973 oil embargo. In a 1974 congressional hearing, Shepherd accompanied NTSB Chair John Reed, who testified that fatalities on natural gas lines alone had increased from sixteen to fifty-nine between 1969 and 1973. There were twenty-four fatal natural gas pipeline accidents in 1974. Alarmingly, Reed also warned that during the same period, the total number of major oil pipeline leaks or failures that caused fatalities was much greater. Numbers were up from 1,285 in 1972 to 1,477 in 1974.[74]

Reports illustrated that pipeline accidents were largely civilian tragedies, killing mostly people unaffiliated with oil production.[75] And prophetically, a full year before the Denver City accident, Reed and Shepherd identified many of the issues that contributed to the tragedy. Reed in particular testified that insufficient training for pipeline personnel delayed shutdowns during emergencies and blamed oil companies for not adequately warning surrounding communities: "We believe more needs to be done to acquaint customers and others at risk of the hazards, because we continue to find that the problem is not sufficiently recognized." They called for a national hazard education program focused on oil and gas infrastructure.[76] While the NTSB lacked the authority to enforce specific regulations, their suggestions were on trend with the era's national push for public safety awareness. However, Congress did not implement a national pipeline awareness campaign. Instead, in early 1975, Sweedler and Shepherd's office was expanded to include a full Pipeline Safety Division, tasked with safety inspections for all interstate pipelines. Later that year, the Hazardous Materials Transportation Act again expanded the NTSB's jurisdiction, tasking the board with monitoring rural gathering pipelines within individual states, not just larger pipelines that crossed state borders.

In this context, while still hamstrung by limited resources and enforcement ability, the NTSB's arrival in Denver City stepped on the toes of not just ARCO, but also local independents, small producers, and Texas regulators who were concerned about the organization's sweeping jurisdiction. Just five years earlier, in 1970, Texas oil producers had watched in alarm as President Nixon signed the National Environmental Protection Act (NEPA) and established the EPA. The EPA, and later the NTSB, joined OSHA in oil industry oversight. The Clean Air Act and subsequent federal water-quality acts only increased the federal presence, as officials seemingly focused only on the industry's risks to health and safety and ignored its many economic risks. This was a particular problem in the Permian Basin, where a desire for federal attention to economic unfairness, especially for independent oil producers, had permeated local politics for decades.

A perception that both state and federal governments were controlled by the interests of major oil companies had sparked the creation of organizations including the powerful Mid-Continent Oil and Gas Association, the Permian Basin Petroleum Association, and the Texas Independent Producers and Royalty Owners Association (TIPRO). For these and other groups, health and safety could not be separated from tense, long-standing debates about regulation, resource management, and local sovereignty.[77] In an interview with the *Lubbock Avalanche Journal*, John Wagner of the Texas Mid-Continent Oil and Gas Association suggested that potential new pipeline regulations would be "a very tough order that will require greatly increased expense in administrative costs." Another West Texas independent described adhering to potential new rules as a "physical impossibility," and Lubbock oil producer J. Roy McCoy predicted that regulation would produce a "blizzard of papers" and the TRRC would need to put up "a new building to process the papers."[78] Their stance was clear—safety regulation inhibited the ability of small producers to function, and enforcement produced needless delays and insurmountable logistical challenges.

However, as the NTSB's limited staffing implied, despite the sweeping regulatory and investigative apparatuses promised by the creation of OSHA and the EPA, most assessment and enforcement of environmental hazards remained the purview of state and local authorities in 1975. Perhaps reflecting the local political power of Texas oil companies or indicative of national economic pressures, OSHA and the Texas Department of Public Safety (TDPS) fined ARCO only $1,125 for inadequately training its employees about the dangers of H2S, poor employee respiratory equipment, and insufficient monitoring gear. Although other members of the Patton family would later sue ARCO for $1 million, no public charges were brought against the company for the civilian deaths.[79] ARCO seemingly found the fine acceptable. The company's internal investigation noted the pipeline's technical problems and did not publicly contest the findings from OSHA and TDPS.[80]

OSHA, the NTSB, and TDPS set the task of creating and enforcing new pipeline regulations to the TRRC, a key ally of local producers. In a study of the TRRC, sociologist David Prindle characterized the organization as a "producer advocacy agency rather than a consumer advocate."[81] History bears this out.[82] The TRRC's historically feather-light touch when addressing workplace hazards and environmental contamination reflected a long-standing relationship between Texas oil producers and the nominally regulatory body. In this and other moments of crisis, TRRC regulators openly favored Texas oil producers rather than displaying concerns about resource waste, environmental damage, or an obligation to consumers.[83] In particular, the economic concerns of independent oil producers—which included opposition to the multinationals, localized control over oil resources, and an acceptance of a high level of environmental risk—were paramount.

Proceedings from a series of remarkably cordial hydrogen sulfide hearings in Austin were indicative of the TRRC's chosen role. Held in the spring of 1975, the mood was deeply sympathetic to the plight of oil producers. Midland lawyer Tom Sealy questioned J. H. Sullivan, the engineer who designed ARCO's failed experimental pipeline on behalf of the TRRC. Sealy asked Sullivan to explain the pipeline's technical design, but Sullivan also emphasized the nation's economic needs, reminding his listeners that due to "renewed emphasis on producing oil and gas, there are going to be some risks in this endeavor," and he likened the victims of the Denver City tragedy to astronauts killed in the space program.[84]

In a later interview, Arthur Barbeck, chief engineer of the TRRC Oil and Gas Division, gently critiqued the use of H2S in well injection, saying that "if it's got some bugs in it, they need to be ironed out."[85] Altogether, the hearings displayed the TRRC's acceptance of environmental risks as inherent to the industry that it was intended to regulate, and TRRC officials expressed sympathy for oil companies that felt pressured by the possibility of outside regulation. Later, according to the *Texas Monthly*, during a TRRC meeting to discuss possible new regulations, one administrator remarked, "My God, [we] already had OSHA inspectors looking over [our] shoulders at every move."[86] This panicked focus on the economic impact of environmental risk reduction was echoed in the popular press.

Such a perspective was probably not shared by all members of the industry. Period OCAW discussions about H2S and oil industry air contamination sounded very different. During OCAW's information-gathering tour ahead of OSHA's founding legislation, attendees discussed H2S at length. Interviewees painted a picture of a known and feared hazard with a cumulative, long-term impact on worker health. At a 1970 OCAW public health seminar in Houston, an unnamed refinery worker asked OCAW health investigator Glen Paulson to describe the acceptable levels of human exposure to H2S. The worker was concerned because he felt unsafe encountering the gas regularly while working at a Gulf Coast oil refinery. In response, Paulson defined H2S as a slow-numbing agent that "can reach such levels that it actually acts as a general nervous-system poison and kills somebody, usually by stopping his breathing."[87] Unlike TRRC officials five years later, who described H2S as well known and well managed, Paulson linked long-term, low-level exposure to chronic lung diseases, especially emphysema. He also singled out the common practice of burning off H2S waste at refineries and pointed out that the practice created large amounts of sulfur dioxide, which was a common, deadly urban air pollutant.[88]

Further, unlike the individualized risk assessment described by W. C. Faulkner, Tom Merrill, and Permian Basin oil producers in the local press, the OCAW hearings described industry workers as collectively dissatisfied with institutional responses. For example, in other 1970 OCAWU testimony, Bill Ricks, secretary-treasurer of OCAW Local 4023 in Port Arthur, described his entire refinery crew walking off the job for hours at a time to avoid mass exposure to H2S released from sour crude.[89] For at least some workers, H2S was considered a serious problem.

Three months after the tragedy, in April 1975, the TRRC amended its Texas Administrative Code to include a new Rule 36, which imposed significant changes to pipeline management. Updates included the required labeling of hazardous gas lines, better security and warning systems at pipelines, and the creation of formal contingency plans in emergencies. The amendment also prohibited the placement of pipelines carrying H2S within 500 feet of highways or dwellings. This rule could be amended through a TRRC hearing.[90] These changes were written by James Smith, assistant director of field operations for the TRRC Oil and Gas Division and a former TRRC field engineer in West Texas. Smith worked in close cooperation with oil producers, publishing these updates only after an ARCO-led investigation during the spring of 1975.[91] ARCO had also worked in tandem with the Texas Department of Public Safety (TDPS), the TRRC, and federal investigators from OSHA and the NTSB. Rule 36 was enforced by permit beginning in 1976. That same year, the TRRC tightened regulations for the handling and use of H2S in any oil and gas operations.[92]

In 1976, just before Rule 36 was to go into effect, Smith was brought into a seminar in Odessa to placate industry representatives.[93] Local press lauded his industry ties, reassuring readers that he was "trained as an oilman." Smith, a graduate of Abilene High School in West Texas and the Petroleum Engineering Department at Texas A&M University, was clearly aware of the local opposition to oversight.[94] He also probably understood the real dangers posed by H2S. His competing allegiances were on display during the seminar. Smith downplayed the risks posed by H2S for his audience and implied that the new rules were simply a public relations effort: "What we [the TRRC and the oil industry] have to do is convince the public not to worry about hydrogen sulfide because the industry is taking care of the situation."

While describing new requirements for signage and fencing around hazardous pipelines, Smith explained that the goal was to prevent general panic and cultivate trust in the industry as experts on the danger: "In all these areas of the act we are dealing with the predictable hazard concerning the public." He also articulated TRRC goals as developing industry-led regulatory structures that would not hurt smaller producers. He downplayed the scope of TRRC oversight, explaining a plan to let the industry set testing requirements for the allowable H_2S content of oil wells, pipelines, and tanks. Further, Smith explained that this would help the TRRC avoid "creat[ing] a whole new bureaucracy."[95]

Smith's industry credentials and soft-pedaling were a comparative success. Just one day earlier, local oil producers were less cordial toward representatives from the new federal agencies. Mike Shopenn was tasked at the meeting with answering questions about the new regulations. While the content of his presentation was not recorded by the press, he was joined by Robert Simmons, area director of the Lubbock OSHA office. Simmons started his presentation on the defensive, saying, "Most think OSHA is controversial and others simply don't like it, but OSHA is here and OSHA is controversial."[96] Unable or unwilling to cater to the economic concerns of oil producers, he had clearly been prepared for a hostile audience.

The regulatory response to the Denver City tragedy had a conflicted legacy. As indicated by the vocal protestations of antiregulatory pundits in West Texas, TRRC's Rule 36 was a comparatively strong effort to reduce oil's public health risks. This decision required locally unpopular regulation to prevent future tragedy. However, federal officials left the creation of these new regulations up to the notoriously pro-industry TRRC during a period of national energy crisis, once again allowing the Texas oil industry essentially to regulate itself. A focus on public awareness-raising instead of mandating clear exposure standards meant that the state response was also a consolatory effort to paper over ongoing and well-known hazards in the name of expanded production. Throughout the process of debating, writing, and approving the new regulations, the needs, concerns, and fears of differing groups within the oil industry fundamentally influenced public discourse surrounding the tragedy and its resulting regulatory policy. These same oil producers and oil workers responded to the Denver City tragedy in the context of major political changes across the state and the nation. Their reactions were indicative of such broader trends.

RISK, DEREGULATION, AND DEPENDENCE

Sociologists writing in the 1970s identified the oil and gas industry as one of the central economic pillars of a rising Sun Belt economy. A big-tent political and economic alliance that stretched from Georgia to California, the Sun Belt represented a growing coalition of resurgent social conservatives, segregationists, libertarians, and even some growth-minded progressives. Sun Belt municipal leaders and regional boosters were united in their support for select industries, including agriculture, defense, advanced technology, real estate and construction, tourism and leisure, and oil production.[97] These were all industries that hinged on constant market growth and access to cheap land and other natural resources.[98] Case in point—it would have been hard for Sun Belt boosters to deny the singular importance of Permian Basin geology and natural resource infrastructure to the Texas economy. And with natural resource exploitation and resulting environmental risks under increased scrutiny in the 1970s, representatives from these industries increasingly turned to popular politics to cultivate allies and power. Significantly, scholars describe a political and social consensus that emerged in Sun Belt cities during this period. Residents "internalized the pro-growth, antiregulatory, free market assurances of venture capitalism and sought to limit the reach of the federal state in sectors that did not serve these interests."[99] While used most often by scholars to describe trends in urban politics, such a perspective also extended to the largely rural Permian Basin through oil producers' responses to risk—particularly the individualized and antiregulatory responses to economic and environmental hazards cultivated for over fifty years on drilling rigs, in mobile engineering offices, and in Midland office towers.

Even as Texas boosters touted Houston's and San Antonio's business-friendly tax policies and federal defense dollars as key to their emergence as new Sun Belt metropolises, in the era of political transition and the energy crisis, the Permian Basin remained a linchpin for the Texas economy and its politics. Permian Basin sour crude was the economic and political fuel that maintained Texas's rapid expansion and the political impact of the Permian Basin financial and technical successes anticipated statewide deregulatory trends.

With such local, state, and national implications, a lot was riding on the promises of continued oil abundance made by ARCO and other operators in the late 1960s. Although Permian Basin oil production peaked in 1973, investors, speculators, and wildcatters continued to bet big in the region later in the decade, relying on secondary and enhanced recovery methods to keep oil flowing.[100] For example, after record years in 1975 and 1976, the 1978 annual report from the Parker Drilling Company in the Permian

Basin proudly boasted that the region continued to be "the pioneer deep drilling area of the nation."[101] The region had always been an extractive economy, but the oil crisis had only strengthened its dependence on creative and increasingly widespread resource intensification for economic survival. And by the end of the 1970s, these trends looked simultaneously more stable and riskier than ever.

Neither Rule 36 nor the presence of new federal agencies removed all of oil's public safety risks. Workers, maintenance crews, and members of the general public continued to be injured and killed in unlucky encounters with its vast infrastructure. NTSB records from that period revealed continued Texas pipeline fatalities. In October 1975, six months after the Denver City tragedy, three workers were killed and two injured by a pipeline explosion at a gas processing plant in Goldsmith, Texas.[102] About one year later, in 1976, five were killed by a vapor cloud and resulting fire emanating from a liquid natural gas pipeline leak near the small Panhandle town of Whitharral.[103] In February 1977, a gas pipeline explosion killed two and injured another member of a repair crew outside Munday, Texas, north of the Permian Basin.[104] Later that year, a pipeline contractor hit an unmarked propane line in Sterling City, Texas. With propane leaking into the air, an unsuspecting driver nearby started the engine of his truck. The resulting explosion severely burned the driver, ultimately killing him.[105]

During the same period, some Texas oil workers sought to apply new federal regulations to advocate for better health and safety precautions and increased compensation for injury or death. In 1977, the *Odessa American* recorded that a group of undisclosed parties began a short-lived, $300,000 lawsuit against El Paso Products Company, seeking damages for health problems caused by long-term exposure to toxic chemicals at its Odessa petrochemical plant.[106] Similarly, between 1975 and 1979, OCAW representatives continued to rally Permian Basin oil workers, having some limited successes as an advocate for health and safety. However, the industry's overwhelming dominance made it difficult for these and other groups to gain widespread support. Midge Erskine described Permian Basin oil's political power during this period as stifling most environmental legal action: "I know in one case, the foreman of the jury told the jury that they could not find that oil company guilty. They had to say they were innocent on a case because everybody worked . . . for an oil company or they had a family member that worked for an oil company and they would lose their jobs. It's just that simple."[107] In the late 1970s, it was a truism in Texas that oil money dominated Texas politics and Texas industry—literally from the ground up.

In 1975, oilmen controlled the Denver City government, and most of these officials easily avoided political fallout from the tragedy and subsequent investigation. For example, after the H2S tragedy, Denver City mayor Ed Gayle did not seek reelection in May 1975. Of the four mayoral candidates, retired oil-field worker J. P. Garner and Shell Oil electrician J. H. Power had close ties to oil.[108] Despite his connection to the H2S controversy, Robert Edgar Self Jr. was elected to the Denver City council in 1975.[109] Further, Hoyt Starling was a former ARCO employee and Yoakum Country Sheriff Ike Toler was also a retired oil-field worker. Similarly, Texas House Representative E. L. Short of Tahoka was a wealthy rancher with diversified business holdings who represented the rural Permian Basin and South Plains, including Yoakum County and Denver City. He had vocally supported the TRRC's H2S investigation and subsequent regulation.[110] A conservative Democrat, Short expressed a vocal commitment to Rule 36, but that did not indicate a lack of support for oil producers. In speeches, he indicated that further federal intervention in Texas oil procedures would not win him reelection, but he needed to balance the needs of powerful oil producers against environmental threats to voters.

Similar industry alliances were seen in other West Texas oil communities, especially Midland and Odessa, where most appointed officials and civic leaders worked in oil or had in the past. For example, a 1970 article announcing that EPNG plant manager W. T. Edwards had been elected vice president of El Paso Products, the *Odessa American* also informed readers that Edwards was the past president of the Odessa Chamber of Commerce, Odessa Kiwanis Club, Permian Basin Petroleum Association, Southern Little League, and Odessa Country Club.[111]

Perhaps unsurprisingly, an array of elected and appointed officials touted their workplace experience in oil as providing administrative credentials. This extended from regional TRRC investigators in the Permian Basin to the halls of the legislature in Austin. Such oil industry connections were not necessarily indicative of corruption, although the Texas legislature was notorious for its bribery schemes and collusion. Rather, it meant that oil's responses to risk, danger, regulation, and financial and public health uncertainty influenced the regulatory and public responses to all major issues, ranging from regional water shortages to pipeline disasters to statewide economic planning. More specifically, with workplace dangers cast as individual problems natural to the oil industry and to the region, and with federal regulators alternately described as violators of immutable states' rights and bureaucratic inhibitors to natural-resource profits, a tendency to understand federal regulations as unnecessary and intrusive easily became the political and cultural consensus.

Texas Governor Dolph Briscoe, a Democrat, was elected in 1973 at the start of the oil crisis and served until 1979. He swept into power on promises of transparency and reform. However, aside from instigating a new statewide Open Records Act, Briscoe was largely a hands-off governor in practice, content to allow his appointees, largely pulled from the oil industry, to navigate the energy crisis, fend off federal oversight over Texas oil, and allocate a ramp-up in state oil tax revenues. Echoing the oil lobby, the governor generally advocated for a less-is-more approach that minimized regulation of any kind. According to Briscoe, "It is not the duty or function of government to solve all the problems that exist in today's society."[112] However this was not simply his personal opinion. In 1976, *Texas Monthly* reporter Griffin Smith Jr. speculated that Briscoe "might be in touch with a genuine, and rising, public desire to restrain government's apparently limitless growth, a desire that may be the coming thing in contemporary politics."[113] Briscoe, the product of a state economy steeped in the logic of oil extraction, was indicative of a broader Sun Belt aversion to social reformist policy and any constraints on financial speculation.

Briscoe was a rancher from the small town of Uvalde in South Texas. A friend to Texas independents, he embodied the era's trends in Sun Belt political leadership. With holdings of more than 600,000 acres, Briscoe was the largest individual landowner in Texas and a well-known civic presence. President of the Texas and Southwestern Cattle Raisers Association, president of the Texas State Chamber of Commerce, and owner of the First State Bank of Uvalde, he maintained many oil wells on his massive property. Through his large investment portfolio, Briscoe was an old-money Texas elite. He also embodied the speculative land- and resource-heavy economy of the new Sun Belt. While not trained in petroleum science, he sat on the National Petroleum Council and chaired the Interstate Oil Compact Commission (IOCC), which coordinated voluntary oil conservation among US states.[114]

Although he was not publicly quoted on the issue, in such roles Briscoe probably agreed with Texas Representative Milton Fox of Houston, a petroleum engineer who in 1975 dismissed the possibility of TRRC safety standards that might change oil production practice: "Scrubbing hydrogen sulfide out of the gas is extremely expensive. If we came up with some half-baked legislation saying everybody has to sweeten the gas in West Texas, we'd just shut them down."[115] For Fox, an industry insider, it was clear that oil's environmental risks were impossible to remove without hurting the oil economy. As a result, the dangers of oil were simply endemic to the region and to the industry.

Fox, Briscoe, and the leaders of the TRRC understood oil resources as both economically pivotal and politically central to Texas's place in the Sun Belt coalition. Case in point—the same year that TRRC's Rule 36 went into effect, Texas regulators began a sustained campaign to reduce federal restrictions on oil profits. This was a key goal that united the often-feuding members of TIPRO, the Permian Basin Petroleum Association, and the Mid-Continent Oil and Gas Association.[116] TIPRO in particular, led by Wichita Falls oil producer Netum Steed, shared a consensus that regulation of the industry was ill advised.[117] In 1976, the TRRC backed their cause, once again banging the drum of state resource sovereignty in an attempt to leverage the importance of Texas oil into policy change. In November 1976, TRRC Chair Jim Langdon, former chief justice of the Court of Civil Appeals in El Paso, announced that he was cutting the state's allowable oil extraction quota from 100 percent to 99 percent.[118] While 1 percent was mostly a symbolic move and would no longer send global prices spiraling, it was an attempt to remind federal officials of Texas's control over a strategic resource. In Washington, this sparked protests that Texas regulators were manipulating prices on behalf of Texas producers. The reason for this move became clear in the summer of 1977, as Langdon appeared before Congress to oppose higher taxes on oil profits and argued for an end to federal oil price caps.[119]

Langdon was a relatively new Briscoe appointee. However, he joined others in the TRRC, such as the previous chair Ben Ramsey, who shared similar perspectives. Ramsey had also supported Texas control over natural resources and the reduction of oil taxes. He fought OCAW and other labor unions over social welfare programs and desegregation, putting him at odds with the Johnson administration and in line with most conservative Southern Democrats of the day.[120] Ramsey retired in 1977. Briscoe replaced him with oil industry insider Jon Newton, a member of the TIPRO Senior

Advisory Council and past member of both the Texas Mining Council and the IOCC. Newton had deep industry knowledge, which Briscoe hoped would help lead Texas oil producers through the era of crisis. He also supported the deregulatory push.

At their 1977 annual meeting in San Antonio, TIPRO members such as Austin-based oil speculator William Koch and longtime Midland resident and former John F. Kennedy appointee Jerome O'Brien considered the newly elected US president, Jimmy Carter, a particular enemy.[121] In 1976 speeches, Carter had articulated "energy conservation" as central to economic revitalization.[122] Such a phrase flew in the face of how Texas oil producers understood resource management. In a 1977 speech that harkened back to the energy debates of the 1930s, TRRC commissioner Langdon harshly criticized the idea of conservation as an attack on the Texas economy and way of life. He exclaimed before an audience of oil producers, "There is no indication that Texas has any prospect of receiving a fair 'shake' from the energy policies proposed at the federal level. . . . Texas depends on the oil and gas industry and must continue to do everything within reason to maintain and to expand exploration for and development of these resources."[123] Langdon articulated a competing definition of resource conservation that was tied to constant growth: "The concept of conservation in Texas [is] where the ideal is to increase the availability of energy for those purposes for which the energy is most useful to humanity."[124] For Langdon and other Texas legislators who equated political and economic power with "energy independence," the constant increase in production of a fundamentally finite resource was both necessary and possible, so long as oil producers were given adequate market incentives.[125]

Significantly, in the nation's premier extractive zone, political and industry leaders called on regulators to instead preserve the economic playing field by minimizing economic barriers to competition and setting safeguards against unfair advantages.[126] Throughout the Sun Belt, such connections easily translated beyond oil, with risk being a natural and necessary part of the oil-fueled economy. For the belabored President Carter, incremental deregulation seemed to be a good compromise. Even as he famously installed solar panels on the White House and angered oil producers with talk of consumer energy conservation, the president also instigated regulatory rollbacks in numerous industries, including trucking, banking, commercial air travel, and the further deregulation of oil prices.

Such efforts were an attempt to fix the era's economic problems by encouraging competition and were remarkably similar to the cries coming from oil independents over the previous several decades.

As Texas oil producers basked in their renewed importance, the interdependence of the global oil industry was again highlighted in 1979, as the Iranian Revolution resulted in yet another oil shortage for US consumers. Prices spiked again to the excitement of domestic oil producers. However, despite Langdon's bluster on behalf of Texas oil royalties, it was clear that the global oil industry had slipped out of US control.[127] In response, Carter began the process of fully deregulating oil prices, a gift to Permian Basin producers that longed for further profits.[128] Oil production in the Permian Basin reached a peak in 1980 after seven years of constant expansion.[129] That same year, Ronald Reagan handily won the entirety of West Texas in the 1980 presidential election, supported by powerful Permian Basin Republican and TIPRO founder H. J. Porter.[130] The election signaled a statewide Republican shift that would become only more pronounced over the rest of the twentieth century.

In 1981, Reagan fully deregulated the US crude oil market for the first time. Domestic prices quickly rose to $31.77 per barrel, matching OPEC market prices; and this was met with thunderous applause in the Permian Basin.[131] The next year, the TRRC returned the Texas allowable extraction quota to 100 percent.

CONCLUSION

The Last Boom?

At the height of the oil industry boom of the 1970s, Texas, and especially West Texas, seemingly represented a new order. Politicians and business leaders touted Texas as the heart of the rising Sun Belt, which would be the catalyst for American economic revitalization, rolling back regulatory constraints on industry and allowing markets to better regulate financial activity and daily workplace practices.[1] Locally, such calls were in part based on evidence from the oil industry's specific history and its promise of future exponential growth. After all, technological development had made Permian Basin oil exploration continuously profitable for decades in spite of the limitations of climate and geology. Physical risks could seemingly be overcome or sufficiently cushioned by the application of enough capital and new technologies. However, cracks were starting to show. Land was central to the oil economy, but the decades-long intensification of resource extraction and energy use required its simultaneous abstraction into balance-sheet line items and engineering reports. Such abstraction hastened regional environmental depletion.

Simultaneously, oil employees at all levels and in all branches of the industry engaged in battles between workers and management over safety and access to profit that were fundamentally contestations over the boundaries of acceptable industry risks. However, such push and pull existed against the inextricable backdrop of the exploitation of finite natural resources and the true cost of cheap energy. In this context, local tolerance for risk was put to the test in the early 1980s as another industry bust swept through the region. The downturn would continue for over a decade and leave a lasting mark on the entire Texas economy.

After seven years of sharp increases, global oil prices began to flatline in the late 1970s. Supply had skyrocketed as domestic oil producers spent the preceding decade expanding drilling operations. By the mid-1970s, Permian Basin drilling contractors began dipping into their savings to cover rising operating costs. Hoping to maintain production estimates, they took out increasingly large—and increasingly risky—loans, which regional banks were more than happy to provide. It was clear that this system could survive for only so long.[2] At the time, US oil pundits and the popular press blamed both decreases in consumption brought about through 1970s calls for energy conservation and Organization of Petroleum Exporting Countries (OPEC) market manipulation for the declining prices. However, the problem was multifaceted. Domestic production had spiked compared to previous decades. In particular, production in the Prudhoe Bay oil field in Alaska began in 1977, competing with Permian Basin and offshore producers for domestic markets. This created a new oil glut, which by the early 1980s contributed significantly to dramatic price fluctuations, reminiscent of the 1930 crisis. In 1983, oil prices began to drop.[3] Permian Basin oil producers were devastated seemingly overnight, especially the vocally anti-regulatory West Texas independents.[4] Prices did not bottom out until 1986.

This process caused a cascading economic collapse in Texas as loans came due and oil producers were unable to pay their debts to banks and other financial institutions. Oil companies filed for bankruptcy across Texas, with the impact hitting across all economic levels. The average income in the Permian Basin plummeted as oil companies laid off most of their employees. This created a growing hole in the Texas economy. Oil and gas employment decreased by one-third between 1982 and 1994. The oil industry contracted from one-quarter of the total Texas economy in 1981 to around 12 percent by 1991.[5] While most US consumers enjoyed the return to low energy prices, the sudden price drop was catastrophic for oil workers in the Permian Basin, where most of the region's oil-dependent and contract-based workforce maintained no savings or pension plans. While continued global consumption and the rise of new hydraulic fracturing technologies later renewed the Permian Basin boom, the threat of oil busts has also dogged the region into the twenty-first century, and pundits and scholars have called into question unilaterally positive assessments of the Sun Belt's oil-fueled economic miracle.[6]

Indicatively, the impact of the 1980s bust was felt for decades. A comparison between the 1980 and 1990 US Censuses reveals the decadelong impact of the regional downturn. In 1990, seven years after the first drop in oil prices, statewide Texas poverty levels remained at a staggering 20.4 percent, up from 14.6 percent in 1980. Midland County showed a starker downturn, with poverty rates rising sharply from 6.2 percent in 1980 to 14.5 percent in 1990. Populations in West Texas counties decreased as oil workers left for other cities or other industries, exacerbating the decline of small towns throughout the state. Particularly hard hit was West Odessa, an industrial exurb near Odessa made up almost entirely of working-class oil-field personnel. In 1985, three-quarters of the population lived in rented mobile homes, with a poverty rate of 24 percent.[7] High risk, for these workers, had not produced high reward.

As oil companies closed and individuals filed for bankruptcy, the crisis had a ripple effect across local financial institutions, embodied by the 1984 collapse of the First National Bank of Midland.[8] This venerable banking champion of West Texas independents and other small-time oil prospectors was established in 1902 in neighboring Odessa, but had quickly relocated to Midland. At its height in the mid-1970s, the First National Bank of Midland was the largest independent bank in the United States, providing massive, no-collateral loans to small, exploratory operations like the short-lived Arbusto Energy, founded in 1979 by future US President George W. Bush at the peak of the boom.

Throughout the 1970s, the First National Bank of Midland had spent wildly on real estate and other oil-dependent assets. In 1976 the bank opened a new fourteen-story headquarters. The building housed the bank's 650-piece art collection, which included works from the famous landscape painters John James Audubon and Thomas Moran.[9] Later that year, bank leaders dreamed even bigger, buying land to erect two forty-story skyscrapers in downtown Midland and drawing up plans to construct a multiblock Bank of Midland Center. The local press supported such perpetual expansion, even as it was built on shaky ground, dependent on waning local oil supplies and the fragility of global oil prices. As a result many were blindsided when the bottom fell out quickly in October 1984. The *New*

York Times reported the "second largest commercial bank failure in US history."[10] While well-connected oil companies like Arbusto would successfully offset their debts through mergers and buyouts, most small oil companies and individual depositors simply defaulted, unable to pay back the ailing bank. In the aftermath, the bank's assets, including two Rolls-Royces, the sizable art collection, and Hollywood movie rights, were seized by the Federal Deposit Insurance Corporation (FDIC) and sold at a liquidation auction to help cover the bank's more than $1 billion debt. Before the year was out, the land set aside for the Bank of Midland Center was converted into a parking lot.

In a cruel irony, a century of antimonopoly lobbying and resistance to outsider regulatory stabilization in the name of comparative autonomy had ultimately made the Permian Basin less equipped to weather such widespread bust. In the aftermath, a wave of buyouts and industry consolidations in the early 1980s hastened the decline of local independents.[11] In this context, it might seem remarkable that local representatives would defend the industry's long-standing aversion to risk-reducing regulations. However, in 1984, when Kingdon R. Hughes, regional vice president of the Independent Petroleum Association of America (IPAA), was asked to comment on FDIC representatives' public disdain for the First National Bank of Midland's lending practices, he simply lamented, "The big frustration is that they don't know the oil business."[12] While probably an effort to avoid criticizing members of the IPAA during a moment of crisis, there is a marked disconnect between Kingston's reaction and the scope of the industry disaster.

As this book shows, oil's extractive economy encouraged an abstract understanding of risk that privileged immediate economic concerns over dangers to long-term public health or the environment. This was not due to lack of knowledge or attention. Rather, in a process begun by nineteenth century ranchers, the acquisition and sale of diversified natural resources became building blocks for an economy dependent on the constant application of new technologies that only intensified the use of those resources. Further, while the technologies of oil extraction were applied the world over, and the Permian Basin became a training ground for managers and engineers throughout the industry, the seemingly mundane specifics of region and ecology shaped the processes of extraction and efforts to regulate the industry. While Permian Basin oil producers worked hard to overcome isolation and a harsh landscape, they employed new infrastructures that only created new environmental problems for locals. Crucially, throughout this process, the wild success and extreme longevity of Permian Basin oil cast a long shadow over twentieth-century Texas. As certain risks became natural, others were considered unacceptable in a shifting give-and-take that spanned the entire century. Wealth from Permian Basin oil helped to fuse the state's long-standing resource nationalism with a pro-business, antiregulatory agenda that enshrined economic risk, rather than resource conservation, public health, or workplace safety, as the chief concern of state regulators and policymakers. This required a selective understanding of oil's many dangers, which often butted up against energy production's central role in the daily life of oil communities and the reality of a globalizing industry.

Significantly, the 1980s bust did not mean that the industry's physical presence simply disappeared, as with its evaporated profits. The sudden drop in prices created immediate changes on paper—and resulted in deeply uncertain financial futures—but defunct drilling operations could not quickly remove hazards such as the millions of gallons of oil in pipelines, refineries, and storage facilities. Out-of-work oil-field hands did not plug up the thousands of wells drilled in Permian Basin sand, nor did they stop the extreme usage of subsurface water consumed by surviving operations. During and after the bust, Permian Basin workers continued to wrestle with leaking hydrogen sulfide (H2S), failed natural gas lines, contaminated water, and other problems, even as they faced mass layoffs, bankruptcy, and financial precarity.

Local regulators' attention to the industry's environmental impact also did not end with bust, instead decline revealed an array of new problems that industry representatives were even less well equipped to handle. For example, *Odessa American* reporter Pat Weir contacted the Texas Water Commission in 1981 after receiving several phone calls from an anonymous source claiming to work at the Odessa Petrochemical Plant. In a letter to Weir, this source expressed concern about the plant's negligent water treatment practices, saying, "Know this though, they know what they are doing but after reading my letter so will you." The source accused the plant of contaminating local groundwater with massive amounts of benzene, nonsulfur inhibitors, and other chemicals. A 1983 memo from the environmental quality specialist Gary Raven to Robert Fleming, director of enforcement at the Texas Commission for Environmental Quality, revealed that the Water Commission only reluctantly followed up on these accusations. Raven had been assigned to the case in 1982 after the abrupt resignation of Robert Bradshaw, the agent previously assigned to the case. After conducting tests of the water table near the plant, two years after the original complaint, Raven recorded no evidence of such hazards in the local groundwater and recommended further monitoring.[13] The Water Commission ultimately recorded no violations, and Pat Weir never published his investigation. Seemingly, the chaos of industry bust meant that the case was not a top priority.

The situation looked different more than ten years later. In 1995, the Odessa branch of the NAACP took over an ongoing class action lawsuit filed in 1991 by South Odessa residents against the petrochemical processors Shell, Rexene, and Dynagen.[14] The lawsuit accused the companies of gross negligence, declaring that inadequate waste disposal and air emissions equipment at the Odessa Petrochemical Complex were responsible for breathing problems and increased cancer rates among people living in the predominately Black and Hispanic neighborhood.[15] The NAACP cited Dynagen's failure to fully address the more than five hundred safety violations—including unsafe wastewater disposal practices and unchecked air contamination from daily chemical burn-offs—that had been found by the Environmental Protection Agency (EPA), Occupational Safety and Health Administration (OSHA), and state regulators in 1988. Then, in an abrupt reversal of its past policies, the state fined Dynagen $1.4 million and ordered it to update its waste disposal equipment immediately.[16] As late as 1994, Dynagen had installed little of the court-ordered emissions control equipment.

The NAACP lawsuit gained international attention, with commentators calling into question the safety of not just the neighborhood, but all the 200,000 people living in the Odessa/Midland metro area. In 1997, after rejecting an initial lump-sum settlement, the NAACP won its case. Between 850 and 2,100 plaintiffs received an undisclosed monetary settlement, and Dynagen was forced to install $12 million worth of pollution control equipment.[17] Odessa gained a dubious reputation as "the most polluted city in America," and descriptions of the "Odessa syndrome"—a malady that included sore throats and eyes, headaches, nausea, and bloody noses—proliferated in the popular press.[18]

Exemplified by such stories, the resource-based, speculative economy seen in the Permian Basin was both location specific and similar across a twentieth-century, global network of extractive industrial production. Scholars have shown that twentieth century resource economies required complex infrastructures and large-scale land acquisition. Control over key resources, including water, timber, or minerals, within specific property boundaries was crucial to extracting profit, which justified the high cost of developing land.[19] As land, ecologies, and environments were abstracted into numbers on a balance sheet, similar processes were increasingly applied to individuals as all property, and all parts of life, became financial assets, ready for development and subject to market forces. Such "financialization" reframed all risks in economic terms and required a constantly-increasing supply of energy and resources to maintain.[20] Indicatively, if we see the past hundred years of Permian Basin history as a story of energy intensification, in which more and more energy and resources were expended in the name of producing profits for royalty holders and investors, we might understand the Permian Basin's expansive oil fields, complex processing networks, and sun-swept cities, as well as its salty groundwater and polluted air, as physical evidence of the consequences of American capitalism in the twentieth century.[21] This cycle began before oil was discovered in the region and has continued through the bust years of the 1980s and defined the fracking revolution of the 2010s.

Of course, the bankers, speculators, investors, and oil company employees who lived and worked within this system did not simply trade environmental degradation for economic expansion. Based on personal experience and workplace tradition, oil was synonymous with the local landscape and the local economy. The perceived needs of the oil industry, the beleaguered juggernaut that controlled Texas economic and political development, were synonymous with the needs of the community. West Texas oil producers provided cultural, economic, and regulatory justification for these trends. They also became key players in a national political sea-change. We can see the impact of these systems at the state and federal levels, with regulators and elected officials occupying unavoidable positions within this altered economy. Even as Texas oil waned in the 1980s and 1990s, Sun Belt support for deregulation and excitement for market-based guardrails swept the nation. Government risk-reduction systems were dismantled and many others privatized across the country.[22]

In 1994, former Permian Basin oil speculator George W. Bush made his first run for state office, winning election for governor in 1995 against the incumbent, Ann Richards. To counter his East Coast connections and Ivy League pedigree, Bush wore a cowboy hat, spoke in a Texas accent, and regularly referenced his cultural connections and business experience in the capital of oil finance, Midland, Texas, in his campaign speeches. In 1999, while still Texas governor, Bush reinforced this image. He built a ranch on land formerly owned by a German hog farmer near Crawford, in Central Texas. The 3,000-square-foot home and surrounding grounds did not produce cattle or oil for market, but it was a meeting place for boosters, advisors, and visiting dignitaries. It was synonymous with Bush's self-consciously West Texan persona.

As governor, George W. Bush not only bore the legacy of his father's presidency but also embodied the promise of decades of deregulatory agitation from Texas oil independents. While Bush's campaign promise to legalize concealed handguns received much fanfare and his explicit appeals to evangelical Christianity represented a departure from traditional political rhetoric, he also implemented an oil industry–backed push to deregulate state electricity markets.[23] In 2010, against a backdrop of yet another regional oil boom, this deregulation would result, perhaps surprisingly, in the rapid expansion of renewable energy in West Texas as market-minded ranchers and oil speculators sought further uses for their vast landholdings.

That same year, in September 2010, a memorial was erected in Denver City commemorating those killed in the 1975 H2S tragedy. The mother of Clara Peevy, one of the victims, had begun petitioning the city for the memorial in 1997. A rose granite monument was placed at the intersection of Texas Highway 83 and Texas Highway 214, just inside the city limits across from a Pizza Hut. The monument listed the names of the nine victims and contained a carefully neutral explanation of events: "This memorial is dedicated to the nine individuals who quickly perished from H2S Poisoning . . . these are the individuals who are deeply missed by family and friends."[24] Organizers intentionally placed the monument just feet away from an earlier marker memorializing the economic importance of West Texas oil. Both are overshadowed by a looming pump jack, painted black and red.

NOTES

INTRODUCTION: NATURAL RISK

1. Michael Ratner and Carol Glover, "U.S. Energy: Overview and Key Statistics," Congressional Research Service, Washington, DC, June 27, 2014, https://fas.org/sgp/crs/misc/R40187.pdf.
2. For a discussion of this concept, see Steve Lerner, *Sacrifice Zones: The Front Lines of Toxic Chemical Exposure in the United States* (MIT Press, 2010). See also Christopher Jones, *Routes of Power: Energy and Modern America* (Harvard University Press, 2016). For other examples, see William Cronon, *Nature's Metropolis: Chicago and the Great West* (Norton, 1991); Barbara Hahn, *Making Tobacco Bright: Creating an American Commodity, 1617–1937* (Johns Hopkins University Press, 2011); Jeffrey G. Williamson, *Trade and Poverty: When the Third World Fell Behind* (MIT Press, 2011); and Sven Beckert, *Empire of Cotton: A Global History* (Vintage, 2014).
3. This has been common throughout the history of the industry; see Brian Frehner, *Finding Oil: The Nature of Petroleum Geology* (University of Nebraska Press, 2011); Alex Beasly, "Exporting Service: Houston and the Globalization of Oil Expertise, 1945–2008" (PhD diss., Yale University, 2015); Hugh Gorman, *Redefining Efficiency: Pollution Concerns, Regulatory Mechanisms, and Technological Change in the U.S. Petroleum Industry* (University of Akron Press, 2001).
4. For big-picture studies of this process, see Matt Huber, *Lifeblood: Oil, Freedom and the Forces of Capital* (University of Minnesota Press, 2013); and Timothy Mitchell, *Carbon Democracy: Political Power in the Age of Oil* (Verso, 2011).
5. For examinations of how these overlapping layers shaped American industry, see Andrew Needham, *Power Lines: Phoenix and the Making of the Modern Southwest* (Princeton University Press, 2014); Thomas Andrews, *Killing for Coal: America's Deadliest Labor War* (Harvard University Press, 2010); Sarah Alisabeth Fox,

Downwind: A People's History of the Nuclear West (University of Nebraska Press, 2014); Trish Kahle, *Energy Citizenship: Coal and Democracy in the American Century* (Columbia University Press, 2024).

6. State-making and the rise of statistical analysis went hand-in-hand. See Dan Bouk, *How Our Days Became Numbered: Risk and the Rise of the Statistical Individual* (University of Chicago Press, 2015); Julia Moses, *The First Modern Risk: Workplace Accidents and the Origins of European Social States* (Cambridge University Press, 2018).
7. This was a complex process. See Barbara Allen, *Uneasy Alchemy: Citizens and Experts in Louisiana's Chemical Corridor Disputes* (MIT Press, 2003); and Donald W. Rogers, *Making Capitalism Safe: Workplace Safety and Health Regulation in America, 1880–1940* (University of Illinois Press, 2009).
8. For a theoretical account of this negotiation, see Ulric Beck, *Risk Society: Toward a New Modernity* (Sage, 1992); and Arwen Mohun, *Risk: Negotiating Safety in American Society* (Johns Hopkins University Press, 2013).
9. Christopher W. Chagnon et al., "From Extractivism to Global Extractivism: The Evolution of an Organizing Concept," *Journal of Peasant Studies* 49, no. 4 (2022): 760–92. For key works on oil's community impact, see Brian Black, *Petrolia: The Landscape of America's First Oil Boom* (Johns Hopkins University Press, 2003); Robert Vitalis, *America's Kingdom: Mythmaking on the Saudi Oil Fronter* (Stanford University Press, 2006); and Mitchell, *Carbon Democracy*.
10. For similar case studies, see Brian James Leech, *The City That Ate Itself: Butte, Montana and Its Expanding Berkeley Pit* (University of Nevada Press, 2018); and Joel B. Goldsteen, *Danger All Around: Waste Storage Crisis on the Texas and Louisiana Gulf Coast* (University of Texas Press, 2009).
11. Paul Sabin, *Crude Politics: The California Oil Market, 1900–1940* (University of California Press, 2004); Karen Merrill, "Texas Metropole: Oil, the American West, and U.S. Power in the Postwar Years," *Journal of American History* 99, no. 1 (June 2002): 197–207; William R. Childs, *The Texas Railroad Commission: Understanding Regulation in America to the Mid-Twentieth Century* (Texas A&M University Press, 2005); Walter Keene Ferguson, *Geology and Politics in Frontier Texas, 1845–1909* (University of Texas Press, 2014).
12. Daniel Yergin, *The Prize: The Epic Quest for Oil, Money, and Power* (Free Press, 2008); Brian Black, Karen Merrill, and Tyler Priest, eds., "Oil in American History," *Journal of American History*, 99 (June 2012); Jason P. Theriot, "The Strategic Petroleum Reserve: U.S. Energy Security and Oil Politics, 1975–2005," *Technology & Culture* 49, no. 4 (2008): 1103–4.
13. For accounts of Texas's political history, see Sean P. Cunningham, *Cowboy Conservatism: Texas and the Rise of the Modern Right* (University Press of Kentucky, 2010); Jeff Roche, *The Political Culture of the New West* (University Press of Kansas, 2008); and Roger M. Olien and Diana Davids Hinton, *Wildcatters: Texas Independent Oilmen* (Texas A&M University Press, 2007).
14. Work on the intertwined political and labor history of Hispanic Texas is a flourishing field. See Gabriela Gonzalez, *Redeeming La Raza: Transborder Modernity, Race, Respectability, and Rights* (Oxford University Press, 2017); Max Krochmal, *Blue Texas: The Making of a Multiracial Democratic Coalition in the Civil Rights Era* (University of North Carolina Press, 2016); Emilio Zamora, *The World of the Mexican Worker in Texas* (Texas A&M University Press, 2000); Monica Perales,

Smeltertown: Making and Remembering a Southwest Border Community (University of North Carolina Press, 2010); and Arnoldo De Leon, *Tejano West Texas* (Texas A&M University Press, 2015).

15. For example, see Bethany Moreton, *To Serve God and Walmart: The Making of Christian Free Enterprise* (Harvard University Press, 2009); Bartow Elmore, *Citizen Coke: The Making of Coca-Cola Capitalism* (Norton, 2014); and Darren Dochuk, *Anointed with Oil: How Christianity and Crude Made Modern America* (Basic Books, 2019).
16. Much of this work has focused on case studies from the Global South, but not all. See Miguel Tinker Salas, *The Enduring Legacy: Oil, Culture, and Society in Venezuela* (Duke University Press, 2009); Michael J. Watts, "A Tale of Two Gulfs: Life, Death, and Dispossession Along Two Oil Frontiers," *American Quarterly* 64, no. 3 (2012): 437–67; and Joseph Pratt, Martin Melosi, and Kathleen Brosnan, eds., *Energy Capitals: Local Impact, Global Influence* (University of Pittsburgh Press, 2014).
17. For an overview of the field, see Arwen P. Mohun, "Constructing the History of Risk: Foundations, Tools, and Reasons Why," *Historical Social Research/Historische Sozialforschung* 41, no. 1 (155) (2016): 30–47. See also Uwe Lubken and Christof Mauch, "Uncertain Environments: Natural Hazards, Risk and Insurance in Historical Perspective," *Environment and History* 17, no. 1 (2011): 1–12. Risk history scholarship is dominated by disaster histories; for key examples, see Ted Steinberg, *Acts of God: The Unnatural History of Natural Disaster in America* (Oxford University Press, 2000); and Jacob A. C. Remes, *Disaster Citizenship: Survivors, Solidarity, and Power in the Progressive Era* (University of Illinois Press, 2016).
18. Cultural studies scholars might call these "regimes of truth." Michel Foucault, *Discipline and Punish* (Gallimard, 1975). See also Theodore Porter, *Trust in Numbers* (Princeton University Press, 1995).
19. Oil's social history is built of rich oral history accounts. See Bobby Weaver, *Oilfield Trash: Life and Labor in the Oil Patch* (Texas A&M University Press, 2010); Gerald Lynch, *Roughnecks, Drillers, and Tool Pushers* (University of Texas Press, 1991); and Paul F. Lambert, *Voices from the Oil Fields* (University of Oklahoma Press, 1984). See also Thomas Eastabrook, *Labor-Environmental Coalitions: Lessons from a Louisiana Petrochemical Region* (Baywood, 2007).
20. Melissa A. Thomasson, "From Sickness to Health: The Twentieth-Century Development of the Demand for Health Insurance," *Journal of Economic History* 60, no. 2 (2000): 504–8; Scott Gabriel Knowles, *The Disaster Experts: Mastering Risk in Modern America* (University of Pennsylvania Press, 2013).
21. Key works include Stephanie Lemangier, *Living Oil: Petroleum Culture in the American Century* (Oxford University Press, 2014); Robert Johnson, *Carbon Nation: Fossil Fuels and the Making of American Culture* (University Press of Kansas, 2014); and Imre Szeman and Dominic Boyer, *Energy Humanities: An Anthology* (Johns Hopkins University Press, 2017).
22. Capitalism's environmental history is a rich and growing field. See Cedric Johnson, *The Neoliberal Deluge: Hurricane Katrina, Late Capitalism, and the Remaking of New Orleans* (University of Minnesota Press, 2011); Susanna Bohme, *Toxic Injustice: A Transnational History of Exposure and Struggle* (University of California Press, 2014); and Martin Melosi, *Effluent America: Cities, Industry, Energy, and the Environment* (University of Pittsburgh Press, 2001).

1. REIMAGINING SANTA RITA

1. Martin W. Schwettmann, "Santa Rita: The University of Texas Oil Discovery," Texas State Historical Association, Austin, 1943, Folder 1, Box 3k8, "Oral History of the Texas Oil Industry," Briscoe Center for American History, Austin, Texas.
2. Julia Cauble Smith, "Santa Rita Oil Well," in *Handbook of Texas Online*, published June 15, 2010, http://www.tshaonline.org/handbook/online/articles/doso1; Schwettman, "Santa Rita"; "Vignettes from the Colorful History of Oil," n.d., Oral Histories of the Texas Oil Industry Collection, Briscoe Center for American History, Austin, Texas.
3. Schwettmann, "Santa Rita."
4. Schwettmann, "Santa Rita."
5. "Centennial Oil Stamp," US Postal Service, 1959; Unknown, *Odessa Texas Oil Field Mural*, Ector County Courthouse, n.d., Odessa, Texas; *The Rookie*, directed by John Lee Hancock (Walt Disney Pictures, 2002).
6. Harold F. Williamson, Ralph L. Andreano, and Carmen Menezes, "The American Petroleum Industry," in *Output Employment and Productivity in the United States After 1800*, ed. Dorothy S. Brady (American Petroleum Institute, 1966), 349–404.
7. *Statistical Bulletin, API Facts and Figures*, American Petroleum Institute (API), New York, 1932, Trade Literature Collection, Hagley Museum and Library.
8. The self-taught geologist and independent oil prospector Pattillo Higgins tapped Spindletop, discovering oil despite all professional or scientific advice. Boosters spread this story throughout the nation. For example, see "Fortunes in Oil," *Norton Courier*, Norton, Kansas, May 18, 1922, 8. Higgins became a household name and Texas folk hero. AP, "Spindletop Discoverer Dies at 92," *Corpus Christi Caller-Times*, Corpus Christi, Texas, June 6, 1955, 30.
9. Today, there is no federal public land in Texas and very little land is state owned. Thomas L. Miller, *The Public Lands of Texas, 1519–1970* (University of Oklahoma Press, 1972).
10. In 1897, a second rail line was built linking West Texas with the Midwest, New Mexico, and Mexico. After the turn of the century, the Kansas City, Mexico and Orient Railway was laid across the Permian Basin. Paul H. Carlson and Bruce Glasrud, *West Texas: A History of the Giant Side of the State* (University of Oklahoma Press, 2014), 21.
11. Arnoldo De Leon, *Tejano West Texas* (Texas A&M University Press, 2015).
12. Carlson and Glasrud, *West Texas*.
13. John D. Alexander, oral history interview by Richard Mason, October 20, 1982, Texas Tech University Special Collections, Lubbock, Texas.
14. Finas Wade Horton, "A History of Ector County, Texas" (MA thesis, University of Texas, 1950).
15. Personal archival materials of Bobby Weaver, oil industry folklorist, examined by author in 2018.
16. Barney Hubbs, oral history interview by Richie Cravens, July 8, 1977, Texas Tech University Special Collections, Lubbock, Texas; Carlson and Glasrud, *West Texas*, 69.
17. Texas Permian Historical Society, *Odessa Texas U.S.A.* (Texas Permian Historical Society, 1961).

18. William R. Childs, *The Texas Railroad Commission: Understanding Regulation in America to the Mid-Twentieth Century* (Texas A&M University Press, 2005).
19. Alexander, oral history interview.
20. Alexander, oral history interview.
21. Henrietta M. Larson and Kenneth Wiggins Porter, *History of Humble Oil and Refining Company: A Study in Industrial Growth* (Harper, 1959).
22. "Investigation of Trusts: Hearings Before the United States House Committee on Manufactures, Fiftieth Congress, First Session, on Mar. 8–10, 12, 23, 1888" (US Government Printing Office, 1888).
23. In the 1880s, a group of lawyers and journalists including economist Simon Sterne, Ohio oil producer turned author George Rice, author-cum-activist Henry Demarest Lloyd, and journalist Ida Tarbell, led the charge against the industry. Rice gained national attention for a series of pamphlets, including "The Standard Oil Company: Its Dishonest Tricks Exposed," 1882; "Railroad Discrimination as Given to the Standard Oil Trust," n.d.; and "Black Death," New York, 1888. Henry Demarest Lloyd also opposed Standard Oil on starkly moralistic terms in *Wealth Against Commonwealth* (Harper, 1894). "The History of the Standard Oil Company," a series of articles by Ida Tarbell, was published in *McClure's Magazine* between 1902 and 1904. These articles were compiled in book form and then adapted into a play called *The Lion and the Mouse*, which was later published as a novel. "Miss Tarbell Is Not to Go on Stage," *San Francisco Call*, March 17, 1907, 51.
24. *Standard Oil Co. of New Jersey v. United States*, 221 US 1 (1911). Signaling elite sympathy for Standard's arguments, the dissolution of the company did not actually end its oil transport monopoly. It simply forced Standard Oil to break up into several loosely connected, regional corporations—today known as Chevron, Amoco, Mobil, and Exxon. *Oil and Gas Journal—Petroleum Panorama*, A6–A9, Trade Literature Collection, Hagley Museum and Library, Wilmington, Delaware. See also Hugh Gorman, *Redefining Efficiency: Pollution Concerns, Regulatory Mechanisms, and Technological Change in the U.S. Petroleum Industry* (University of Akron Press, 2001), chapter 1.
25. In the 1890s, Texas and Ohio each also filed individual lawsuits against Standard Oil. Gorman, *Redefining Efficiency*, chapter 1.
26. "Experience of Farmers, and Others Owning Land Along Pipe Lines Now in Operation," *Affidavits of Suffering Land Owners, from Devastations Caused by Pipe Line Companies*, State of Pennsylvania, Union County, 1883, Special Collections, Hagley Museum and Library, Wilmington, Delaware.
27. "Dallas, Texas J. Edgar Pew 1924," Box 109, Series 1F Administrative Interoffice (Geographical), Sun Oil Company Records, Hagley Museum and Library, Wilmington, Delaware.
28. Wayne D. Collins, "Trusts and the Origins of Antitrust Legislation," *Fordham Law Review* 81, no. 5 (2013); Frank H. Easterbrook, "Limits of Antitrust," *Texas Law Review* 63, no. 1 (1984): https://appliedantitrust.com/00_basic_materials/week00_supp/easterbrook_limits_antitrust1984.pdf.
29. "Nick Carter Strikes Oil," *Nick Carter Stories*, 11, November 23, 1912; "Struck Oil! Or, The Boy Who Made a Million," *Fame and Fortune Weekly*, 492, Folder "Publication—Magazine-Fame & Fortune Weekly"; "The Bradys and the Beaumont Oil King: Or, Three 'Bad' Men from Texas," *Secret Service Old and Young King*

Brady Detectives, 416, New York, 1907, Folder "Publications-Magazine-Secret Service (1907)"; Box 5, Collection 60, Warshaw Petroleum Collection, Smithsonian Archives Center, Washington, DC.

30. Berte R. Haigh, *Land, Oil and Education* (Texas Western Press, 1986).
31. Natalie Ornish, *Pioneer Jewish Texans* (Texas A&M University Press, 2011), 116.
32. Alexander, oral history interview.
33. Haymon Crupp & Co., El Paso Texas City Directory, 1923, 575. The US censuses of 1930 and 1940 differ on Krupp's country of origin. The 1930 census lists Russia, and the 1940 census lists Lithuania. US Bureau of the Census, *1930 Federal Population Census* (US Government Printing Office, 1930); and US Bureau of the Census, *1940 Federal Population Census* (US Government Printing Office, 1940).
34. Kory Killgo and Kenneth J. Robinson, "The Evolution of Texas Banking," in *Ten-Gallon Economy: Sizing up Economic Growth in Texas*, edited by Pia M. Orrenius, Jesús Cañas, and Michael Weiss (Palgrave Macmillan, 2015), 119–37.
35. Ornish, *Pioneer Jewish Texans*, 117; Schwettmann, "Santa Rita"; "Carl G. Cromwell," San Angelo City Directory, 1931.
36. National Weather Service Forecast Office, "Local Data/Records," National Oceanic and Atmospheric Administration (NOAA), Washington, DC, accessed February 28, 2017, https://www.weather.gov/climate/local_data.php?wfo=hgx.
37. US Census Bureau, *Census of the Population and Housing 1920*, accessed June 5, 2017, https://www.census.gov/prod/www/decennial.html.
38. Richard C. Anderson, "The Contributions of J. A. Udden to an Understanding of Iowa Geology," *Journal of the Iowa Academy of Science* 104, no. 4 (1997): 91–96.
39. Patents, Box 1, Serge Scherbatskoy Papers, Col. 936, Smithsonian Archives Center, Washington, DC.
40. Patents, Box 1, Serge Scherbatskoy Papers, Col. 936, Smithsonian Archives Center, Washington, DC.
41. Elliott Cowden, oral history interview, September 16, 1970, Midland, Texas, Oral History Collection, Permian Basin Petroleum Museum, Midland, Texas.
42. Walter Rundell Jr., *Oil in West Texas and New Mexico: A Pictorial History of the Permian Basin* (Texas A&M University Press, 1982).
43. Gus L. Ford, ed., *Texas Cattle Brands* (Cockrell, 1936); Gil Hinshaw, *Lea, New Mexico's Last Frontier* (Hobbs Daily News-Sun, 1976); H. Allen Anderson, "Cowden Ranch," *Handbook of Texas Online*, uploaded June 12, 2010, http://www.tshaonline.org/handbook/online/articles/apc05.
44. Alexander, oral history interview.
45. Don Worcester, *The Texas Longhorn: Relic of the Past, Asset for the Future* (Texas A&M University Press, 1987); Paul H. Carlson, *Texas Woolybacks: The Range Sheep and Goat Industry* (Texas A&M University Press, 1982).
46. W. C. Arnold, *Cattle, Cotton, Corn: A History of Central Texas Middle-Class Ranches, 1880–1930* (Texas Tech University Press, 2022); Terry G. Jordan, "Early Northeast Texas and the Evolution of Western Ranching," *Annals of the Association of American Geographers* 67, no. 1 (1977): 66–87.
47. C. C. Slaughter Cattle Company Records, Southwest Collection, Texas Tech University.
48. "Memorial and Biographical History of Dallas County" (Lewis Publishing, 1892); "Bank Changes and Consolidations in Texas in the Last Thirty Days," *Clifton Record*, Clifton, Texas, January 24, 1930, 5.

49. John R. Wunder, *Working the Range: Essays on the History of Western Land Management and the Environment* (Greenwood, 1985), 90.
50. David J. Murrah, *C. C. Slaughter, Rancher, Banker, Baptist* (University of Texas Press, 1981).
51. "Give Cup to Scharbauer," *Abilene Reporter-News*, December 27, 1934, 7.
52. These families joined the University of Texas as the largest landholders in the region. In the 1880s, the university was deeded several thousand acres by the state of Texas to defray the cost of higher education in Texas. The land would be considered largely worthless until the discovery of oil in the 1920s. Todd Houck, *The University Lands: Resources and Higher Education in Texas, 1838–1996* (Windy Fox, 2011).
53. "Give Cup to Scharbauer."
54. "Contract on Additional Hotel Is Let," April 21, 1929, *Abilene Reporter-News*, 12. Ira Yates, a small landholder in Pecos County, speculated in a variety of industries, including dry goods, even as he continued his ranching operations. Roger M. Olien and Diana Davids Hinton, *Wildcatters: Texas Independent Oilmen* (Texas A&M University Press 2007), chapter 1.
55. Cecil Bickley, oral history interview, January 1981, Texas Tech University Special Collections, Lubbock, Texas.
56. Henderson K. Yoakum, *History of Texas: From Its First Settlement in 1685 to Its Annexation to the United States in 1846* (Redfield, 1855); Barnes F. Lathrop, *Migration into East Texas, 1835–1860: A Study from the United States Census* (Texas State Historical Association, 1949); Texas General Land Office, First Census of Austin's Colony, 1826 (Dolph Briscoe Center for American History, University of Texas at Austin).
57. Alexander, oral history interview.
58. "Lucas Oil Geyser," Box 6, Col. 60, Warshaw Petroleum Collection, Smithsonian Archives Center, Washington, DC.
59. Classified ads, *Odessa News and Ector County News*, August 16, 1927, 7.
60. John Edward Brantley, *History of Oil Well Drilling* (Gulf Publishing, 1971) 1474.
61. *Statistical Bulletin, API Facts and Figures*.
62. *Statistical Bulletin, API Facts and Figures*; US Treasury Department, *Statistics of Income from Returns of Net Income for 1925*, US Government Printing Office, 1927, accessed June 28, 2017, https://www.irs.gov/pub/irs-soi/25soirepar.pdf.
63. This trend would continue for the next several decades. In 1935, the Gulf Production Company set a new drilling record in Upton County, Texas, at 12,786 feet. In 1944, Phillips Petroleum set a record in Pecos County, at 15,279 feet, and again in 1945 in Brazos County, at 16,655 feet. The height of this drilling arms race was reached in 1958, as Phillips Petroleum spent ten years drilling to an astonishing depth of 25,340 in Pecos County. J. Brewster, "Record Pecos Deep Wells Make Major Strides," *Drill Bit* 29, no. 6 (1980).
64. Olien and Hinton, *Wildcatters*, 45; see also *Census of Population and Housing 1920*, US Census Bureau, accessed June 1, 2017, https://www.census.gov/prod/www/decennial.html.
65. For example, the Hendricks Field was approximately twenty miles from the Texas and Pacific Railroad. Untitled Railroad Map, Grizwald Map Collection, Permian Basin Petroleum Museum, Midland, Texas.

66. Contracts, Folder "Drilling Contracts 12/1953–10/1954," Box 83-021, C. J. Red Davidson Collection, Special Collections, Permian Basin Petroleum Museum, Midland, Texas.
67. American Petroleum Institute (API), *Petroleum: The Story of an American Industry* (American Petroleum Institute, 1935), 34, Hagley Museum and Library, Wilmington, Delaware.
68. In 1931, the worst year of the Depression, oil was priced at $0.65 per barrel. This would result in a royalty profit of approximately $237.25 per year in 1931 dollars. In 2017 dollars, this would come to $3,802.29. Many West Texas wells were financed using joint stock companies. Whatever company owned the extraction equipment used in the well was considered the well operator and typically received the most equity in the well. The operator was legally considered the owner of the well, but the profits were divided among several parties. Older wells attached to pumps produced on average less than one barrel per day, making the profits for the individual stakeholder even smaller. Oil price data comes from *API Statistical Bulletin 1930–1940*, American Petroleum Institute (API), Special Collections, Hagley Museum and Library, Wilmington, Delaware.
69. Oil Leases, Folder "Cummins Area Lease Assignments and Misc Ector County TX 83-021," Box 3, C. J. Red Davidson Collection, Permian Basin Petroleum Museum, Midland, Texas.
70. Carl D. Estes, oral history interview, May 20, 1970, Monahans, Texas, Oral History Collection, Permian Basin Petroleum Museum, Midland, Texas.
71. "Ira Yates Had Faith in Arid Land," *Odessa American*, 119.
72. In an effort to house the dozens of prospectors who arrived after the initial boom, Ira Yates donated 152 acres to the boomtown of Redbarn, which sprung up on his property. Samuel D. Myres, *The Permian Basin: Petroleum Empire of the Southwest*, 2 vols. (Permian, 1973, 1977).
73. By 1927, fifty-five major oil companies had leased over two million acres of land in Pecos County. H. S. Hunter, "Pecos County Oil Lands Find Unprecedented Sale," *El Paso Herald*, December 8, 1927, 1. As of 2009, the Yates Field, which had produced over one billion barrels of oil, covered over 26,400 acres. As of 2017, the field still produced oil.
74. James Wheat of Loving County remembered that his father broke his suffering farmland into five-acre sections, with the plan to lease rights to different oil companies on each section. James J. Wheat and George Clayton, oral history interview, July 17, 1970, Mentone, Loving County, Texas, Oral History Collection, Permian Basin Petroleum Museum, Midland, Texas, 3.
75. For those who did not drill their own water wells, a Mr. Melton sold water by the barrel. E. N. Beane, oral history interview, June 1970, Crane, Texas, Oral History Collection, Permian Basin Petroleum Museum, Midland, Texas, 15–16. In the 1920s, some Permian Basin landholders, desperate for cash, sold the mineral rights to their land, ultimately ceding control to oil companies. This would cause resentment between oil companies and landholders in future decades.
76. Samuel D. Myres, *The Permian Basin: Era of Discovery* (Permian, 1973), chapter 9; Elliott Cowden and Holt Jowel, oral history interview, September 16, 1970, Oral History Collection, Permian Basin Petroleum Museum, Midland, Texas; Letters—Royalty Payments, Folder "Cummins Area: Correspondence Ector County, TX 83-021

C. J. Red Davidson," Box 83-021 3 of 4, C. J. Red Davidson Collection, Permian Basin Petroleum Museum, Midland, Texas.

77. *API Statistical Bulletin 1930–1940*.
78. Alexander, oral history interview.
79. For example, James J. Wheat remembers that his father sold most of his mineral rights after falling on hard times. Wheat and Clayton, oral history interview, 16.
80. Deeds, Folder "Cummins Area, Ector County TX Title Abstracts 83-021 C. J. Red Davidson," Box 83-021 3 of 4, C. J. Red Davidson Collection, Permian Basin Petroleum Museum, Midland, Texas; George R. Bentley and Carl D. Estes, oral history interview, May 20, 1970, Monahans, Texas, Oral History Collection, Permian Basin Petroleum Museum, Midland, Texas; Cowden and Jowel, oral history interview, September 16, 1970, Midland Texas, Oral History Collection, Permian Basin Petroleum Museum, Midland, Texas, 9.
81. Cowden and Jowel, oral history interview, 9.
82. Scott Nelson, *A Nation of Deadbeats: An Uncommon History of America's Financial Disasters* (Vintage, 2013); David Hochfelder, "'Where the Common People Could Speculate': The Ticker, Bucket Shops, and the Origins of Popular Participation in Financial Markets, 1880–1920," *Journal of American History* 93, no. 2 (2006): 335–58.
83. "New Firms Here," *Odessa News*, November 1, 1927, 1.
84. US Bureau of the Census, *1940 Federal Population Census*.

2. A TOUGH, GREEDY, BRAWLING TIME AND PLACE

1. Associated Press, "Town Spared as Explosion Fires Tanks," *Atlanta Constitution*, January 28, 1928, 1.
2. "Wichitan Dead McCamey Blast," *Wichita Falls Times*, January 28, 1928, 1; "Great Oil Fire Burns out at M'Camey," *Austin Statesman*, January 28, 1928, 2; "McCamey Fire out with Large Loss: One Man and $100,000 Loss from Blaze," *Austin American*, January 29, 1928, 10; "Damage Half Million and One Known Dead in Blast at McCamey," *Galveston Daily News*, January 28, 1928, 1.
3. "New Texas Oil Town Makes a Holiday When 12 Exploding Tanks Take Little Toll," January 28, 1928, *New York Times*, 11.
4. "Wichitan Dead McCamey Blast."
5. "Damage Half Million and One Known Dead in Blast at McCamey."
6. For example, the statements of earnings and balance sheets of the High Test Oil Company illustrate very tight profit margins. Box 3, Majewskey Papers, University of Wyoming. Later human resources departments discuss historical trends. See "Human Resources Employee Relations: R&D Supervisors Manual ca. 1950," Exxon Mobil Historical Collection, Box 2.207/E39, Briscoe Center for American History, Austin.
7. Nancy Ethie Eagleton, *On the Last Frontier: A History of Upton County, Texas* (Texas Western Press, 1971); Richard R. Moore, *West Texas After the Discovery of Oil* (Pemberton, 1971).
8. Roger M. Olien and Diana Davids Hinton, *Oil Booms: Social Change in Five Texas Towns* (University of Nebraska Press, 1982).

9. Mody C. Boatright, *Tales from the Derrick Floor: A People's History of the Oil Industry* (University of Nebraska Press, 1982), 218; "Oil Man 'Shoots' out Fatal Gas Fire," *Daily Press*, Newport News, Virginia, May 28, 1927, 1; "Use Dynamite to Stop Texas Gas Well Fire," *New York Times*, May 28, 1927, 3.
10. The rotary drill was first patented in 1845 and rose to fame in 1901 as the drill that produced the well-known Lucas Gusher at Spindletop. However, because the rotary was more complex and more expensive, cable tool still outnumbered rotary in most of the United States as late as the late 1940s. It would take until 1951 for rotary to supplant cable tools. According to midcentury engineers and industry historians, the twentieth-century oil industry was defined by the switch from cable tool to rotary drilling technology. John Edward Brantley, *History of Oil Well Drilling* (Gulf Publishing, 1971); Samuel D. Myres, *The Permian Basin: Petroleum Empire of the Southwest*, 2 vols. (Permian, 1973, 1977); Martin W. Schwettmann, *The Discovery and Early Development of the Big Lake Oil Field* (MA thesis, University of Texas, 1941).
11. US Bureau of Labor Statistics, *Wages and Hours of Labor in the Petroleum Industry 1920*, US Government Printing Office, Bulletin of the United States Bureau of Labor Statistics, No. 297, 1920.
12. American Petroleum Institute (API), *History of Petroleum Engineering: A Publication of the American Petroleum Institute* (American Petroleum Institute, 1961).
13. "Radio, Dynamite, used in Locating Hidden Pools," *Odessa American*, November 14, 1930, 8; "New Methods to Find Salt Domes," *New York Times*, April 3, 1925, 3; API, *History of Petroleum Engineering*; Brantley, *History of Oil Well Drilling*.
14. Boatright, *Tales from the Derrick Floor*, 225.
15. Boatright, *Tales from the Derrick Floor*, 174.
16. Boatright, *Tales from the Derrick Floor*, 225.
17. Boatright, *Tales from the Derrick Floor*, 189.
18. Boatright, *Tales from the Derrick Floor*, 174.
19. "Burns Prove Fatal to Three Oilfield Workers," *Waxahache Daily Light*, September 9, 1929, 1.
20. Boatright, *Tales from the Derrick Floor*, 184.
21. Martin W. Schwettmann, *Santa Rita: The University of Texas Oil Discovery* (Texas State Historical Association, 1958).
22. Boatright, *Tales from the Derrick Floor*, 107. See also "Subject File 1948: American Petroleum Institute—Committee on Safety," Box 29, Majewski Papers, American Heritage Center, University of Wyoming, Laramie.
23. John D. Alexander, oral history interview by Richard Mason, October 20, 1982, Texas Tech University Special Collections, Lubbock.
24. "Subject File 1948: American Petroleum Institute—Committee on Safety," Box 29, Majewski Papers, American Heritage Center, University of Wyoming, Laramie; General Petroleum Corporation, "Industrial Relations 1940–1943," Box 2.207/E214, Exxon Mobil Historical Collection, Briscoe Center for American History, Austin.
25. Bruce Ashburn, oral history interview by Paul Patterson, April 29, 1968, Special Collections, Texas Tech University, Lubbock.
26. Alexander, oral history interview.
27. Richard Mason, oral history interview by Walter Boren, January 23, 1980, Special Collections, Texas Tech University, Lubbock.

28. Boatright, *Tales from the Derrick Floor*, 176.
29. For example, O. J. Lawson relayed with derision workers carrying lighted lanterns and striking matches that could have ignited the nearby gas. He also remembered that oil storage tanks were regularly placed very close together to save space and admitted that workers in the industry recognized that there was no good way to protect such tightly packed tanks from igniting. Boatright, *Tales from the Derrick Floor*, 172, 194. See also "Subject File 1948: American Petroleum Institute—Committee on Safety," Box 29, Majewski Papers, American Heritage Center, University of Wyoming, Laramie; General Petroleum Corporation, "Industrial Relations 1940–1943."
30. For scholarly accounts of this debate, see Joseph Giacomelli, *Uncertain Climes: Debating Climate Change in Gilded Age America* (University of Chicago Press, 2023); Tom McCarthy, "The Coming Wonder? Foresight and Early Concerns About the Automobile," *Environmental History* 6, no. 1 (2001): 46–74; Alan Derickson, "Naphtha Drunks, Lead Colic, and the Smelter Shakes: The Inordinate Exposure of Immigrant Workers to Occupational Health Hazards at the Turn of the Twentieth Century," *Journal of American Ethnic History* 37, no. 2 (2018): 37–61; Christopher Sellers, "Factory as Environment: Industrial Hygiene, Professional Collaboration and the Modern Sciences of Pollution," *Environmental History Review* 18, no. 1 (1994): 55–83. See also Melanie Kiechel, *Smell Detectives: An Olfactory History of Nineteenth-Century Urban America* (University of Washington Press, 2017); Joel A. Tarr and Jeffrey K. Stine, eds., "Special Issue on Technology, Pollution, and the Environment," *Environmental History Review* 18, no. 1 (1994); Christine M. Rosen and Joel A. Tarr, eds., "Special Issue Devoted to the Environment and the City," *Journal of Urban History* 20, no. 3 (1994).
31. Similar trends took place in other oil-producing centers. See Nigel Anthony Sellars, *Oil, Wheat and Wobblies: The Industrial Workers of the World in Oklahoma, 1905–1930* (University of Oklahoma Press, 1998); Nancy Quam-Wickham, "'Cities Sacrificed on the Altar of Oil': Popular Opposition to Oil Development in 1920s Los Angeles," *Environmental History* 3, no. 2 (1998): 189–209.
32. Mark Aldrich, "Safety First Comes to the Railroads, 1910–1939," *Railroad History*, no. 166 (1992): 6–33.
33. John Fabian Witt, "The Transformation of Work and the Law of Workplace Accidents, 1842–1910," *Yale Law Journal* 107, no. 5 (1998): 1467–502; Carl Hookstadt et al., "Workmen's Compensation," *Monthly Labor Review* 9, no. 5 (1919): 266–338.
34. Nate Holdren, *Injury Impoverished: Workplace Accidents, Capitalism, and Law in the Progressive Era* (Cambridge University Press, 2020); Jonathan Levy, *Freaks of Fortune: The Emerging World of Capitalism and Risk in America* (Harvard University Press, 2012); Bertram Edises, "Multiplicity of Remedies in the Field of Industrial Accident Law," *California Law Review* 21, no. 5 (1933): 430–59.
35. Raynal C. Bolling, "The United States Steel Corporation and Labor Conditions," *Annals of the American Academy of Political and Social Science* 42 (1912): 38–47; Hookstadt et al., "Workmen's Compensation."
36. Lewis L. Gould, *Progressives and Prohibitionists: Texas Democrats in the Wilson Era* (University of Texas Press, 1973).
37. Aldrich, "Safety First"; Price Fishback and Shawn Kantor, *A Prelude to the Welfare State: The Origins of Workers' Compensation* (University of Chicago Press, 2000).

38. Trish Kahle, *Energy Citizenship: Coal and Democracy in the American Century* (Columbia University Press, 2024).
39. Seung-Wook Kim and Price V. Fishback, "Institutional Change, Compensating Differentials, and Accident Risk in American Railroading, 1892–1945," *Journal of Economic History* 53, no. 4 (1993): 796–823; Herbert K. Abrams, "A Short History of Occupational Health," *Journal of Public Health Policy* 22, no. 1 (2001): 34–80.
40. This was a reissue of an earlier manual published by Standard Oil in 1909 called *Rules for Guidance of Employees and for Safe-Guarding the Receiving Handling and Distributing of Petroleum Products*. S. S. Joslin Jr., "History of Socony Mobil's Safety Program," Pauisboro Refinery, January 23, 1965, Folder "Mobil Historical Collection Corporate Administration," Exxon Mobil Collection 2.207 E33, Briscoe Center for American History, Austin.
41. Joslin, "History of Socony Mobil's Safety Program."
42. International Association of Oil Field, Gas Well, Refinery Workers of America, *International Oil Worker: Official Publication of the International Association of Oil Field, Gas Well and Refinery Workers of America* (The Association, Vol. 5, no. 8, 1934). See also *CIO News, Oil Workers Edition* (Oil Workers International Union, 1938).
43. "Rules and Regulation Governing Working Conditions of Field Employees," General Petroleum Corporation of California, 1934, 20, Exxon Mobil Historical Collection, 2.207 Box E33, Briscoe Center for American History, Austin.
44. "Industrial Relations 1940–1943," Folder "General Petroleum Corporation," Box 2.207/E214, Exxon Mobil Historical Collection, Briscoe Center for American History, University of Texas, Austin.
45. "Playing Safe and Keeping Well at Beaumont," *Magnolia News*, October 1931, 16, Briscoe Center for American History, Box 2.207 E33, Exxon Mobil Collection, Briscoe Center for American History, Austin.
46. "Playing Safe and Keeping Well."
47. "Break Ground for Refinery," *Abilene Daily Reporter*, July 1, 1928, 5.
48. For example, see 1924 correspondence between field officers in Beaumont, Dallas, and Sun Oil headquarters. Series 1F Interoffice Correspondence, Sun Oil Company Records, Hagley Museum and Library, Wilmington, Delaware.
49. This number steadily increased, with the use of contractors jumping from 70 percent to 75 percent between 1942 and 1943. By 1966, contract labor made up 97 percent of oil drilling operations. Brantley, *History of Oil Well Drilling*, 1486; US Department of Labor, *Wages and Hours of Labor in the Petroleum Industry 1920*.
50. Alexander, oral history interview.
51. During the 1920s and 1930s, it took between thirty and one hundred days to drill a well between 2,000 and 3,000 feet. E. N. Beane, oral history interview, Crane, Texas, June 1970, Oral History Collection, Permian Basin Petroleum Museum, Midland, Texas. By the 1960s, this number had been cut to approximately thirty days to drill a 3,000-foot well and put it into production. Brantley, *History of Oil Well Drilling*, 7.
52. US Department of Labor, *Wages and Hours of Labor in the Petroleum Industry 1920*.
53. Fred Jennings, oral history interview, Goose Creek, June 19, 1952, Oral History of the Texas Oil Industry, Briscoe Center for American History, University of Texas at Austin.

54. E. N. Beane, oral history interview, Crane, Texas, June 19, 1970, Oral History Collection, Permian Basin Petroleum Museum, Midland, Texas, 14.
55. *Mud*, Box 25, API Photo and Film Collection, Collection 711, Smithsonian Archives Center, Washington, DC. See also Farm Security Administration/Office of War Information, Black and White Negatives, Prints and Photographs Online Collection, Library of Congress, accessed March 14, 2014, http://www.loc.gov/pictures/collection/fsa/.
56. Bobby Weaver, *Oilfield Trash: Life and Labor in the Oil Patch* (Texas A&M University Press, 2010).
57. E. E. Brackens, oral history interview, July 16, 1970, Wink, Texas, Oral History Collection, Permian Basin Petroleum Museum, Midland, Texas, 2; George W. Ramer, oral history interview, February 12, 1970, McCamey, Texas, Oral History Collection, Permian Basin Petroleum Museum, Midland, Texas, 14. Photographs from the 1920s also illustrate these harsh traveling conditions. The American Petroleum Institute (API), the Sun Oil Company, and the Office of War Information all developed archives of images depicting scenes such as roughnecks braving sandstorms on foot and isolated derricks half-buried in shifting dunes. John Vachon, *Andrews County, Texas, Oil Field in Sand Hills Country*, November 1942, Farm Security Administration/Office of War Information, Black and White Negatives, Prints and Photographs Online Collection, Library of Congress, accessed March 14, 2014, http://www.loc.gov/pictures/item/owi2001014517/PP/.
58. Michael McLeaish, who grew up in the Gulf Oil camp, summed up the isolated lifestyle: "They say fences made good neighbors. Well, we didn't have any fences." This statement recalled a lack of privacy in his oil camp community of about fifty people. David A. Johnson, "Boomtown: Oil Shaped Permian Basin, Changed World," *Odessa American*, March 10, 2012.
59. E. E. Brackens, oral history interview, July 16, 1970; *Tents and Shacks*, Box 14, API Photo and Film Collection, Collection 711, Smithsonian Archives Center, Washington, DC. See also Diana Davids Hinton, "Creating Company Culture: Oil Company Camps in the Southwest, 1920–1960," *Southwestern Historical Quarterly* 111, no. 4 (2008): 371–87.
60. Compared to the Permian Basin, most American wells were only 2,500 to 7,000 feet on average by the early 1930s. In 1930, the average drilling cost per well in the United States was approximately $22,000. API Facts and Figures, Hagley Museum and Library, Wilmington, Delaware; Brantley, *History of Oil Well Drilling*, 38.
61. US Department of Labor, *Wages and Hours of Labor in the Petroleum Industry 1920*.
62. F. Arthur Stout and Joseph W. Graybeal, oral history interview, Oral History Collection, Permian Basin Petroleum Museum, Midland, Texas, 14; Folder "Human Resources: Wages and Salaries General 1883–1998," Box 2.207/E46 Exxon Mobil Historical Collection, Briscoe Center for American History, University of Texas, Austin.
63. US Department of Labor, *Handbook of Labor Statistics* (US Government Printing Office, 1936), 916; see also Bruce Ashburn, oral history interview by Paul Patterson, April 29, 1968, Texas Tech Special Collections, Lubbock.
64. Nancy Quam-Wickham, "Rereading Man's Conquest of Nature: Skills, Myths, and the Historical Construction of Masculinity in Western Extractive Industries," in *Boys and Their Toys: Masculinity, Class and Technology in America*, ed. Roger Horowitz (Routledge, 2001), 91–108.

65. "Men Who Make Magnolia . . .," *Magnolia News*, December 1950, 14, Box 2.207 E224, Exxon Mobil Collection, Briscoe Center for American History, Austin.
66. Boatright, *Tales from the Derrick Floor*, 199.
67. Alexander, oral history interview.
68. Alexander, oral history interview.
69. Jennings, oral history interview.
70. Weaver, *Oilfield Trash*.
71. Texas Wills and Probate Records, Tom Green County, Ancestry.com. *Texas, U.S., Wills and Probate Records, 1833–1974* (Ancestry.com Operations, 2015); Myres, *The Permian Basin*; Schwettmann, *Santa Rita*.
72. Chandler Davidson, *Race and Class in Texas Politics* (Princeton University Press, 1990).
73. Alexander, oral history interview.
74. Abrams, "A Short History of Occupational Health."
75. After 1942, farmers and ranchers in West Texas used Bracero program immigrants as both ranch hands and seasonal farm labor. Noncitizens and limited by their exploitative contracts, these workers largely did not unionize. See Neil Foley, "Mexicans, Mechanization, and the Growth of Corporate Cotton Culture in South Texas: The Taft Ranch, 1900–1930," *Journal of Southern History* 62, no. 2 (1996): 275–302.
76. Barney Hubbs, oral history interview by Richie Cravens, July 8, 1977, Texas Tech University Special Collections, Lubbock.
77. Joe Conger, oral history interview by Paul Patterson, August 3, 1970, Texas Tech Special Collections, Lubbock.
78. Alexander, oral history interview.
79. Alexander, oral history interview. Similarly, Dee Locklin remembers working with Bud Barfield, a cowboy turned roughneck, in Reagan County oilfields. Dee Locklin, oral history interview, McCamey, Texas, February 13, 1970, Oral History Collection, Permian Basin Petroleum Museum, Midland, Texas, 2.
80. Alexander, oral history interview.
81. Boatright, *Tales from the Derrick Floor*, 121.
82. George Bentley, oral history interview, May 20, 1970, Monahans, Texas, Oral History Collection, Permian Basin Petroleum Museum, Midland, Texas.
83. Allen W. Hamill, oral history interview by William A. Owens, September 2, 1952, Tulsa, Oklahoma, Oral History of the Texas Oil Industry Collection, Briscoe Center for American History, University of Texas, Austin.
84. Terry G. Jordan, "A Century and a Half of Ethnic Change in Texas, 1836–1986," *Southwestern Historical Quarterly* 89, no. 4 (1986): 385–422; Melinda C. Miller, "Land and Racial Wealth Inequality," *American Economic Review* 101, no. 3 (2011): 371–76; Foley, "Mexicans, Mechanization, and the Growth of Corporate Cotton Culture in South Texas"; Armando Alonzo, *Tejano Legacy: Rancheros and Settlers in South Texas, 1734–1900* (University of New Mexico Press, 1998).
85. Henry Alexander Wiencek, *Oil Cities: The Making of North Louisiana's Boomtowns, 1901–1930* (University of Texas Press, 2024).
86. "History," *Odessa American*, December 19, 1999, 2.
87. Olien and Hinton, *Oil Booms*, chapter 5. US Census recordings for race and ethnicity were spotty during the 1920s and 1930s. While the census did include categories

for "White," "Negro," and "Mexican Origin," its records state that such information is "unavailable" for most West Texas counties, instead including only numbers for total population and the gender breakdown. US Census Bureau, *Census of the Population and Housing 1920, 1930*, accessed June 5, 2017, https://www.census.gov/prod/www/decennial.html.

88. "Quanah Oil Mill Puts up Homes for Workmen," *Times Record News*, Wichita Falls, Texas, August 3, 1927, 2.
89. Fred W. Viehe, "The Social-Spatial Distribution in the Black Gold Suburbs of Los Angeles, 1900–1930," *Southern California Quarterly* 73, no. 1 (1991): 33–54; Gregg Andrews, "Black Working-Class Political Activism and Biracial Unionism: Galveston Longshoremen in Jim Crow Texas, 1919–1921," *Journal of Southern History* 74, no. 3 (2008): 627–68.
90. Texas labor organizing in the 1920s and 1930s was mostly concentrated in cities, especially San Antonio, and often linked to pushback against racial and ethnic discrimination. Max Krochmal and Todd Moye, *Civil Rights in Black and Brown: Histories of Resistance and Struggle in Texas* (University of Texas Press, 2021). See also Monica Perales, *Smeltertown: Making and Remembering a Southwest Border Community* (University of North Carolina Press, 2010); and Max Krochmal, *Blue Texas: The Making of a Multiracial Democratic Coalition in the Civil Rights Era* (University of North Carolina Press, 2016).
91. Bentley, oral history interview, 36; W. M. Allman and Mrs. Allman, oral history interview, June 19, 1970, Crane, Texas, Oral History Collection, Permian Basin Petroleum Museum, Midland, Texas, 30.
92. Al Lowman, "Bell Cord Rutherford: Cowboy Quixote of the West Texas Plains; Or, Some Shards from Our Storytelling Past," *Southwestern Historical Quarterly* 104, no. 4 (2001): 495–513; Slim Willet, "Johnny Don't Drill Anymore," *Texas Oil Patch Songs by Slim Willet*, Winston LP 1040, 1959.
93. Folder "Hughes Tool Co.," Trade Literature Collection, Smithsonian Archives Center. See also Nathan Rosenberg, "Technological Change in the Machine Tool Industry, 1840–1910," *Journal of Economic History* 23, no. 4 (1963): 414–43.
94. Soon after, the Sharp Machine was developed and patented to mix mud for drilling, and drilling mud became a complex mixture of chemicals over time. Boatright, *Tales from the Derrick Floor*, 18.
95. James S. Abercrombie and Harry S. Cameron, "Blow-out Preventer," US Patent 552,522, filed April 14, 1922, and issued January 12, 1926; "Cameron First Ram-Type BOP an ASME Historical Mechanical Engineering Landmark," ASME International, 2003.
96. Brantley, *History of Oil Well Drilling*.
97. Roger M. Olien and Diana Davids Hinton, *Wildcatters: Texas Independent Oilmen* (Texas A&M University Press, 2007).
98. According to Mody Boatright, "At the beginning of the century the driller was directly dependent upon his senses. He surmised what was going on under the ground largely by the feel of the cable, or by the sound and speed of the rotary." Boatright, *Tales from the Derrick Floor*, 225.
99. George T. Abel, Charles Vertrees, Berte Haigh, and S. D. Myres, oral history interview, Midland, Texas, February 2, 1971, Oral History Collection, Permian Basin Petroleum Museum, Midland, Texas.

100. Abel et al., oral history interview, 200.
101. During the 1920s, there was also a wave of experimentation in core-sampling technologies. Instead of reading mud in slush pits, core sampling allowed drillers to take rock or mud samples as the drill was running to test the geological composition at the bottom of the oil well. Like the rolling rock cutter bit, such core-sampling technology was developed on the job. According to one oral history, one Mr. Robicheaux designed one of the first down-hole testing technologies, called a "core barrel." The core barrel was attached to a chain and then dropped down the drill pipe. It landed in a hole in the middle of the drill bit and collected down-hole mud as the drill was used. The core barrel could be drawn up without requiring the entire drill to be removed from the hole. To search specifically for subsurface salt, drillers would send down a core barrel filled with water saturated with salt. Once a salt dome was identified, drillers estimated the edges of the dome and attempted to drill as close to the middle of the formation as possible. Boatright, *Tales from the Derrick Floor*, 216.
102. In one instance, former driller Curt G. Hammil remembered using a convenient herd of cattle to churn up enough mud to keep the drill in operation. Boatright, *Tales from the Derrick Floor*, 18.
103. Brantley, *History of Oil Well Drilling*, chapter 5.
104. For example, George Bentley, a contractor who prepared prospective well sites for drilling, described his laborious and complex daily activities setting up a well for long-term production. While he encountered hazards, he appreciated autonomy. George R. Bentley, oral history interview at Monahans, May 20, 1970, Oral History Collection, Permian Basin Petroleum Museum, Midland, Texas, 12.
105. Boatright, *Tales from the Derrick Floor*, 62.
106. William Wolfe and Anna Wolfe, oral history interview, February 12, 1970, McCamey, Texas, Oral History Collection, Permian Basin Petroleum Museum, Midland, Texas, 25.

3. THE INFRASTRUCTURE OF MODERNITY

1. James S. Hudnall, "Geology and Economic Importance of the East Texas Field," *Oil Weekly*, July 31, 1931.
2. Wallace Scot McFarlane, "Oil on the Farm: The East Texas Oil Boom and the Origins of an Energy Economy," *Journal of Southern History* 83, no. 4 (2017): 853–88.
3. A representative 1929 article in the *Austin Statesman* breathlessly stated that Texas Land Commissioner J. T. Robison keeps a shotgun in his desk "as only a precaution." "Oil Scrapbooks," Box 3L425, Briscoe Center for American History, Austin. For analogous histories of the environmental impact of boom and bust, see Brian Black, *Petrolia: The Landscape of America's First Oil Boom* (Johns Hopkins University Press, 2003); and Henry Alexander Wiencek, *Oil Cities: The Making of North Louisiana's Boomtowns, 1901–1930* (University of Texas Press, 2024).
4. Diana Davids Hinton and Roger M. Olien, *Oil in Texas: The Gusher Age, 1895–1945* (University of Texas Press, 2002).
5. Hale B. Soyster, "Review of the Petroleum Industry in the United States," Circular 11, US Department of the Interior, US Government Printing Office, 1934.

6. "Oil Output Far Exceeds Demand," *Abilene Morning Reporter-News*, July 28, 1929, 15.
7. API Committee on Public Affairs, *Petroleum Facts and Figures, Centennial Edition* (American Petroleum Institute, 1959), API Photo and Film Collection, Box 116, Smithsonian Archives Center.
8. Julia Cauble Smith, "The East Texas Oilfield," in *Handbook of Texas Online*, accessed March 20, 2017, published by the Texas State Historical Association, http://www.tshaonline.org/handbook/online/articles/doe01.
9. API Committee on Public Affairs, *Petroleum Facts and Figures, Centennial Edition*.
10. Soyster, "Review of the Petroleum Industry in the United States."
11. Soyster, "Review of the Petroleum Industry in the United States."
12. Black, *Petrolia*; Brian Frehner, *Finding Oil: The Nature of Petroleum Geology* (University of Nebraska Press, 2011).
13. "Oil Remakes West Texas," *El Paso Evening Post*, October 24, 1929, C49.
14. "Witnesses Reveal Present and Future Possibilities of New Rail Territory," *Lubbock Morning Avalanche*, April 3, 1929, 10.
15. "Little Oil Is Being Turned into Storage," *Abilene Reporter News*, April 14, 1929, 5.
16. "Gulf Pipe Line from Hendricks Pool to Monacans Is Completed," *Abilene Reporter News*, April 21, 1929, 5.
17. Petroleum Administration for War (PAW), *A History of the Petroleum Administration for War*, Series 10: Arthur E. Pew Jr. Engineering and Development, Sun Oil Company Collection, Hagley Museum and Library, Wilmington, Delaware. Photos from the American Petroleum Institute (API) give visual evidence of the physical labor involved in pipeline construction before 1950. *Pipelaying*, Box 20, Collection 711, API Photo and Film Collection, Smithsonian Archives Center, Washington, DC; Hugh Gorman, *Redefining Efficiency: Pollution Concerns, Regulatory Mechanisms, and Technological Change in the U.S. Petroleum Industry* (University of Akron Press, 2001), 87.
18. *Delivery*, Photographs, Box 4, API Photo and Film Collection, Collection 711, Smithsonian Archives Center, Washington, DC. See also "National Seamless Pipeline," *National Tube Company Bulletin*, No. 23, 1940, Trade Literature Collection, Hagley Museum and Library, Wilmington, Delaware; "Building the Pipe Line," 1950, Folder 3, "Blasting: Dynamite in Use," Series IV, Box 3, DuPont Company Product Information photographs, Audiovisual Collections and Digital Initiatives Department, Hagley Museum and Library, Wilmington, Delaware.
19. George S. Wolbert, *American Pipe Lines: Their Industrial Structure, Economic Status and Legal Implications* (University of Oklahoma Press, 1952); "Pipelines-Workers-Tong Gang," Box 20, API Photo and Film Collection, Collection 711, Smithsonian Archives Center, Washington, DC.
20. "Welding Torch Sets off Pipeline Explosion: Six Killed," *Abilene Daily Reporter*, January 19, 1937.
21. William Wolfe and Anna Wolfe, oral history interview, February 12, 1970, McCamey, Texas, Oral History Collection, Permian Basin Petroleum Museum, Midland, Texas, 21–22.
22. "Cowden Awarded $15.00 an Acre by Jury Here," *Odessa American*, April 6, 1934, 1.
23. John D. Alexander, oral history interview by Richard Mason, October 20, 1982, Texas Tech University Special Collections, Lubbock.

24. Clyde Barton, oral history interview, July 15, 1970, Kermit, Texas, Oral History Collection, Permian Basin Petroleum Museum, Midland, Texas, 18.
25. Barton, oral history interview, 18.
26. Gorman, *Redefining Efficiency*.
27. Prissy Neill, "McCamey's Million Barrel White Elephant," *Texas Historian*, September 1976; Roger M. Olien and Diana Davids Hinton, *Oil Booms: Social Change in Five Texas Towns* (University of Nebraska Press, 1982).
28. Wolbert, *American Pipe Lines*.
29. Telegrams from J. Howard Pew to J. Edgar Pew, June 1941, Collection 10, Box 97, Folder 892.116 DIS.1 War Emergency Pipeline 1941–1945, Sun Oil Company Collection A. E. Pew Jr., Hagley Museum and Library, Wilmington, Delaware.
30. American Petroleum Institute (API), *Petroleum: The Story of an American Industry* (American Petroleum Institute, 1935).
31. PAW, *A History of the Petroleum Administration for War*.
32. PAW, *A History of the Petroleum Administration for War*.
33. Wolbert, *American Pipe Lines*.
34. "Oil Showing in Stonewall Test," *Abilene Reporter News*, April 29, 1938.
35. "Men Who Make Magnolia," *Magnolia News*, 12–14, Box 2.207 E224, Exxon Mobil Historical Collection, Briscoe Center for American History.
36. "Humble Safety Campaign Gets Results in '39," *Odessa American*, January 3, 1940, 1; Wolbert, *American Pipe Lines*.
37. Roger M. Olien and Diana Davids Hinton, *Wildcatters: Texas Independent Oilmen* (Texas A&M University Press, 2007), 69.
38. "Humble Safety Campaign Gets Results in '39," 1.
39. Wolbert, *American Pipe Lines*. See also Christopher Casteneda and Clarence M. Smith, *Gas Pipelines and the Emergence of America's Regulatory State: A History of Panhandle Eastern Corporation, 1928–1993* (Cambridge University Press, 1996).
40. "Oil Men Ask Law to Control Pipelines; Moody Insists Bill Must Attain Aim," February 27, 1930, *Austin Statesman*, 1. "Regulation of Pipelines to Solons," March 3, 1930, *Austin Statesman*, 1; "Oil Industry: Big Man Fights Little Man, Third Group Opposes Both, Confusing Code-Making," *Newsweek*, August 5, 1933, 20–22.
41. Correlative rights in Texas were officially upheld in court. Rights-holders Mabel and Frank Elliff were awarded damages to their potential profit from oil extraction after an oil well neighboring their property blew out, allowing oil in the commonly shared pool to evaporate. *Elliff v. Texxon Drilling Co.*, 146 Tex. 575 (Tex. 1948).
42. E. N. Beane, oral history interview, June 19, 1970, Crane, Texas, Permian Basin Petroleum Museum, Midland, Texas, 10.
43. Alexander, oral history interview.
44. William R. Childs, "The Transformation of the Railroad Commission of Texas, 1917–1940: Business-Government Relations and the Importance of Personality, Agency Culture, and Regional Differences," *Business History Review* 65, no. 2 (1991): 285–344.
45. David F. Prindle, *Petroleum Politics and the Texas Railroad Commission* (University of Texas Press, 1980), 7.
46. Ross S. Sterling and Ed Kilman, *Ross Sterling, Texan* (University of Texas Press, 2007).
47. "Statement by Wolters," October 16, 1931, cited in East Texas Chamber of Commerce, "Martial Law in East Texas," undated pamphlet, 52, Box 3F59, Sterling Papers.

48. William R. Childs, *The Texas Railroad Commission: Understanding Regulation in America to the Mid-Twentieth Century* (Texas A&M University Press, 2005); "More Operators Close Wells," *Longview (Texas) Daily News*, July 22, 1931, 1.
49. Childs, *The Texas Railroad Commission*, 154; Gorman, *Redefining Efficiency*, chapter 6; "Standard Oil's Strangle Hold," 1923, Texas Oil Industry Scrapbooks, Briscoe Center for American History, University of Texas, Austin; Olien and Hinton, *Wildcatters*, chapter 3.
50. Historians have shown that battles over Texas oil regulation in the Depression era were deeply intertwined with debates over states' rights and the ongoing legacy of the Civil War. Roger M. Olien and Diana Davids Hinton, *Oil and Ideology: The Cultural Creation of the American Petroleum Industry* (University of North Carolina Press, 2000), chapter 1; Childs, *Texas Railroad Commission*, 153; Matthew Ware Coulter, "Taming the East Texas 'Black Giant': Ernest O. Thompson and Illusions of Independence, 1930–1935," *Southwestern Historical Quarterly* 123, no. 3 (2020): 292–315.
51. Childs, *The Texas Railroad Commission*; Coulter, "Taming the East Texas 'Black Giant.'"
52. "1860–1964, Progress in the Permian Basin of West Texas," Box 3G314, Olin Wellborn Nichols Culberson Papers, Briscoe Center for American History, Austin.
53. Samuel D. Myres, *The Permian Basin: Petroleum Empire of the Southwest*, 2 vols. (Permian, 1973, 1977). Yates was an extreme example. The Hendricks Field, also in West Texas, had over five hundred competing leases. However, the East Texas Field took this to extremes. In 1930, the field had over one thousand leases. Julia Cauble Smith, "Hendrick Oilfield," in *Handbook of Texas*, uploaded June 15, 2010, https://tshaonline.org/handbook/online/articles/doho3; Julia Cauble Smith, "The East Texas Oilfield," in *Handbook of Texas*, uploaded June 12, 2010, https://tshaonline.org/handbook/online/articles/doeo1.
54. Myres, *The Permian Basin*.
55. H. H. King, "Revise Basis of Proration in Yates Field," *Oil Weekly* 49, no. 10 (May 25, 1928): 45.
56. Olien and Hinton, *Wildcatters*, 47.
57. Before the 1930s, attempts at oil regulation were typically implemented on a field-by-field basis. Depending on the state, industry or state officials would attempt to enforce rules that limited the number of wells allowed in a single field. Most of these efforts were unsuccessful. Sharon O. Flanery and Ryan J. Morgan, "Overview of Pooling and Unitization Affecting Appalachian Shale Development," Steptoe & Johnson PLLC, Charleston, West Virginia; Gorman, *Redefining Efficiency*, chapters 3 and 4.
58. Cooperation in the Yates Field was held up nationally as an example of rational, free-market risk management that could be used nationally to solve the looming problem. Sam Ashburn, "Yates Pool-Wightiest of Producing Areas," *Lubbock Avalanche-Journal*, September 23, 1928, 5; "Increase for Oil Is Asked," *Lubbock Morning Avalanche*, August 31, 1932, 4.
59. Associated Press, "Oil Operators Invited to Big Dallas Meet," *Longview (Texas) News-Journal*, June 6, 1931, 1.
60. Associated Press, "Oil Production in U.S. on Increase," *Brownsville (Texas) Herald*, July 4, 1929, 19.

61. Howard Barrett, "Yates Field, Texas' Busiest Spot," *Abilene Morning Reporter-News*, December 25, 1927, 15.
62. Olien and Hinton, *Wildcatters*, chapter 3.
63. "Oil Compact Is Praised by Col. Thompson," *Pampa (Texas) Daily News*, November 11, 1936, 3; William R. Childs, "Texas, the Interstate Oil Compact Commission, and State Control of Oil Production: Regionalism, States' Rights, and Federalism During World War II," *Pacific Historical Review* 64, no. 4 (1995): 567–98.
64. "Oil Commission Asked to Dallas: Thompson Satisfied with Interstate Compact," *Austin American*, December 15, 1935, 2.
65. American Petroleum Institute (API), "Statistical Bulletin, 1932–1940," Hagley Museum and Library, Wilmington, Delaware.
66. "Outside Tests Hold Interest in Ector," *Abilene Reporter-News*, December 9, 1934, 10.
67. This process, called a "farm out," became an increasingly common way for large oil companies to avoid risky oil speculation. Olien and Hinton, *Wildcatters*, chapter 4.
68. John Brewer, "Gaines County Cedar Lake Pool Gets Second Producer," *Abilene Reporter-News*, December 3, 1939, 6.
69. Clippings, Box 76, Harvey O'Conner Collection, Walter Reuther Library, Detroit.
70. "U.S. May Drop Price Fixing Plan on Oil," *Pittsburgh Press*, November 21, 1933, 27.
71. Harold Ickes Papers, Secretary of the Interior Files, Boxes 112 and 113, Library of Congress. See also Stephen J. Randall, "Harold Ickes and United States Foreign Petroleum Policy Planning, 1939–1945," *Business History Review* 57, no. 3 (Autumn 1983): 367–87.
72. Barry Mackintosh, "Harold L. Ickes and the National Park Service," *Journal of Forest History* 29, no. 2 (1985), https://npshistory.com/publications/jfh-v29n2-78-84.pdf.
73. See also Harold Ickes, "Fighting Oil," Newberry Library, Chicago; Associated Press, "Ickes Returns East, Leaving API Meeting Facing Difficulties," *Corsicana (Texas) Semi-Weekly Light*, November 16, 1934, 19; Harold Ickes, *Fightin' Oil* (Knopf, 1943). For a summary of this history, breaking oil legislation into four periods (extractive anarchy, conservation regulation, buyouts, and unitization), see Gary Libecap and James L. Smith, "The Economic Evolution of Petroleum Property Rights in the United States," *Journal of Legal Studies* 31, no. S2 (June 2002): S589–S608.
74. Gorman, *Redefining Efficiency*, chapter 6.
75. In 1933, Ickes backed the Marland Bill, calling for federal regulation of oil production. In 1934, he again began pushing for further oil conservation legislation through the failed Thomas-Disney Bill. This move called for some in the industry to call for Ickes to resign. Ickes, *Fightin' Oil*.
76. "Removal of Ickes as Oil Chief Urged," *New York Times*, November 25, 1934, N7.
77. "Major Companies Blamed for Many Ills of Oil Industry," *Abilene Reporter-News*, December 9, 1934, 10; J. Howard Marshall II, *Done in Oil: An Autobiography*, ed. Robert L. Bradley Jr. (Texas A&M University Press, 2000).
78. Legislation Files, 1903–1952, Boxes 144–145, Tom Connally Papers 1896–1952, Library of Congress, Washington, DC.
79. Gerald Nash, *United States Oil Policy, 1890–1964: Business and Government in Twentieth-Century America* (University of Pittsburgh Press, 1968).
80. Nash, *United States Oil Policy*.
81. Ickes, *Fightin' Oil*.

82. Axtel Byles, "A Petition to the Congress of the United States, Submitted by the American Petroleum Institute," American Petroleum Institute (API), 1935, Special Collections, Hagley Museum and Library, Wilmington, Delaware.
83. In the article, the Mid-Continent Oil and Gas Association provided numerous statistics reminding locals that the oil industry made up the majority of the tax base for oil-producing states. "At W. T. C. of C. Convention—J. C. Hunter Discusses Unequal Tax Burden Imposed on Oil," *Abilene Reporter-News*, April 26, 1938, 17.
84. See William Boyd, *The Slain Wood: Papermaking and Its Environmental Consequences in the American South* (Johns Hopkins University Press, 2015), 20; Omer Aloni, *The League of Nations and the Protection of the Environment* (Cambridge University Press, 2021), chapter 4.
85. Olien and Hinton, *Oil and Ideology*, 121.
86. Susan Jane M. Brown, " 'The Forest Must Come First': Gifford Pinchot's Conservation Ethic and the Gifford Pinchot National Forest—the Ideal and the Reality," 11 *Fordham Environmental Law Review* 137 (1999).
87. Mark Fiege, *The Republic of Nature: An Environmental History of the United States* (University of Washington Press, 2012), chapters 4 and 6.
88. J. E. Redburn, "World Move to Stabilize Oil Industry Adis [sic] West Texas," *Abilene Morning Reporter-News*, April 14, 1929, 5.
89. US Bureau of Mines, "Review of the Petroleum Industry in the United States," US Department of the Interior, Washington, DC, 1934, 8.
90. Harold Ickes, "A New Day for Conservation," address at the American Game Conference Banquet, New York, January 22, 1935.
91. Franklin D. Roosevelt, *The Public Papers and Addresses of Franklin D. Roosevelt* (Macmillan, 1941), 138.
92. Randall, "Harold Ickes and United States Foreign Petroleum Policy Planning."
93. Sarah T. Phillips, *This Land, This Nation: Conservation, Rural America, and the New Deal* (Cambridge University Press, 2007).
94. John A. Adams, *Damming the Colorado: The Rise of the Lower Colorado River Authority, 1933–1939* (Texas A&M University Press, 2000).
95. API, *Petroleum*.
96. "4 Completions in County for 4,976.03 Barrels," *Odessa American*, September 7, 1938, 8; Mark Aldrich, *Safety First: Technology, Labor, and Business in the Building of American Work Safety, 1870–1939* (Johns Hopkins University Press, 1997).
97. Telegram, Folder "Ruth Bennet #1 Correspondence Yoakum County TX 83-021 C. J. Red Davidson," C. J. Red Davidson Collection, Permian Basin Petroleum Museum, Midland, Texas.
98. The local press described similar problems across Pecos County in the 1920s. For example, see Howard Barrett, "Yates Field, Texas' Busiest Spot," *Abilene Morning Reporter-News*, December 25, 1927, 15.
99. "Objectives of Year Assigned to Committees," *Abilene Reporter-News*, June 15, 1938, 3.
100. Clippings, Box 76, Harvey O'Conner Collection, Walter Reuther Library, Detroit.
101. "Objectives of Year Assigned to Committees," *Abilene Reporter-News*, June 15, 1938, 3.
102. "WTCC Fires Guns in Freight Rates Battle," *Abilene Reporter News*, May 15, 1939, 1; *Hearing Before Temporary National Economic Committee, Pursuant to Pub Res*

113, 5th Cong., 76th Cong., 2d & 3d Sess., Parts 14-17A 7376, 7588, 7652, 1939–1941, Trade Literature Collection, Hagley Museum and Library, Wilmington, Delaware; Wolbert, *American Pipe Lines*, 3.

103. In 1940, such statements spurred the US Justice Department to formally announce its intention to use antitrust laws to divest all pipelines from major oil companies. Although divestiture was postponed due to the outset of war, congressional opposition to pipeline monopolies continued. US Congress, Temporary National Economic Committee (TNEC), TNEC Hearings, 7103–7104, Records of the Temporary National Economic Committee, US National Archives, Washington, DC.
104. US Congress, Temporary National Economic Committee (TNEC), TNEC Hearings, 7103–7104, 1938–1941, Records of the Temporary National Economic Committee, US National Archives, Washington, DC.
105. Hinton and Olien, *Oil in Texas*, chapter 9.
106. API, *Petroleum*, 25.
107. "Pipelines Planned to Relieve Threatened East Coast Shortage," *World Petroleum*, date unknown, 28–31, Box "A. E. Pew Jr., Box 97—War Emergency Pipeline," Series 10, Sun Oil Company Collection, Hagley Museum and Library, Wilmington, Delaware.
108. Shell Oil Company, *Pipeline Construction Laying Pipe*, n.d., Box 19, Collection 711, API Photo and Film Collection, Smithsonian Archives Center, Washington, DC; Box 19, Collection 711, API Photo and Film Collection, Smithsonian Archives Center.
109. Magnolia sped up this pipe-building trend only after the war, building five more lines connecting remote Texas fields between 1947 and 1955. Reports, Folder "History of the Magnolia Pipeline Company," Box E222, Exxon Mobil Collection 2.207, Briscoe Center for American History, University of Texas; Wolbert, *American Pipe Lines*.
110. Telegrams from J. Howard Pew to J. Edgar Pew, June 1941, Folder "892.116 DIS.1 War Emergency Pipeline 1941–1945, A. E. Pew Jr.," Collection 10, Box 97, Sun Oil Company Collection, Hagley Museum and Library, Wilmington, Delaware.
111. PAW, *A History of the Petroleum Administration for War*.
112. PAW, *A History of the Petroleum Administration for War*.
113. *Important Facts About Texas Oil*, 5th ed., January 1943, Texas Mid-Continent Oil and Gas Association, Dallas.
114. PAW, *History of the Petroleum Administration for War*, 25.
115. Hinton and Olien, *Oil in Texas*, chapter 9.

4. WATER RUNS OUT IN THE "TALL CITY"

1. "Bibliographic File—Fred T. Hogan," Permian Basin Petroleum Museum, Midland, Texas; "Fred T. Hogan Helped Put Midland on Oil Industry Map," *Midland Reporter Telegram*, May 10, 2003.
2. Garth Jones, "Population Increases Cause Greater Drains on Inadequate Waters," *The Austin Statesman*, July 19, 1947, 4.
3. "Lack of US Funds Curbs Solving Water Shortage," *The Austin Statesman*, January 20, 1948, 7; "5 West Texas Cities Ask Colorado River Water," *The Austin American*, August 4, 1946, 7.

4. American Petroleum Institute (API), *API Facts and Figures*, Collection 711, Box 116, API Photo and Film Collection, Smithsonian Archives Center, Washington, DC.
5. "A Trip to the Oklahoma City Oil Field," September 8, 1929, Oklahoma City Chamber of Commerce, Box 6, Collection 60, Warshaw Petroleum Collection, Smithsonian Archives Center, Washington, DC.
6. Transcript, oral history interview, Dr. Myres, Berte Haigh, and J. Ben Carsey at Houston, October 9, 1970, Oral History Collection, Permian Basin Petroleum Museum, Midland, Texas.
7. James J. Wheat and George Clayton, oral history interview, July 17, 1970, Mentone, Loving County, Texas, Oral History Collection, Permian Basin Petroleum Museum, Midland, Texas, 13–14.
8. Wheat and Clayton, oral history interview.
9. Diana Davids Hinton, "Creating Company Culture: Oil Company Camps in the Southwest, 1920–1960," *Southwestern Historical Quarterly* 111, no. 4 (2008): 369.
10. These key reservoirs ran dry in 1968.
11. Odessa grew from a population of 2,407 to 9,573 between 1930 and 1940. US Census Bureau, Census of the Population and Housing 1940, accessed June 5, 2017, https://www.census.gov/prod/www/decennial.html.
12. *Odessa, Texas: City Directory, 1938–1939* (Lloyd's National Directory, 1938).
13. Joanna Hadjicostandi, "Historical Growth of African Americans in Odessa, Texas," *National Forum of Multicultural Issues Journal* 12, no. 1 (2015).
14. Jones, "Population Increases Cause Greater Drains on Inadequate Waters."
15. "What 'Unlimited Water for Odessa' Plan Means to You," *Odessa American*, November 13, 1950, 7.
16. *Midland Reporter Telegram*, January 1, 1942, 9.
17. Jones, "Population Increases Cause Greater Drains on Inadequate Waters."
18. Suburban expansion continued as golf course gated communities were built to the north of town in the late 1970s and early 1980s. These communities were called Saddle Club North and Green Tree Country Club Estates. Susan Orlean, "A Place Called Midland," *The New Yorker*, October 16, 2000, https://www.newyorker.com/magazine/2000/10/16/a-place-called-midland, 128.
19. "Five Cities Present Pleas for Upper Colorado Water Grants," *The Austin American*, October 13, 1946, 32.
20. "Water Permits Issue Debated," *The Austin Statesman*, October 14, 1946, 3.
21. John Williams, *The Untold Story of the Lower Colorado River Authority* (Texas A&M University Press, 2016).
22. Jones, "Population Increases Cause Greater Drains on Inadequate Waters."
23. "Sewage May Be One Answer to State's Water Shortage," *The Austin Statesman*, November 20, 1947, 9.
24. "Sewage May Be One Answer to State's Water Shortage."
25. "Rains Soak West Texas," *The Austin American*, May 11, 1947, 1.
26. "Sweetwater and Trent Flooded by Heavy Rains: Much of West Texas Gets Badly Needed Drought-Breaking Rain," *The Austin American*, October 26, 1947, 1.
27. "What 'Unlimited Water for Odessa' Plan Means to You."
28. Williams, *The Untold Story of the Lower Colorado River Authority*.
29. "Parley Called on New Water Code," *The Austin American*, July 25, 1948, 1.

30. By 1949, it was legal to establish voluntary conservation districts, which could impose limitations on private water holders. However, this law was rarely enforced. Otis W. Templer, "Texas Ground Water Law: Inflexible Institutions and Resource Realities," *Ecumene* 10 (April 1978).
31. The by-then-venerable Board of Water Engineers was renamed the Texas Water Commission in 1962 as an umbrella organization for these different groups. Timothy L. Brown, "A Primer for Understanding Texas Water Law," Legislative Reference Library of Texas, 29 (Austin, 2006); Williams, *The Untold Story of the Lower Colorado River Authority*.
32. Oral histories record little objection to either unitization or water flooding among regional landowners or urban administrators. Elliott Cowden and Holt Jowel, interview, September 16, 1970, Midland, Texas, Oral History Collection, Permian Basin Petroleum Museum, Midland, Texas; George R. Bentley, interview, May 20, 1970, Monahans, Texas, Oral History Collection, Permian Basin Petroleum Museum, Midland, Texas.
33. Samuel D. Myres, *The Permian Basin: Era of Advancement* (Permian, 1977).
34. This sand allows for only 15 percent of the oil trapped within it to be extracted using traditional drilling methods. John Edward Brantley, *History of Oil Well Drilling* (Gulf Publishing, 1971).
35. Boxes 1–2, Arthur Harvey Papers 1938–1963, American Heritage Center, University of Wyoming.
36. It is now known that the area contained approximately ten billion barrels of oil. Julia Cauble Smith, "Spraberry-Dean Sandstone Fields," in *Handbook of Texas Online*, uploaded June 15, 2010, https://tshaonline.org/handbook/online/articles/dosqw.
37. Myres, *The Permian Basin*.
38. By comparison, between 1955 and 1960, the average US well depth came only to 4,236 feet. American Petroleum Institute (API), *API Facts and Figures 1959–1967*, Collection 711, Box 116, API Photo and Film Collection, Smithsonian Archives Center, Washington, DC.
39. In 1955, nationwide average per-well drilling costs were $65,500. API, *API Facts and Figures 1959–1967*.
40. Roger M. Olien and Diana Davids Hinton, *Wildcatters: Texas Independent Oilmen* (Texas A&M University Press 2007).
41. Tim Parker, "Oil Causes Host Spectacular Texas Cities Growth," *The Austin Statesman*, December 8, 1949, 20; Virginia Paty, "Midland . . . Deep in the Heart of Texas Oil." *The Sun*, February 1948, 1.
42. "Texas Water District Raises $11,750,000 Through Sale of Bonds," *Wall Street Journal*, February 28, 1951, 11.
43. "Many Texas Cities Wailing for Water," *Odessa American*, July 15, 1951, 1.
44. C. L. Dowell, *Dams and Reservoirs in Texas: History and Descriptive Information* (Texas Water Commission Bulletin 6408, Austin, 1964).
45. US Census Bureau, *Census of Population—Texas 1960, Vol. I*, accessed July 21, 2015, https://www.census.gov/prod/www/decennial.html.
46. According to the US Census, the population of Midland in 1950 was 21,713. By 1960, the population of the Midland urbanized area was 63,274. US Census Bureau, *US Census of the Population—1960*, accessed June 6, 2017, https://www.census.gov/prod/www/decennial.html.

47. "Population Boom Seen at Midland and Odessa," *The Austin American*, June 7, 1959, 1.
48. "Texas Building Boom Rolling in High Gear: Early-Spring Spurt of Private Homes Adds to Record Total," *The Austin American*, February 16, 1947, 5; "Texas Building Boom Rolling Along at $1,000,000 per Day," *The Austin American*, January 19, 1947, 5.
49. Ron Tyler, ed., *The New Handbook of Texas*, Vol. 4 (Texas State Historical Society, 1996), 706–10.
50. *Midland City Directory 1955* (Hudspeth's Directory Company, 1955). See also Bill Modisett, ed., *Historic Midland* (Historical-Publishing Network Lammert Publications, 1998), 43–73.
51. "Lubbock," Emporis, accessed January 19, 2017, https://www.emporis.com/city/101489/lubbock-tx-usa.
52. Richard B. Wright, "Urban Centers of West Texas," in *West Texas: A History of the Giant Side of the State*, ed. Paul H. Carlson and Bruce A. Glasrud (University of Oklahoma Press, 2007), 161.
53. Harbert Parmet, *George Bush: The Life of a Lone Star Yankee* (Transaction, 2010), 78.
54. *Midland City Directory 1955*.
55. John Leffler, "Midland, TX," in *Handbook of Texas*, uploaded June 15, 2010, https://tshaonline.org/handbook/online/articles/hdm03.
56. "Black Oilers Win Two Weekend Games," *Odessa American*, August 11, 1947, 3; Midland City Council, *Midland City Plan*, 1950; Jack Gale, "Midland Will Be Suburb of Odessa, Says 100 Committee," *Odessa American*, March 17, 1948, 1; "Odessa Building Shatters All Previous Marks," *Odessa American*, December 31, 1950, 1.
57. Texas and Pacific Oil Company, *TP Voice*, July–August 1965, 4, Hagley Museum and Library, Wilmington, Delaware.
58. Jennifer Klein, *For All These Rights: Business, Labor, and the Shaping of America's Public-Private Welfare State* (Princeton University Press, 2003); Jennifer Klein, "The Politics of Economic Security: Employee Benefits and the Privatization of New Deal Liberalism," *Journal of Policy History* 12, no. 1 (2004): 48; Karen Orren, *Corporate Power and Social Change: The Politics of the Life Insurance Industry* (Johns Hopkins University Press, 1974).
59. Caley Horan, *Insurance Era: Risk, Governance, and the Privatization of Security in Postwar America* (MIT Press, 2021), chapter 4; Thomas Hanchett, "Financing Suburbia: Prudential Insurance and the Post–World War II Transformation of the American City," *Journal of Urban History* 26, no. 3 (2000): 312–28. See also Robert Fishman, *Bourgeois Utopias: The Rise and Fall of Suburbia* (Basic Books, 1987); Kenneth T. Jackson, *Crabgrass Frontier: The Suburbanization of the United States* (Oxford University Press, 1985); Keeanga-Yamahtta Taylor, *Race for Profit: How Banks and the Real Estate Industry Undermined Black Homeownership* (University of North Carolina Press, 2019).
60. "New Homes Add Spurt to Texas Building Boom: Record-Breaking Pace Rolls Past $100,000,000 Mark," *The Austin American*, March 9, 1947, 21.
61. Based on US Census records, aggregate household wages in the Permian Basin remained approximately three times higher than the state average of $1,546 for the duration of the 1950s. In 1960, the average household wages in Texas were $4,058.

Midland's average household wages were much higher, at $6,936, and Odessa's were $6,128. US Census Bureau, "Average Household Wages," *US Census of Population and Housing*, accessed July 21, 2015, https://www.census.gov/prod/www/decennial.html.

62. US Census Bureau, "Average Unemployment," *US Census of Population and Housing, 1960*, accessed July 21, 2015, https://www.census.gov/prod/www/decennial.html.
63. Manager, Texas Employment Commission, Midland, April 15, 1957, in Dickinson Weber, "A Comparison of Two Oil City Business Centers (Odessa-Midland, Texas)," (Dissertation, University of Chicago, 1958), 35.
64. Eunice Grier and George Grier, "Case Studies in Racially Mixed Housing 3: Midland Texas," in *Princeton Conference on Equal Opportunity in Housing* (Washington Center for Metropolitan Studies, 1962). In 1950, the median Midland income was $1,546, and it increased to $4,058 by 1960. US Census Bureau, *US Census of the Population—1960*.
65. The state average was $4,058. "Tables," Folder "Statistical Records: 1965," Box 2E200, Mid-Continent Oil and Gas Association Records, Briscoe Center for American History, University of Texas, Austin.
66. Texas and Pacific Oil Company, *TP Voice*, 4.
67. Parker, "Oil Causes Host Spectacular Texas Cities Growth."
68. James Collett, *Images of America: Midland* (Arcadia, 2010), 121.
69. Weber, "A Comparison of Two Oil City Business Centers."
70. US Bureau of the Census, "General Social and Economic Characteristics, Texas," in *US Census of the Population—1960*, accessed June 6, 2017, https://www.census.gov/prod/www/decennial.html.
71. US Bureau of the Census, "General Social and Economic Characteristics, Texas."
72. Midland housed 1,350 families who identified as nonwhite and 600 "unrelated individuals," making up about 10 percent of the population. US Bureau of the Census, "General Social and Economic Characteristics, Texas."
73. The 1960 Midland City Directory listed two churches with Spanish names: the Iglesia Bautista Immanual, at 1800 N. Lincoln, and the Primera Iglesia Bautiste Oriente, at 1609 E. Orchard Lane. The directory also lists Our Lady of Guadalupe Catholic Church, at 1401 Garden Lane, and the Mexican Baptist Mission, at 501 N. Tyler. "Churches," in *Midland City Directory 1960–1961* (R. W. Byram, 1960), Permian Basin Petroleum Museum, Midland, Texas, 120–21.
74. Jimmy Patterson, *A History of Character: The Story of Midland, Texas* (Abell-Hanger Foundation, 2014).
75. "The Oil Fields of Odessa, TX," from Delma Abalos, oral history interview with Todd Moye, Karen Wisely, and Joel Zapata, July 14, 2016, Odessa, Texas, Civil Rights in Black and Brown Interview Database, https://crbb.tcu.edu/clips/2259/the-oil-fields-of-odessa-tx, accessed August 14, 2025.
76. According to the US Census, the average median family income across demographics in 1960 was $6,936. The state average was $4,058. Although segregation was more pervasive in Midland than in other urban areas, median nonwhite income was significantly higher in several other Texas cities. US Census Bureau, "Income," in *US Census of the Population—1960*, accessed June 6, 2017, https://www.census.gov/prod/www/decennial.html.
77. US Census Bureau, "Income."
78. Grier and Grier, "Case Studies in Racially Mixed Housing 3: Midland Texas," 18.

79. Grier and Grier, "Case Studies in Racially Mixed Housing 3: Midland Texas." Racial tensions remained high in the city for the next decade. "School Integration," from Gene Collins, oral history interview, July 8, 2016, Odessa, Texas, Civil Rights in Black and Brown Interview Database, https://crbb.tcu.edu/clips/3824/school-integration-3, accessed August 14, 2025.
80. Michelle Nickerson and Darren Dochuk, eds., *Sunbelt Rising: The Politics of Space, Place, and Region* (University of Pennsylvania Press, 2011); Bradley R. Rice and Richard M. Bernard, eds., *Sunbelt Cities: Politics and Growth Since World War II* (University of Texas Press, 1984).
81. Bradford Luckingham, *The Urban Southwest: A Profile History of Albuquerque, El Paso, Phoenix, Tucson* (Texas Western Press, 1982); Marc Reisner, *Cadillac Desert: The American West and Its Disappearing Water* (Penguin, 1993); Christopher J. Manganiello, *Southern Water, Southern Power: How the Politics of Cheap Energy and Water Scarcity Shaped a Region* (University of North Carolina Press, 2017). See also Richard A. Earl and Robert Czerniac, "Sunbelt Water War: The El Paso–New Mexico Water Conflict," *Social Science Journal* 33, no. 4 (1996): 359–79; Andrew Needham, *Power Lines: Phoenix and the Making of the Modern Southwest* (Princeton University Press 2014).
82. D. B. Knowles, "Ground-Water Resources of Ector County," Texas Board of Water Engineers, Bulletin 5210, 1952, 16.
83. "$3,170,000 Issue Sold by Texas Community," *New York Times*, March 21, 1953, 28.
84. "Water Supply Discovered in Midland Area," *The Austin Statesman*, December 14, 1956, 17.
85. "Midland, Texas, Issue Voted," *Wall Street Journal*, March 29, 1957, 11.
86. Richmond F. Brown and Donald C. Signor, "Artificial-Recharge Experiments and Operations on the Southern High Plains of Texas and New Mexico," USGS Water Resources Investigation 10–73, May 1973, https://pubs.usgs.gov/wri/wri10-73/pdf/wri10-73.pdf.
87. Seemingly in response, Midland's municipal water authority constructed a new one-million-gallon, aboveground water reservoir that same year and developed plans for more. Robert L. Martin, *The City Moves West: Economic and Industrial Growth in Central West Texas* (University of Texas Press, 1969), 143.
88. "Population Boom Seen at Midland and Odessa."
89. "Midland's Water Sources," City of Midland, accessed August 15, 2025, https://www.midlandtexas.gov/170/Midlands-Water-Sources.
90. Twelve elementary schools, three junior high schools, a new junior/senior high school, and fourteen other school buildings were built to accommodate a student population that had expanded from 25,000 to approximately 60,000 by 1960. *Texas Almanac and State Industrial Guide, 1952–1953* (A. H. Belo, 1952); John Howard Griffin, *Land of the High Sky* (First National Bank of Midland, 1959), 163–80.
91. The Midland Central YMCA opened its doors just north of downtown in 1959. Weber, "A Comparison of Two Oil City Business Centers."
92. "Churches," in *Midland City Directory 1955* (Hudspeth's Directory Company, 1955); also see "Churches."
93. *World Petroleum Report: 1955*, Edition II (Mona Palmer, 1955), 202.
94. *World Oil*, XLIV, 7 (Gulf Publishing, 1957), 120.
95. *The Oil and Gas Journal*, LV, 4 (1957), 165.

96. *Petroleum Development and Technology in 1926* (Petroleum Division AIME, American Institute of Mining and Metallurgical Engineers, 1927).
97. Olien and Hinton, *Wildcatters*, 51.
98. Unitization was initially promoted in the 1920s by the Federal Oil Conservation Board and the American Bar Association as a method to thwart the rule of capture laws and promote oil resource conservation. Bruce M. Kramer and Patrick H. Martin, *The Law of Pooling and Unitization*, 3rd ed. (Matthew Bender, 1970).
99. Gary D. Libecap and Steven N. Wiggins, "The Influence of Private Contractual Failure on Regulation: The Case of Oil Field Unitization," *Journal of Political Economy* 31, no. S2 (June 2002): S589–S608; Olien and Hinton, *Wildcatters*, 116.
100. James C. Tanner, "Petroleum Push," *Wall Street Journal*, July 20, 1959, 1.
101. L. G. Huntley, "Possible Causes of the Decline of Oil Wells and Suggested Methods of Prolonging Yield," US Bureau of Mines (US Government Printing Office, 1913), 29, Box 6, Warshaw Petroleum Collection, Collection 60, Smithsonian Archives Center, Washington, DC.
102. Mody C. Boatright, *Tales from the Derrick Floor: A People's History of the Oil Industry* (University of Nebraska Press, 1982), 223; Associated Press, "Nitro Explosion Kills Three Men," *Dallas Morning News*, April 15, 1927.
103. Hugh S. Taylor, *The A B C's of Science in Oil Recovery* (American Petroleum Institute, 1927), 11, Box 6, Warshaw Petroleum Collection, Collection 60, Smithsonian Archives Center, Washington, DC.
104. H. C. Miller, *The Function of Natural Gas in the Production of Oil* (American Petroleum Institute, 1929).
105. "Huge Program to Save Texas Oil Revealed," *The Austin American*, June 15, 1947, 5.
106. Permian Basin experiments in unitization had been lauded as a revolutionary solution to unregulated and wasteful production in the late 1920s. The API and the US Bureau of Mines, as well as federal regulators and the Texas Railroad Commission, all advocated increased well spacing to preserve the life of producing oil fields. Miller, *The Function of Natural Gas*, 5.
107. Austin Bureau, "Basin Is Tops in Unitization Pacts for Texas Fields," *Odessa American*, October 9, 1952, 4.
108. Reports, Folder "Vickers Petroleum Products Annual Report 1953," Company Annual Reports, Permian Basin Petroleum Museum, Midland, Texas.
109. Olien and Hinton, *Wildcatters*, 114.
110. "Dow Chemical Hydraulic Fracturing Release," Press Release, Box 66, API Photo and Film Collection, Collection 711, Smithsonian Archives Center, Washington, DC.
111. A series of droughts in the late 1940s had increased the use of irrigation on farms statewide. Associated Press, "Drought Shown Need for Reservoirs, Engineers Say," *Odessa American*, September 8, 1946, 5.
112. "The Rise of Lake J. B. Thomas, Part One," *Snyder News*, August 8, 2020, https://www.thesnydernews.com/news/rise-lake-jb-thomas-part-one.
113. "Scurry County's Canyon Reef Oil Field," State Historical Survey Committee, Snyder, Texas, 1967.
114. James H. Banks and John E. Babcock, *Corralling the Colorado: The First Fifty Years of the Lower Colorado River Authority* (Eakin, 1988).
115. "Engineering Study of the Welch Field San Andreas, August 1958," Folder "Welch Field Engineering Committee Reports 1957–1959 83-021 C J Red Davidson," Box

83-012, Box 3, C. J. "Red" Davidson Collection, Permian Basin Petroleum Museum, Midland, Texas.
116. "1962 Frac Recs for Crane County—Cost Estimates," Folder "H R Henderson A-1, Well File, Crane County TX 83-021 C J Red Davidson," Box 83-021 Box 2, C. J. "Red" Davidson Collection, Permian Basin Petroleum Museum, Midland, Texas.
117. "Canadian Oil Firm Buys Acreage and 35 Wells in Texas," *Wall Street Journal*, July 5, 1952, 4.
118. "Chase Manhattan Trust Unit Buys Texas Mineral Interests," *Wall Street Journal*, March 25, 1957, 7.

5. AN OILMAN IS NOT A UNION MAN

1. "American Petrofina Buys Cosden Corp," *New York Times*, May 1, 1963, 55.
2. "Sub-Lease Between American Petrofina, Inc. and Cosden Oil & Chemical Co., April 29, 1963," Box 9, Folder 2, Cosden Petroleum Corporation Collection, Collection #S218, Southwest Collection, Texas Tech University, Lubbock.
3. "District 4 & 5," Box 9-45, OCAWU Records, Special Collections, University of Colorado, Boulder.
4. "Alfred Goodson," Obituaries, Crowder Funeral Home, accessed August 15, 2025, https://www.crowderfuneralhome.com/obituaries/alfred-goodson/; Matthew M. Day, *Refiner on the Rise: How the Cosden Petroleum Corporation's Refinery Bucked the Trend of Imports and Charted a Path for Survival amid Changing Conditions for the Petroleum Industry (and Did It in 1950s West Texas)* (independently published, 2024).
5. In 1965, Midland County boasted the second-highest wages statewide. "Texas Oil Data, 1965," Box 2E200, Mid-Continent Oil and Gas Association Records, Briscoe Center for American History, University of Texas, Austin. By the 1990s, the Sprayberry-Dean Field alone had produced approximately 924.4 million barrels of oil.
6. Robert Gottlieb, *Forcing the Spring: The Transformation of the American Environmental Movement* (Island, 1993); Robert Gordon, "'Shell No!': OCAW and the Labor-Environmental Alliance," *Environmental History* 3, no. 4 (1998): 460–87; Charles Noble, *Liberalism at Work: The Rise and Fall of OSHA* (Temple University Press, 1986), 70–77.
7. In 1933, Texas refineries processed 218,145,000 barrels of crude petroleum and natural gas. By 1941, this number had increased to 436,000,000 barrels. "Important Facts About Texas Oil," January 1943, Texas Mid-Continent Oil and Gas Association, Warshaw Petroleum Collection, Smithsonian Archives Center, Washington, DC, 12.
8. George Ramer, oral history interview, February 12, 1970, McCamey, Texas, Oral History Collection, Permian Basin Petroleum Museum, Midland, Texas, 10.
9. Nancy Ethie Eagleton, *On the Last Frontier: A History of Upton County, Texas* (Texas Western Press, 1971); William Wolfe and Anna Wolfe, oral history interview, February 12, 1970, McCamey, Texas, Oral History Collection, Permian Basin Petroleum Museum, Midland, Texas, 25; E. N. Beane, oral history interview, 1970, Crane, Texas, Oral History Collection, Permian Basin Petroleum Museum,

Midland, Texas, 4; Dr. Myres, Bertie Haigh, and Ben Carsey, oral history interview, Oral History Collection, Permian Basin Petroleum Museum, Midland, Texas, 4–5.

10. William A. Owens, "First Teakettle in Texas," DuPont Chemical Division, Briscoe Center for American History, University of Texas, Austin; "Gasoline," Chemical Profiles, Agency for Toxic Substances and Disease Registry, https://www.atsdr.cdc.gov/toxprofiles/tp72-c4.pdf, accessed August 15, 2025.
11. Magnolia Petroleum Company Refining Division, "Fundamentals of Refining," 1953, Folder "Exploration and Producing," Box 2.207/E221, Exxon Mobil Historical Collection, Briscoe Center for American History, University of Texas, Austin; Socony-Vacuum, Folder "General Petroleum Corporation Histories 1932–1958," General Petroleum, Folder "General Petroleum Corporation News Clippings, 1955–1990," Box 2.207/E214, Exxon Mobil Historical Collection, Briscoe Center for American History, University of Texas, Austin; *Ref—Workers—p Removing Petrol. Coke from Cracking Still*, 1930, Box 23, Collection 711, API Photo and Film Collection, Smithsonian Archives Center, Washington, DC.
12. "Masters of Molecules: The Story of Petroleum Refining," The Texas Company, 1944, Box 6, Warshaw Center Petroleum Collection, Smithsonian Archives Center, Washington, DC, 9–12.
13. Postwar, many of these federal facilities were sold at auction to private industry, often at cost. Such wartime expediency dramatically sped up the construction of Texas petrochemical and refining infrastructure. For example, construction on the Neches Butadiene Products Company at Port Neches, Texas, was finished in 1944. Although the federal government oversaw construction of the plant and two adjacent copolymerization plants, the connected plants were operated by Gulf Oil, the Atlantic Refining Company, the Pure Oil Company, Socony-Vacuum Oil, and the Texas Company, which collaborated during the war on the development of rubber substitutes and other synthetics. Petroleum Administration for War (PAW), *History of the Petroleum Administration for War*, Series 10: Arthur E. Pew Jr. Engineering and Development, Sun Oil Company Collection, Hagley Museum and Library, Wilmington, Delaware, 193, 213.
14. Gustav Egloff, "The Cracking of California Gas Oil and Fuel Oil," 1930; Alfred Fisher, "Cracked Gasses to Bring Higher Prices," Universal Oil Products Company, Chicago, n.d.; Gustav Egloff, "The Cracking Art," Chicago: Universal Oil Products Company, 1930–1931 1932, Box 7, Collection 60, Warshaw Petroleum Collection, Smithsonian Archives Center, Washington, DC.
15. *Important Facts About Texas Oil*, 5th ed., January 1943, Texas Mid-Continent Oil and Gas Association, Dallas.
16. "History of Magnolia Pipeline Company," Folder "Magnolia Petroleum Company: Histories Folder 1," Box 2.207/E222, Exxon Mobil Historic Collection, Briscoe Center for American History, Austin.
17. "District 4 & 5," Box 9-45, OCAWU Records, Special Collections, University of Colorado, Boulder.
18. "District 4 & 5," Box 9-45, OCAWU Records, Special Collections, University of Colorado, Boulder.
19. Press Releases, Folder "Mobil Corporation: Subject Files Affiliates Mobil Chemical Company Phosphorus Division," Press Releases, Folder "Mobil Corporation: Subject Files Affiliates Mobil Chemical Company Plastics Division," Box 2.207/F122,

Exxon Mobil Historical Collection, Briscoe Center for American History, University of Texas at Austin; "Industrial Relations 1940–1943," Folder "General Petroleum Corporation," Box 2.207/E214, Exxon Mobil Historical Collection, Briscoe Center for American History, University of Texas, Austin.

20. Manuals, Folder "Human Resources Employee Relations: R&D Supervisors Manual ca. 1950," Box 2.207/E39, Exxon Mobil Historical Collection, Briscoe Center for American History, University of Texas, Austin.
21. Notes, Folder "BP 78-4109," Box 10, OCAW Tony Mazzocchi Collection; "Notebook," Box 1, OCAW Tony Mazzocchi Collection, Special Collections, University of Colorado, Boulder.
22. "Notebook," Box 1, OCAW Tony Mazzocchi Collection, Special Collections, University of Colorado, Boulder; "Union News," Box 5 1968–69, Archives, Walter Reuther Library, Detroit.
23. Flow Charts, Folder "Exploration and Producing," Box 2.207/E221, Exxon Mobil Historical Collection, Briscoe Center for American History, University of Texas, Austin.
24. Skin exposure to benzene resulted in rashes and the removal of fats from the skin. According to Paulson, this created a "very gross chemical change in the structure of the skin." Glen Paulson, *Conference Proceedings*, 30, Tony Mazzocchi Collection, OCAWU Records, Special Collections, University of Colorado, Boulder.
25. Paulson, *Conference Proceedings*, 30.
26. "The Shift from U.S. Production of Commodity Petrochemicals to Value-Added Specialty Chemical Products and the Possible Impact on U.S. Trade," Report on Investigation No. 332-183, US International Trade Commission (US Government Printing Office, April 1985).
27. Gordon H. Turrentine, "Newsmakers in the Texas Gulf Coast Chemical Empire: 1955," *Analysts Journal* 12, no. 2 (1956): 109–15.
28. Jesse Owens left public service in 1953 to work for the El Paso Natural Gas Corporation. "Harold Downs Wins Odessa Mayor's Job," *Odessa American*, April 7, 1954, 1; "Record Vote Seen for City Election," *Odessa American*, March 30, 1952, 1.
29. Hall of Fame Files, Permian Basin Petroleum Museum, Midland, Texas; "Noel, Rodman, Lasting Partnership Started with a Handshake," *Odessa American*, March 29, 2003.
30. According to the 1950 US census, the combined population of both Ector and Midland counties was only 67,800. US Census Bureau, "Characteristics of the Population—1950," in *Census of Population and Housing*, accessed July 21, 2015, https://www.census.gov/prod/www/decennial.html.
31. Frank Mangan, *The Pipeliners: The Story of El Paso Natural Gas* (Guynes, 1977).
32. US Census Bureau, *Census of the Population—1960*, accessed June 6, 2017, https://www.census.gov/prod/www/decennial.html.
33. "Texas Almanac: City Population History from 1850–2000," https://www.texasalmanac.com/drupal-backup/images/CityPopHist%20web.pdf, accessed August 14, 2025.
34. Charles W. Howe, "Water Resources and Regional Economic Growth in the United States, 1950–1960," *Southern Economic Journal* 34, no. 4 (1968): 477–89.
35. While most research was into the creation of cheap 1,000-octane fuel for fighter jets, the development of synthetic rubber and plastic had a lasting impact. "Copper

and Brass in the Petroleum Industry," Box 6, Collection 60, Rubber, Warshaw Petroleum Collection, Smithsonian Archives Center, Washington, DC.

36. In June 1941, Secretary of the Interior Harold Ickes sent a memo to leaders of the largest American oil companies, alerting them that all patents filed in the United States by enemy combatants were suspended for the duration of World War II. Telegrams from J. Howard Pew to J. Edgar Pew, June 1941, Folder "892.116 DIS.1 War Emergency Pipeline 1941–1945," Box 97, A. E. Pew Jr., Collection 10, Sun Oil Company Collection, Hagley Museum and Library, Wilmington, Delaware. See also Correspondence, Boxes 82 and 86, A. E. Pew Jr., Sun Oil Company Collection, Series 10, Hagley Museum and Library, Wilmington, Delaware. For an environmental history of plastics and other synthetics, see Jeffrey L. Meikle, "Material Doubts: The Consequences of Plastic," *Environmental History* 2, no. 3 (1997): 278–300.

37. "Cracking" refers to a variety of processes that break hydrocarbons into their component parts. Beginning in the late 1930s, several companies began experimenting with chemical additives that increased cracking efficiency. Along with the preexisting Houndrey process, several new cracking processes were developed in the 1950s, the beneficiaries of government funding. *The Petroleum Refiner: Oil Centennial Issue*, January 1959, Hagley Museum and Library, Wilmington, Delaware; Gustav Egloff, "The Cracking Art in 1928–1929"; "American Society for Testing Materials Report of Committee D-2," 1932, Box 7, Collection 60, Warshaw Petroleum Collection, Smithsonian Archives Center, Washington, DC.

38. "West Texas Plants," Photographs, Box 42, API Photo and Film Collection, Collection 711, Smithsonian Archives Center, Washington, DC. For a history of natural gas production, see Charles Blanchard, *The Extraction State: A History of Natural Gas in America* (University of Pittsburgh Press, 2021).

39. Norman L. Morrow, "The Industrial Production and Use of 1,3-Butadiene," *Environmental Health Perspectives* 86 (1990): 7–8.

40. "New Plant to Produce More Geon," *Goodchemco News* 4: 9, B. F. Goodrich Chemical Company, September 1950, Box 2, Collection 60, Rubber, Warshaw Collection, Smithsonian Archives Center, Washington, DC.

41. Reports, Folder "El Paso Natural Gas Co Annual Reports 1948–1954," Company Annual Reports, Permian Basin Petroleum Museum, Midland, Texas.

42. Folder "El Paso Natural Gas Co Annual Reports 1948–1954"; Folder "El Paso Natural Gas Co. Service Awards 1979–1988," Company Annual Reports, Permian Basin Petroleum Museum, Midland, Texas.

43. Joel A. Tarr, "Toxic Legacy: The Environmental Impact of the Manufactured Gas Industry in the United States," *Technology and Culture* 55, no. 1 (2014): 107–47; Mangan, *The Pipeliners*.

44. *Gas Fields in West Texas: Symposium*, Vol. 3 (West Texas Geological Society, 1977).

45. "Texas Oil Data, 1965," Box 2E200, Mid-Continent Oil and Gas Association Records, Briscoe Center for American History, University of Texas, Austin.

46. "El Paso Natural Gas Products Co. Grew with Odessa," *Odessa American*, February 26, 1965, 2B; Folder "El Paso Natural Gas Annual Reports 1948–1954," Company Annual Reports, Special Collections, Permian Basin Petroleum Museum, Midland, Texas.

47. "TCEQ WST IHW 30142 Reports MF307606 Hydrogeological Investigation at the Xylene Tank Area Facility 28," Microfiche, Archive, Texas Commission for Environmental Quality, Austin.

48. "El Paso Products Odessa, Tex," Folder "04-662," Box 35, OCAW District 4 & 5, OCAWU Records, Special Collections, University of Colorado, Boulder.
49. "Protecting the Environment," from oral history interview with Gene Collins, July 8, 2016, Odessa, Texas, Civil Rights in Black and Brown Interview Database, https://crbb.tcu.edu/clips/3814/protecting-the-environment; John E. Matthews, "Industrial Reuse and Recycle of Wastewaters," 1980, Robert S. Kerr Environmental Research Laboratory, Office of Research and Development, US Environmental Protection Agency, Washington, DC.
50. "TCEQ WST IHW 30142 Correspondence MF307609 1–16 (Pre 1985)," Microfiche Archives, Texas Commission for Environmental Quality, Austin.
51. Dan M. Wells, Robert M. Sweazy, and George A. Whetstone, "Long-Term Experiences with Effluent Reuse," *Water Pollution Control Federation Journal* 51, no. 11 (1979): 2641–48; J. Eller, D. L. Ford, and E. F. Gloyna, "Water Reuse and Recycling in Industry," *American Water Works Association Journal* 62, no. 3 (1970): 149–54.
52. Joseph Santodonato et al., "Investigation of Selected Potential Environmental Contaminants: Styrene, Ethylbenzene, and Related Compounds," Final Report, Office of Toxic Substances, US Environmental Protection Agency (EPA), May 1980.
53. Paulson, *Conference Proceedings*, 30.
54. Neil Carman, oral history interview, February 23, 2008, Conservation History Association of Texas, https://texaslegacy.org/transcript/neil-carman/, accessed August 14, 2025.
55. Santodonato et al., "Investigation of Selected Potential Environmental Contaminants."
56. "Protecting the Environment," from oral history interview with Gene Collins; Matthews, "Industrial Reuse and Recycle of Wastewaters."
57. "Changes in Community and Politics, Part One," from oral history interview with Joann Littleton, July 6, 2016, Odessa, Texas, Civil Rights in Black and Brown Interview Database, https://crbb.tcu.edu/clips/3065/changes-in-community-and-politics-part-one, accessed August 14, 2025.
58. Carman, oral history interview.
59. For example, Ector High School was opened in 1956 as a predominately "minority-serving institution," and the majority Hispanic student body immediately launched protests against racial discrimination. "Cultural Shock," from interview with Delma Abalos conducted by Todd Moye, Karen Wisely, and Joel Zapata, July 14, 2016, Odessa, Texas, Civil Rights in Black and Brown Interview Database, https://crbb.tcu.edu/clips/2207/cultural-shock, accessed August 14, 2025.
60. "Changes in Community and Politics, Part One," from oral history interview with Joann Littleton.
61. "Protecting the Environment," from oral history interview with Gene Collins.
62. Tyler Priest and Michael Botson, "Bucking the Odds: Organized Labor in Gulf Coast Oil Refining," *Journal of American History* 99, no. 1 (June 2012): 100–110.
63. National Petroleum Council's Committee on Petroleum and Gas Industries Manpower Requirements, "Skills and Occupations of People in the United States Oil and Gas Industries," National Petroleum Council (Washington, DC, 1969).
64. Theodore R. Eck, "The Growth of the Southwestern Petrochemical Industry," *Business Review* 45, no. 6 (June 1960).
65. For an account of this wider history, see Jason Resnikoff, *Labor's End: How the Promise of Automation Degraded Work* (University of Illinois Press, 2022).

66. The multi-industry union formed in response to a bitter 1917 oil-field worker strike at Goose Creek in East Texas, spurred primarily by harsh working conditions. By 1921, the Oil Field, Gas Well, and Refinery Workers had over 30,000 members. James C. Maroney, "The Texas-Louisiana Oil Field Strike of 1917," in *Essays in Southern Labor History*, ed. Gary M. Fink and Merl E. Reed (Greenwood, 1976); Fred Jennings, interview with William A. Owens, June 19, 1952, Goose Creek, Texas, Oral History of the Texas Oil Industry Records, Briscoe Center for American History, University of Texas, Austin. *Oil, Chemical and Atomic Workers International Union AFL-CIO Fact Book*, Publicity Department OCAW-AFL-CIO (October 1956). After a sharp dip in membership during the early years of the Depression, union membership continued to climb throughout the 1930s. In 1948, the OCAW began membership drives in Canada. Folder "Convention Proceedings & Reports," OCAW Collection, Walter Reuther Library, Detroit.
67. "Report on Industrial Relations in the General Petroleum Corporation of California," Industrial Relations Counselors, New York, 1943, 11, Exxon Mobil Historical Collection Box 2.207 E214. As scholars such as Emilio Zamora have shown, Texas had an active labor movement in the postwar era. Activism in oil has been less studied, but it is clear that the refining centers in Port Arthur and Houston were centers for unionization in the state. Emilio Zamora, *Claiming Rights and Righting Wrongs in Texas in Texas: Mexican Workers and Job Politics During World War II* (Texas A&M University Press, 2009). See also Ray Marshall, "Independent Unions in the Gulf Coast Petroleum Refining Industry—the Esso Experience," *Labor Law Journal* 12 (1961): 823–40.
68. "Communication and Public Statements in Connection with the Rate Dispute in Socony-Vacuum's Refineries Beginning in September 1945," Folder "Human Resources," Box 2.207/E46, Exxon Mobil Historical Collection, Briscoe Center for American History, University of Texas, Austin.
69. "Who's Right—and Who's Wrong?," Socony-Vacuum Oil Company, Folder "Human Resources Wages and Salaries 1945 Dispute 1945–1946," Box 2.207 E46, Exxon Mobil Historical Collection, Briscoe Center for American History, University of Texas, Austin; "Average State Membership, Aug 1957–July 1958," Box 4, Otto Pragan Collection, Oil Chemical and Atomic Workers Union, Collection 617, Reuther Library, Wayne State University, Detroit.
70. T. E. C. Bunch, "Odessa Contractors and Labor Unions," *Odessa American*, July 18, 1948, 5.
71. "Analysis of Work Stoppages During 1952," Bulletin No. 1136, US Department of Labor, US Bureau of Labor Statistics, Washington, DC.
72. This was a part of the much larger merger between the American Federation of Labor (AFL) and the Congress of Industrial Organizations (CIO). Philip Taft, "Independent Unions and the Merger," *Industrial and Labor Relations Review* 9, no. 3 (April 1956): 433–46.
73. While the International Chemical Workers Union also represented some American refinery and petrochemical workers, OCAW led most oil industry union action from this point forward. *Oil, Chemical and Atomic Workers International Union AFL-CIO Fact Book.*
74. *Oil, Chemical and Atomic Workers International Union AFL-CIO Fact Book.*

75. For example, see "Dowell Employees Vote Non Union," *Odessa American*, February 17, 1957, 32; and Associated Press (AP), "Strike Threat Hits Lone Star Gas Firm," *Odessa American*, July 4, 1969, 11.
76. "They Are Here," *Odessa American*, May 13, 1957, 12.
77. Press Release, Folder "Human Resources: Education and Training Learning About Computers," Box 2.207/E33, Exxon Mobil Historical Collection, Briscoe Center for American History, University of Texas, Austin.
78. John Wooding, Charles Levenstein, and Beth Rosenberg, "The Oil, Chemical and Atomic Workers International Union: Refining Strategies for Labor," *International Journal of Health Services* 27, no. 1 (1997): 125–38.
79. Wooding et al., "The Oil, Chemical and Atomic Workers International Union."
80. US Department of Labor, "Salaries of Federal Workers, Major Wage Developments, Defense Employment by Region, Representation of Classroom Teachers," *Monthly Labor Review* 91, no. 7 (July 1968).
81. Tyler Priest, "Labor's Last Stand in the Refinery: The Shell Oil Strike of 1962–1963," *Houston History* 4, no. 2 (2008).
82. "Plastic Plant Planned; Rexall Chemical Co. to Build Facility in Chicago Area," *New York Times*, December 7, 1960, 71.
83. "Rexall Starts Polyethylene Plant," *Chemical and Engineering News* 40, no. 8 (February 19, 1962): 24–25.
84. Folder "04-40 Rexall Chemical Company Odessa, Texas Potential: 86," Box 26, OCAW Districts 4 and 5, OCAWU Collection Special Collections, University of Colorado, Boulder.
85. Wooding et al., "The Oil, Chemical and Atomic Workers International Union."
86. For further Texas context, see Bruce A. Glasrud and Jame C. Maroney, *Texas Labor History* (Texas A&M University Press, 2013). For a national story, see Nelson Lichtenstein, *State of the Union: A Century of American Labor* (Princeton University Press, 2002); Ray Davidson, *Challenging the Giants: A History of the Oil Chemical and Atomic Workers Union* (OCAW Denver, 1988); Walter Galenson, *The CIO Challenge to the AFL: A History of the American Labor Movement, 1935–1941* (Harvard University Press, 1960).
87. *Oil, Chemical and Atomic Workers International Union AFL-CIO Fact Book.*
88. Folder "04-66 Rexall Chem Co. Odessa, Tex Potential: 110," Box 26, OCAW Districts 4 and 5, OCAWU Records, Special Collections, University of Colorado, Boulder.
89. These late 1960s efforts reflect the changing ethnic makeup of industrial work in West Texas. Hispanic and Tejano workers had moved to towns and cities throughout the 1930s and 1940s, moving from agricultural or ranch work into more stable employment. By the 1960s, some of their children took jobs in industrial plants such as the Odessa Petrochemical Plant. Hispanic names make up a significant minority of union card holders at the Duval Corporation sulfur mine and processing plant southwest of Odessa. "Folder 04-668 Duval Sulphur Pecos, Texas Potential: 150," Box 35, OCAW Districts 4 and 5, OCAWU Records, Special Collections, University of Colorado, Boulder.
90. *National Labor Relations Board, Petitioner, v. Rexall Chemical Company, a Division of Rexall Drug and Chemical Company*, Respondent, 418 F.2d 603 (5th Cir. 1969).

91. Davidson, *Challenging the Giants*.
92. Gordon, "Shell No!"
93. Ample work has been done theorizing the relationship between risk, safety regulations, and twentieth-century state-making. For example, see Mary Douglas and Aaron Wildavsky, *Risk and Culture: An Essay on the Selection of Technological and Environmental Dangers* (University of California Press, 1983); Ulric Beck, *Risk Society: Toward a New Modernity* (Sage, 1992); and G. Burchell, C. Gordon, and P. Miller, eds., *The Foucault Effect: Studies in Governmentality* (University of Chicago Press, 1991).
94. Arwen Mohun, *Risk: Negotiating Safety in American Society* (Johns Hopkins University Press, 2013); Joseph A. Page, "Consumer Involvement and the Consumer Product Safety Act," *Hofstra Law Review* 2 (1974): 605–18.
95. Thomas A. Chittenden, "A Study of Occupational Safety Responsibility of the Department of Labor" (Washington, DC, 1964), 1, 2, 53–58; Secretary of Labor's Order 12–66, July 19, 1966; Federal Radiation Council Meeting, May 4, 1967, Secretary of Labor files, National Archives, Washington, DC.
96. Christopher W. Wells, ed., *Environmental Justice in Postwar America* (University of Washington Press, 2018); Nancy Quam-Wickham, "An 'Oleaginous Civilization': Oil in Southern California," *Southern California Quarterly* 97, no. 3 (2015): 283–95; Andy McPhee, *The Donora Death Fog: Clean Air and the Tragedy of a Pennsylvania Mill Town* (University of Pittsburgh Press, 2023).
97. Charles Halvorson, *Valuing Clean Air: The EPA and the Economics of Environmental Protection* (Oxford University Press, 2021).
98. Gordon, "Shell No!"
99. In contrast to lukewarm concern for employee health, Hugh Gorman argues that pollution remediation efforts start much earlier at oil refineries across the country. Hugh Gorman, *Redefining Efficiency: Pollution Concerns, Regulatory Mechanisms, and Technological Change in the U.S. Petroleum Industry* (University of Akron Press, 2001), chapter 9.
100. Judson MacLaury, "The Job Safety Law of 1970: Its Passage Was Perilous," *Monthly Labor Review* 104, no. 3 (March 1981): 18–24.
101. John G. Johnson, "Texas Air Control Board," *Handbook of Texas*, 1976.
102. The Walsh-Healey Act listed acceptable exposure levels for 450 chemicals but maintained only fifty inspectors for approximately 23 million US oil, chemical, and atomic workers. Tony Mazzochi, "Hazards in the Industrial Environment—a Conference," Rice Hotel, Houston, February 20–21, 1970, 2, Box 1, Tony Mazzocchi Collection, OCAWU Records, Special Collections, University of Colorado, Boulder.
103. US Congress, House Committee on Education and Labor, "Hearings on the Occupational Safety and Health Act of 1969" (Washington, DC, 1970), 1194.
104. "Protecting the Environment," from oral history interview with Gene Collins.
105. Gordon, "Shell No!," 465.
106. US Department of Labor, "Public Hearing on Proposed Revision of Safety and Health Standards for Federal Supply Contracts," March 17–27, 1964, Department of Labor Library.
107. Les Leopold, *The Man Who Hated Work and Loved Labor: The Life and Times of Tony Mazzocchi* (Chelsea Green, 2007).

108. Pamphlets, Folder "The Ghastly Story of Gas Explosions 1968," Tony Mazzochi, Box 5, Tony Mazzocchi Collection, OCAW Records, Special Collections, University of Colorado, Boulder. OCAW also represented oil tanker drivers, as well as refinery and gasoline plant workers. Associated Press, "Fuel Oil Strike, Epidemic of Flu Endanger New York Inhabitants," *Lubbock Avalanche-Journal*, December 19, 1968. The OCAW was asking for wage increases, as well as improved working conditions. Associated Press, "OCAW on Strike—Supervisory Personnel Operating Refineries," *Odessa American*, January 6, 1969, 19. On January 4, 1969, OCAW began yet another national strike with approximately 60,000 refinery workers nationwide walking off the job, asking for both wage increases and better working conditions.
109. "Foreword," Oil Chemical and Atomic Workers International Union Conference Proceedings, Box 1, OCAW Tony Mazzocchi Collection, Special Collections, University of Colorado.
110. "Foreword."
111. At the Salt Lake City conference, Mazzocci discussed recent studies that showed that 50 percent of asbestos plant workers ultimately died of cancer. "District 2 Conference Proceedings," Salt Lake City, 19; "District 3 Conference Proceedings," Atlanta, 18, Box 1, OCAW Tony Mazzocchi Collection, Special Collections, University of Colorado, Boulder.
112. Harold Smith, Local 8-447, Wood Ridge Chemical Corporation, quoted in "Foreword."
113. Mazzochi, "Hazards in the Industrial Environment—a Conference."
114. "District 7 Conference Proceedings," Fort Wayne, Indiana; "District 4 Conference Proceedings," Houston, Box 1, Tony Mazzocchi Collection, OCAWU Records, Special Collections, University of Colorado, Boulder.
115. Terry L. Thomas et al., "Mortality Patterns Among Workers in Three Texas Oil Refineries," *Journal of Occupational Medicine* 24, no. 2 (1982): 135–41.
116. The Walsh-Healey Act was a part of the National Recovery Administration (NRA), which stipulated that any company receiving more than $100,000 of federal contracts must provide overtime pay to its workers. The act was amended to include that companies must abide by certain minimum safety standards for workers. Charles Noble, *Liberalism at Work: The Rise and Fall of OSHA* (Temple University Press, 1986).
117. For histories of the workplace health and safety movement, see Richard Kazis and Richard Grossman, *Fear at Work: Job Blackmail, Labor and the Environment* (New Society, 1990); Gottlieb, *Forcing the Spring*; Joseph A. Page and Mary-Win O'Brien, *Bitter Wages: Ralph Nader's Study Group Report on Disease and Injury on the Job* (Grossman, 1973).
118. US Congress, House Committee on Education and Labor, "Hearings on Occupational Safety and Health Act of 1969"; US Congress, Senate Committee on Labor and Public Welfare, "Hearings on Occupational Safety and Health Act of 1970," (Washington, DC, 1970).
119. Noble, *Liberalism at Work*, 70.
120. Keeping with trends begun in the 1950s, little debate about industry automation or information about this new wave of national strikes was published in Permian Basin periodicals such as the *Odessa American*, *Lubbock Avalanche*, and *Abilene*

Reporter-News, or in company magazines during the 1960s or 1970s. Over the course of the strike, few articles appeared in the *Odessa American*, the *Lubbock Avalanche*, or the *Abilene Reporter-News*. All were reprints of the same Associated Press story. AP, "OCAW on Strike—Supervisory Personnel Operating Refineries"; AP, "Wage Dispute Idles Petroleum Workers"; Associated Press (AP), "20,000 Texans Join in Walkout," *Abilene Reporter-News*, January 5, 1969, 13.

121. AP, "Wage Dispute Idles Petroleum Workers."
122. With that said, the difference in scale is significant. Harris County had thirty-three plants and Jefferson County had sixteen. Both counties sit within Houston's extended metropolitan area. "Statistical Records: 1965," Box 2E200, Mid-Continent Oil and Gas Association Records, Archives, University of Texas, Briscoe Center for American History, University of Texas, Austin.
123. While there is no date on the document, adjacent text indicates that the list probably dates from the 1960s.
124. Permian Basin Petroleum Directory, 1966, Permian Basin Petroleum Museum, Midland, Texas.
125. "Business Directory," Box 1, Tony Mazzocchi Collection, OCWU Records, University of Colorado, Boulder.
126. Max Krochmal and Todd Moye, *Civil Rights in Black and Brown: Histories of Resistance and Struggle in Texas* (University of Texas Press, 2021); Zamora, *Claiming Rights and Righting Wrongs in Texas*.
127. William Wolfe and Anna Wolfe, interview, February 12, 1970, McCamey, Texas, Oral History Collection, Permian Basin Petroleum Museum, Midland, Texas, 31–32.

6. THE BUCKLE OF THE SUN BELT

1. Rick Scott, "Oil Shortage Now Creating 'Boom Towns,'" *Austin American Statesman*, December 13, 1974, 1.
2. Scott, "Oil Shortage Now Creating 'Boom Towns.'"
3. J. Craig Jenkins and Craig M. Eckert, "The Right Turn in Economic Policy: Business Elites and the New Conservative Economics," *Sociological Forum* 15, no. 2 (2000): 307–38; R. McGreggor Cawley, *Federal Land, Western Anger: The Sagebrush Rebellion and Environmental Politics* (University of Kansas Press,1993); Jacqueline Vaughn Switzer, *Green Backlash: The History and Politics of Environmental Opposition in the U.S.* (Lynne Rienner, 1997); David Helvarg, *The War Gains the Greens: The "Wise-Use" Movement, the New Right, and Anti-Environmental Violence* (Random House, 1994).
4. "Energy Crisis Task Force," Folder "Government Relations: Department History 1956–1988," Box 2.207/E26A, Exxon Mobil Historical Collection, Briscoe Center for American History, University of Texas, Austin.
5. "MGF Oil Proposes Offering," *Securities and Exchange Commission News Digest*, August 28, 1970, Washington, DC, 2.
6. Robert Reinhold, "U.S. Helps Texans Survive Death of Bank," *New York Times*, October 14, 1984, 1; Skip Hollandsworth, "That's Oil, Folks!," *Texas Monthly*, September 2010. Lewis also maintained a 183,000-acre ranch. "Clayton Williams,"

Midlander Magazine, October 1983, Clayton Williams Collection, Haley Memorial Library and History Center, Midland, Texas.

7. "Industry: A Golden Flood Returns," *Time*, 1975.
8. Bradley R. Rice and Richard M. Bernard, eds., *Sunbelt Cities: Politics and Growth Since World War II* (University of Texas Press, 1984); James P. Sterba, "Houston as Energy Capital, Sets Pace in Sunbelt Boom," *New York Times*, February 9, 1976, 1; Box 6 1970–1974, Oil Chemical and Atomic Workers Union News, Reuther Library Archives, Detroit.
9. Reminiscences of H. J. Porter, oral history interview by Maclyn Burg, December 16, 1975, Columbia University Oral History Archives 1975, https://dx.doi.org/10.7916/d8-w2cn-9589.
10. Throughout the 1950s and 1960s, many of the city's leaders were vocal members of the John Birch Society. In 1961, Odessa Mayor J. T. Clark wrote several editorials supporting the society in the local paper. In 1962, the famously anti-integration General Edwin Walker won Odessa's vote for governor over ex–oil industry lawyer John Connally in the Texas Democratic primary. In 1965, the John Birch Society posted a full-page ad in the *Odessa American*. According to one author, throughout the 1960s, the president of the Odessa United States Junior Chamber of Commerce was a paid recruiter for the John Birch Society. Jack Crumpler, "Odessa Member Defends Objectives of Birch Society," *Odessa American*, March 30, 1961, 3; "What Is the John Birch Society? The Truth May Surprise You!," *Odessa American*, December 13, 1965, 21; Larry L. King, "Who's Number One in the Permian Basin?," *Texas Monthly*, June 1975.
11. Rick Perlstein, *Before the Storm: Barry Goldwater and the Unmaking of the American Consensus* (Hill & Wang, 2001); Darren Dochuk, *Anointed with Oil: How Christianity and Crude Made Modern America* (Basic Books, 2019); Joe R. Feagin, "The Global Context of Metropolitan Growth: Houston and the Oil Industry," *American Journal of Sociology* 90, no. 6 (1985): 1204–30; Donald Critchlow, *The Conservative Ascendancy: How the GOP Right Made Political History* (University Press of Kansas, 2007); Bruce Schulman and Julian E. Zelizer, *Rightward Bound: Making America Conservative in the 1970s* (Harvard University Press, 2008); Gary R. Mormino, "Sunbelt Dreams and Altered States: A Social and Cultural History of Florida, 1950–2000," *Florida Historical Quarterly* 81, no. 1 (2002): 3–21; James Morton Turner, "'The Specter of Environmentalism': Wilderness, Environmental Politics, and the Evolution of the New Right," *Journal of American History*, 96, no. 1 (2009): 123–48.
12. "School Integration," from Gene Collins, oral history interview, July 8, 2016, Odessa, Texas, Civil Rights in Black and Brown Interview Database, https://crbb.tcu.edu/clips/3824/school-integration-3.
13. Even with stringent new environmental and workplace safety laws, accidents were not eliminated by the 1970s. For example, according to Warren G. Magnuson, chair of the Senate Commerce Committee, the number of pipeline accident fatalities tripled between 1969 and 1974. During this period, the number of fatalities among workers on natural gas pipelines nationwide increased from sixteen to fifty-nine. Perhaps more alarmingly, in 1974, there were 1,477 major pipeline leaks or failures throughout the United States that resulted in human fatalities. "Pipeline Safety Problems," Congressional Record, Senate, 15774, May 21, 1974, https://www.govinfo.gov/content/pkg/GPO-CRECB-1974-pt12/pdf/GPO-CRECB-1974-pt12-2-2.pdf.

14. Beginning in 1949, despite the sharp increase in US oil production, the United States imported more oil than it exported. This trend did not reverse until 2011. "US Petroleum Product Exports Exceeded Imports in 2011 for the First Time in over Six Decades," US Energy Information Administration, March 7, 2012, https://www.eia.gov/todayinenergy/detail.php?id=5290.
15. Turner, "The Specter of Environmentalism"; Natasha Zaretsky, *No Direction Home: The American Family and the Fear of National Decline, 1968–1980* (University of North Carolina Press, 2007).
16. See Daniel Yergin, *The Prize: The Epic Question for Oil, Money, and Power* (Free Press, 2008); Robert D. Lifset, "A New Understanding of the American Energy Crisis of the 1970s," *Historical Social Research/Historische Sozialforschung* 39, no. 4 (150) (2014): 22–42; Martin V. Melosi, "Energy and Environment in the United States: The Era of Fossil Fuels," *Environmental Review: ER* 11, no. 3 (1987): 167–88.
17. Murray was president of the US marketing and refining division in 1975 and would be appointed Mobil's chief executive officer (CEO) in 1985. A. E. Murray, "Statement by A. E. Murray, Mobil Oil Corporation, to the Joint Legislative Committee on Transportation and Utilities," Mobil Oil Company, Seattle, June 18, 1973, Folder "Government Relations Hearings and Testimonies: Sen. Jackson Hearings 1973–1974," Exxon Mobil Historical Collection, Briscoe Center for American History, University of Texas, Austin.
18. David F. Prindle, *Petroleum Politics and the Texas Railroad Commission* (University of Texas Press, 1980); Lifset, "A New Understanding."
19. Meg Jacobs, *Panic at the Pump: The Energy Crisis and the Transformation of American Politics in the 1970s* (Hill & Wang, 2017).
20. Box 11, EX NR 6 Oil-Natural Gas 1/1973–7/1973, Richard Nixon Presidential Library, Yorba Linda, California.
21. Energy Policy and Conservation Act of 1975, Public Law 94-163 (1975): 103b.1.
22. US Bureau of the Census, Current Industrial Reports Series, *Annual Survey of Oil and Gas*, 1974, MA-13K (74)-1 (Washington, DC: US Government Printing Office, 1976), 1–4; "Active Drilling Rigs Zoom to 4-Year High," *World Oil* 178, no. 3 (February 15, 1979): 85–86; Roger J. Stern, "Oil Scarcity Ideology in US Foreign Policy, 1908–97," *Security Studies* 25, no. 2 (May 2016): 214–57; Matt Huber, *Lifeblood: Oil, Freedom and the Forces of Capital* (University of Minnesota Press, 2013).
23. Box 93, SP (Speeches), Richard Nixon Presidential Library, Yorba Linda, California; Paul Sabin, "Crisis and Continuity in U.S. Oil Politics, 1965–1980," *Journal of American History* 99, no. 1 (2012): 177–86.
24. Box 2E200 and 2E201, Mid-Continent Oil and Gas Association Records, Briscoe Center for American History, University of Texas, Austin. "Alphabetical Index," *Permian Basin Oil Directory 1973* (Burmass Publishing, 1973).
25. For example, OCAW records show starting wages as high as $11 per hour at the Cabot Corp Carbon Black Plant in Pampa, Texas, in 1983. Folder "04-814 Cabot Corp 16-RD-993," OCAW District 4 & 5, OCAWU Records, Special Collections, University of Colorado, Boulder.
26. Box 9-45, OCAW District 4 & 5, OCAW Collection, Special Collections, University of Colorado, Boulder.

27. Mody C. Boatright, *Tales from the Derrick Floor: A People's History of the Oil Industry* (University of Nebraska Press, 1982), 224.
28. Although Gulf Oil improved the technology, the first magnetometer was developed in 1834 by Carl Friedrich Gauss of Germany as a replacement for the compass. "Land Men Follow Geologists' Trail," Folder "General Petroleum Corporation Reference Compilation Folder 2 1950–1954," Box 2.207/E215, Exxon Mobil Historical Collection, Briscoe Center for American History, University of Texas, Austin; "Masters of the Hunt," *Texaco Star Magazine*, 1948, Box 11, Warshaw Petroleum Collection, No. 60, Smithsonian Archives Center, Washington, DC; Patents, Box 8, Serge Scherbatskoy Papers, Collection 936, Smithsonian Archives Center, Washington, DC; Reports, Folders "Haliburton: Annual Reports 1966–1974" and "The TXL Oil Corporation: Annual Reports 1955–1961," Company Annual Reports, Permian Basin Petroleum Museum, Midland, Texas.
29. This is not to say that oil companies hesitated to infringe on these patents. For example, Serge Scherbatskoy spent the majority of the 1980s suing Exxon for patent infringement on his well-logging technology. Correspondence, Box 20, Collection 936 Serge Scherbatskoy Papers, Smithsonian Archives Center, Washington, DC.
30. Samuel D. Myres, *The Permian Basin: Petroleum Empire of the Southwest*, 2 vols. (Permian, 1973, 1977).
31. *Midland City Directory 1955* (Hudspeth's Directory Co., 1955).
32. *Burmass Oil Directory* (Burmass, 1973).
33. "Seismic Operations," Photographs, Box 40, API Photo and Film Collection, Collection 711 and Patents, Box 1, Serge Scherbatskoy Papers, Collection 936, Smithsonian Archives Center, Washington, DC. While rudimentary down-hole testing equipment existed since the 1920s, most geologists used aboveground visual cues to predict where oil was most likely to appear in rock strata. H. C. Miller, *The Function of Natural Gas in the Production of Oil* (American Petroleum Institute, 1929), 13; Trade Literature Collection, Hagley Museum and Library, Wilmington, Delaware; Brian Frehner, *Finding Oil: The Nature of Petroleum Geology* (University of Nebraska Press, 2011).
34. Hollandsworth, "That's Oil, Folks!"
35. A National Petroleum Council study identified the two most significant technological advancements as water injection, or flooding, and hydraulic fracturing. "Impact of New Technology on the Petroleum Industry 1946–1966," National Petroleum Council, 1967; Ralph E. Bailey, "Enhanced Oil Recovery," National Petroleum Council, 1984.
36. "Carbon Dioxide Enhanced Oil Recovery," National Energy Technology Laboratory, US Department of Energy, https://www.netl.doe.gov/sites/default/files/netl-file/CO_2_EOR_Primer.pdf, accessed August 15, 2025.
37. Hoxie Smith, "Epicenter of a Revolution; Part 3," *Permian Basin Oil and Gas Magazine*, May 3, 2012.
38. Folder "Well Completion Records," Box 83-021, Box 1, C. J. "Red" Davidson Collection, Permian Basin Petroleum Museum, Midland, Texas.
39. Drilling Reports, Folder "Drilling Records," Box 2.207/H6, Exxon Mobil Historical Collection, Briscoe Center for American History, University of Texas, Austin; Reports, Folder "Well Completion Records," Box 83-021, Box 1, C. J. "Red" Davidson Collection, Permian Basin Petroleum Museum, Midland, Texas.

40. Well Logs, Folder "H. R. Henderson #A-1, Well File, Crane County TX," Box 83-021, C. J. "Red" Davidson Collection, Permian Basin Petroleum Museum, Midland, Texas.
41. "Cascade Petroleum Company Oil Properties West Texas Evaluation Jan 1, 1956," Folder "Cactus Petroleum Co—Hallie C Day and Royalty No 221 Crane County, TX," Box 83-021, C. J. "Red" Davidson Collection, Permian Basin Petroleum Museum, Midland, Texas.
42. Carl T. Montgomery and Michael B. Smith, "Hydraulic Fracturing: History of an Enduring Technology," *Journal of Petroleum Technology* 62, no. 12 (2010): 26–40; Michael Berry Smith and Carl T. Montgomery, *Hydraulic Fracturing* (CRC Press, 2015).
43. "Future Supply of Oil and Gas from the Permian Basin of West Texas and Southeastern New Mexico," USGS Geological Survey Circular 828 (1980).
44. Texas Railroad Commission (TRRC), Oil and Gas Division, *Annual Reports*, 1969–1981.
45. C. C. Reeves Jr., "Location, Flow and Water Quality of Some West Texas Playa Lake Springs," Texas Tech University Water Resources Center, Lubbock, December 1970.
46. Midge Erskine, interview by David Todd, March 27, 2001, Conservation History Association of Texas, Briscoe Center for American History, University of Texas at Austin.
47. Erskine, interview by David Todd.
48. Folder "San Angelo Standard Times 7/4/1967 Section H," Box 83-021, C. J. "Red" Davidson, Box 4 of 4, C. J. "Red" Davidson Collections, Permian Basin Petroleum Museum, Midland, Texas.
49. "Somber Mood Surrounds Denver City After Tragedy," *Odessa American*, February 4, 1975, 16.
50. "Somber Mood Surrounds Denver City After Tragedy."
51. "Somber Mood Surrounds Denver City After Tragedy"; Robert Borden, "Deaths May Remain Mystery," *Odessa American*, February 3, 1975, 17.
52. Michael Kerr, "Nine Tragic Deaths Stun Town," *Odessa American*, February 3, 1975, 17.
53. Kerr, "Nine Tragic Deaths Stun Town."
54. Karen Malkowski, "Call for Help Came Too Late," *Odessa American*, February 3, 1975, 17.
55. Howard Swindle, "The Deadly Smell of Success," *Texas Monthly*, June 1975.
56. John Wynn, interview by William A. Owens, July 7, 1952, Beaumont, Texas, and Walter Cline, interview by Mody Boatright and Louise Kelly, August 13, 1952, Wichita Falls, Texas, Oral History of the Texas Oil Industry Collection, Briscoe Center for American History, University of Texas, Austin.
57. Frank Hamilton, interview by Mody Boatright, July 29, 1952, Sour Lake, Texas, Oral History of the Texas Oil Industry Collection, Briscoe Center for American History, University of Texas, Austin.
58. Kerr, "Nine Tragic Deaths Stun Town."
59. Webster B. Todd, "National Transportation Safety Board Safety Recommendation Document," July 27, 1976, National Transportation Safety Board (NTSB), Washington, DC.
60. UPI, "Legislature, Commission May Study Value of Working 'Dead' Oil Wells," *Galveston Daily News*, March 3, 1975, 2.

61. Bob Horn, "Handling of Hydrogen Sulfide Gas Studied at State Meets," *Odessa American*, February 15, 1976, 50.
62. Horn, "Handling of Hydrogen Sulfide Gas Studied at State Meets."
63. Swindle, "The Deadly Smell of Success"; Howard Swindle, "Fatal Cloud Cloaks Home," *Lubbock Avalanche-Journal*, February 3, 1975, 1.
64. James Carberry and Douglas Martin, "Insidious Killer: A Lethal Gas Freed in Oil-Gas Production Poses a Rising Hazard: New Techniques in Industry Tend to Widen Exposure to Hydrogen Sulfide Peril," *Wall Street Journal*, December 5, 1975, 1; "Silent Killer Stalks Texas," *Austin American Statesman*, November 20, 1975, A18; "Oil Well Fumes Kill 9 in Texas: Experimental System Ruptures Near House," *Los Angeles Times*, February 3, 1975, A1; "Nine Die Trying to Flee Leaking Gas from Oil Well, *Jerusalem Post*, February 4, 1975, 5.
65. "Safety Programs Talks Scheduled," *El Paso Herald-Post*, September 11, 1974, 19.
66. "Hoyt Starling," *Lubbock Avalanche-Journal*, June 16, 1976, 12.
67. Robert Borden, "Deaths May Remain Mystery," *Odessa American*, February 3, 1975, 17.
68. "Death Well Had Safety Devices," *Odessa American*, February 3, 1975, 17.
69. Charles Jones, *From the Rio Grande to the Arctic: The Story of the Richfield Oil Corporation* (University of Oklahoma Press, 1972).
70. Odd Magne Mathiassen, "CO_2 as Injection Gas for Enhanced Oil Recovery and Estimation of the Potential on the Norwegian Continental Shelf," May 2003, NTNU, chapter 5, http://large.stanford.edu/courses/2013/ph240/salehi2/docs/mathiassen.pdf.
71. In 1977, ARCO merged with the Anaconda Mining Company in the hope of expanding into shale oil extraction. However, the drop in oil prices in the 1980s ended this effort. "Arco Acquires Anaconda After Court Refuses to Bar Tie," *New York Times*, January 13, 1977, 60.
72. "CO_2 Enhanced Oil Recovery, and the Texas Oil and Gas Lawyer," *Holmes Law*, https://www.holmeslawpllc.com/wp-content/uploads/sites/1603174/2021/11/9_CO_2.EOR_.Lawyer-DBA_8-2007.pdf, accessed August 15, 2025.
73. "1970s: Bursting the Pipeline Construction Bubble," *Underground Infrastructure* 76, no. 4 (April 2021); US Congressional Record, Senate, "Pipeline Safety Problems," May 21, 1974, 15780–15783.
74. US Congressional Record, Senate, "Pipeline Safety Problems," May 21, 1974, 15780–15783.
75. US Congressional Record, Senate, "Pipeline Safety Problems."
76. US Congress, Senate Committee on Commerce, Subcommittee on Surface Transportation, "Statement of John H. Reed, Chairman, National Transportation Safety Board; Accompanied by Henry H. Wakeland, Director, Bureau of Surface Transportation Safety; Barry M. Sweedler, Deputy Director, Bureau of Surface Transportation Safety; Henry M. Shepherd, Acting Chief, Pipeline Safety Division; and Fritz L. Puls, General Council," in *Natural Gas Pipeline Safety Act Amendments of 1975* (University of Michigan Library, 1975).
77. Admitting the toxin's widespread prevalence in almost all Permian Basin oil, others predicted that the new regulations would apply to "every drop of oil" produced in the Permian Section. "Area Oilmen Flay Gas Curb Plans," *Lubbock Avalanche-Journal*, May 18, 1975, 1.

78. "Hydrogen Sulfide Controls Disturbing to Oil Officials," *Lubbock Avalanche-Journal*, April 27, 1975, 8.
79. Staff Writer, "Denver City Remembers H2S Tragedy," *Lubbock Avalanche-Journal*, September 14, 2010.
80. ARCO released a statement after the hearings: "Naturally we are aware of hearings and did provide input, but we have no comment with regard to future operations." "Hydrogen Sulfide Controls Disturbing to Oil Officials."
81. In turn, the IOCC and other agencies described the TRRC as little more than a mouthpiece for Texas oil producers. This assessment was backed up by both scholars and industry insiders. Prindle, *Petroleum Politics and the Texas Railroad Commission*.
82. Prindle, *Petroleum Politics and the Texas Railroad Commission*, 161–62. See also Sidney J. Strong, "Application of the Doctrine of Correlative Rights by the State Conservation Agency in the Absence of Express Statutory Authorization," *Montana Law Review* 28, no. 2 (Spring 1967); Clippings, Box 76, Harvey O'Connor Collection, Walter Reuther Library, Detroit.
83. William R. Childs, *The Texas Railroad Commission: Understanding Regulation in America to the Mid-Twentieth Century* (Texas A&M University Press, 2005), 153.
84. Associated Press, "Railroad Commission Hears Testimony About Gas Deaths," *Valley Morning Star*, Harlingen, Texas, March 14, 1975, 14.
85. UPI, "Legislature, Commission May Study Value of Working 'Dead' Oil Wells."
86. UPI, "Legislature, Commission May Study Value of Working 'Dead' Oil Wells."
87. Glen Paulson, Conference Proceedings, Houston, 1969; Tony Mazzocchi Collection, 17, OCAWU Records, Special Collections, University of Colorado, Boulder.
88. This was a national and global problem. M. L. Bell and D. L. Davis, "Reassessment of the Lethal London Fog of 1952: Novel Indicators of Acute and Chronic Consequences of Acute Exposure to Air Pollution," *Environmental Health Perspectives* 109, Suppl. 3 (June 2001): 389–94; Andy McPhee, *The Donora Death Fog: Clean Air and the Tragedy of a Pennsylvania Mill Town* (University of Pittsburgh Press, 2023).
89. Bill Ricks, "District 4 Conference Proceedings," Houston, 1970, Box 1, Tony Mazzocchi Collection, OCAWU Records, Special Collections, University of Colorado, Boulder, 16–17.
90. Docket No. 20–64,973, Texas Legislature (April 17, 1975), https://texreg.sos.state.tx.us/public/readtac$ext.TacPage?sl=R&app=9&p_dir=&p_rloc=&p_tloc=&p_ploc=&pg=1&p_tac=&ti=16&pt=1&ch=3&rl=36.
91. See also Christopher Casteneda and Clarence M. Smith, *Gas Pipelines and the Emergence of America's Regulatory State: A History of Panhandle Eastern Corporation, 1928–1993* (Cambridge University Press, 1996).
92. Texas Railroad Commission Rule 051.02.02.036, 1 Tex. Reg. 1517 (1976).
93. "Hydrogen Sulfide Seminar Slated," *Odessa American*, March 16, 1976, 4.
94. "James Edward Smith," Obituaries, *Tyler Morning Telegraph*, June 1, 2019, https://tylerpaper.com/obituaries/james-edward-smith/article_5366a646-849e-11e9-931b-9fe206f5cc8d.html.
95. Bob Horn, "RRC Representative Spoke Language of Oil Industry," *Odessa American*, March 18, 1976, 37.
96. Bob Horn, "Welfare of Public, Workers Cited at Hydrogen Sulfide Meet," *Odessa American*, March 17, 1976, 23.

97. "Introduction," in Michelle Nickerson and Darren Dochuk, eds., *Sunbelt Rising: The Politics of Space, Place, and Region* (University of Pennsylvania Press, 2011), 8.
98. Scholars have noted the links between Sun Belt economies and cheap natural resources. Huber, *Lifeblood*; Christopher J. Manganiello, *Southern Water, Southern Power: How the Politics of Cheap Energy and Water Scarcity Shaped a Region* (University of North Carolina Press, 2017); Andrew Needham, *Power Lines: Phoenix and the Making of the Modern Southwest* (Princeton University Press 2014).
99. "Introduction," *Sunbelt Rising*. See also Kevin B. Phillips, *The Emerging Republican Majority* (Anchor, 1969); Jerry Hagstrom, *Beyond Reagan: The New Landscape of American Politics* (Norton, 1988).
100. Similar processes were at work in cities throughout the Sun Belt. Andrew Needham, "Sunbelt Imperialism: Boosters, Navajos, and Energy Development in the Metropolitan Southwest," in *Sunbelt Rising: The Politics of Space, Place, and Region*, ed. Michelle Nickerson and Darren Dochuk (University of Pennsylvania Press, 2011), 240–64.
101. Folder "Parker Drilling Company Annual Reports 1977–1982 and Parker Drilling Company Annual Reports 1969–1976," Permian Basin Petroleum Museum, Midland, Texas.
102. "Pipeline Accident Reports—Brief Format, Issue Number 1–1977," National Transportation Safety Board (NTSB), Washington, DC.
103. The subsequent investigation revealed that six other people had been killed by leaks on that pipeline system since 1968. National Transportation Safety Board (NTSB), Safety Recommendations P-76-22 through 25, June 14, 1976; "Blasts Suit Shifted to Federal Court," *Lubbock Avalanche-Journal*, October 15, 1976, 97.
104. Associated Press, "Two Men Killed in Gas Line Blast," *Brownwood Bulletin*, February 23, 1977, 5.
105. "Pipeline Accident Reports—Brief Format, Issue Number 1–1980," National Transportation Safety Board (NTSB), Washington, DC.
106. That same year, the OCAW held yet another failed union drive at the Odessa Petrochemical Complex, this time working to organize employees of Rexene Polymers. Folder "04-661 Rexene Polymers Odessa, Texas," Box 26, OCAW Districts 4 and 5, OCAW Records, Special Collections, University of Colorado, Boulder.
107. Erskine, interview by David Todd.
108. "City Elections Set Throughout West Texas," *Odessa American*, March 9, 1975, 29. Bob Garrett, an assistant manager at a lumber company, won the election in May 1975.
109. "City Elections Set Throughout West Texas."
110. Short had held office since 1969 and focused on issues facing rural Texas. "E. L. Short Wins Representative Post by Large Margin," *Lynn County News*, August 7, 1969, 1; Adam D. Young, "Former South Plains State Lawmaker Short Remembered as Strong Voice for West Texas," *Lubbock Avalanche-Journal*, June 26, 2015; "Rep E L Short Committee Chairman," *Lynn Country News*, February 6, 1975, 1.
111. "Edwards Elevated to Vice President," *Odessa American*, June 26, 1970, 36.
112. In 1973, the legislature passed a series of reforms designed to create greater transparency in government spending and lobbying. In 1974, Dolph Briscoe presided over a failed Texas Constitutional Convention, which would have enshrined a

right-to-work clause in the Texas constitution. Griffin Smith Jr., "Why Does Dolph Briscoe Want to Be Governor?," *Texas Monthly*, February 1976.

113. Smith, "Why Does Dolph Briscoe Want to Be Governor?"
114. Smith, "Why Does Dolph Briscoe Want to Be Governor?"
115. UPI, "Poison Gas Deaths Under Study," *Pampa Daily News*, March 2, 1975, 4.
116. Box 4JC65, TIPRO Collection, Briscoe Center for American History, University of Texas at Austin.
117. Box 4JC2, TIPRO Collection, Briscoe Center for American History, University of Texas at Austin.
118. Statewide Hearing (November 17, 1976), "Texas Oil Output Cut to Spur a U.S. Move," *New York Times*, November 19, 1976, 87; "Statement by Jim C. Langdon, Railroad Commission of Texas, for the 47th Annual Oil Progress, Edition of the Kilgore *News Herald*, May 1977," James C. Langdon Papers, Archives and Information Services Division, Texas State Library and Archives Commission, Austin.
119. Congressional Record—House, 25937, August 1, 1977, https://www.congress.gov/95/crecb/1977/08/01/GPO-CRECB-1977-pt21-1-2.pdf.
120. Attention to their efforts was a reasonable bellwether for the political leanings of state leadership. While there was a team of commissioners at any one time, the TRRC commissioner appointment typically went to retired governors or favored politicians. For specific accounts, see Childs, *Texas Railroad Commission*.
121. "Briscoe to Speak at Tipro Meeting," *Odessa American*, June 5, 1977, 49; "Langdon Says Energy Problems Complicated," *Odessa American*, April 15, 1977, 23; Jerome J. O'Brien, "Carter Program Called Serious Step Backward," *The Oil Daily*, Folder "Press Releases CIPA," Box 2008-10 5 of 16, Jerome O'Brien Collection, Permian Basin Petroleum Museum, Midland, Texas.
122. Jimmy Carter, "Address to the Nation on Energy," April 18, 1977.
123. "Statement by Jim C. Langdon, Railroad Commission of Texas."
124. "Statement by Jim C. Langdon, Railroad Commission of Texas."
125. Charles Homans, "Anthropology of an Idea: 'Energy Independence,'" *Foreign Policy*, no. 191 (2012): 34–35; Melosi, "Energy and Environment in the United States."
126. Needham, "Sunbelt Imperialism."
127. Yergin, *The Prize*; Tyler Priest, "The Dilemmas of Oil Empire," *Journal of American History* 99, no. 1 (2012): 236–51.
128. "Crisis of Confidence," speech of July 15, 1979, Stuart Eizenstat Oral History, January 29, 1982, Miller Center, University of Virginia, https://millercenter.org/the-presidency/presidential-oral-histories/stuart-eizenstat-oral-history.
129. In 1970, Odessa Products branched out into oil exploration and extraction. "Subsidiary of Products Firm Formed," *Odessa American*, September 25, 1970, 11.
130. Porter, oral history interview by Maclyn Burg.
131. This was the highest that oil prices had ever been up to that point. For a more detailed history of this fallout, see Jacobs, *Panic at the Pump*.

CONCLUSION: THE LAST BOOM?

1. For state and national accounts of this process, see Rick Perlstein, *Before the Storm: Barry Goldwater and the Unmaking of the American Consensus* (Hill & Wang, 2001);

Darren Dochuk, *Anointed with Oil: How Christianity and Crude Made Modern America* (Basic Books, 2019); Sean P. Cunningham, *Cowboy Conservatism: Texas and the Rise of the Modern Right* (University Press of Kentucky, 2010); Jeff Roche, *The Political Culture of the New West* (University Press of Kansas, 2008).

2. Roger M. Olien and Diana Davids Hinton, *Wildcatters: Texas Independent Oilmen* (Texas A&M University Press, 2007), chapter 7.
3. In early 1983, global crude oil prices dropped from $34 to $29 per barrel. The next year, prices plummeted as low as $7 per barrel and would stay low for the rest of the decade. Michael Ratner and Carol Glover, "U.S. Energy: Overview and Key Statistics," Congressional Research Service, Washington, DC, June 27, 2014, https://fas.org/sgp/crs/misc/R40187.pdf.
4. Ratner and Glover, "U.S. Energy: Overview and Key Statistics."
5. Lisa Belkin, "Now, It's Remember the Oil Bust!," *New York Times*, August 22, 1989, D1; Colin Eaton, "1980s Oil Bust Left a Lasting Mark," *Houston Chronicle*, August 31, 2016, http://www.chron.com/local/history/economy-business/article/The-1980s-oil-bust-left-lasting-mark-on-Houston-9195222.php.
6. "Introduction," in Michelle Nickerson and Darren Dochuk, eds., *Sunbelt Rising: The Politics of Space, Place, and Region*.
7. US Census Bureau, "1980 of Population Preliminary Reports," accessed July 21, 2015, https://www.census.gov/prod/www/decennial.html; US Census Bureau, "1990 of Population Preliminary Reports," accessed July 21, 2015, https://www.census.gov/prod/www/decennial.html.
8. Robert Reinhold, "US Helps Texans Survive Death of Bank," *New York Times*, 1984, 1.
9. Reinhold, "U.S. Helps Texans Survive Death of Bank."
10. Reinhold, "U.S. Helps Texans Survive Death of Bank."
11. Olien and Hinton, *Wildcatters*, chapter 6.
12. Reinhold, "U.S. Helps Texans Survive Death of Bank."
13. "TCEQ WST IHW Correspondence MF307608 8 of 16_0000," Microfiche, Archive, Texas Commission for Environmental Quality, Austin.
14. In the initial lawsuit against Dynagen, residents asked for $27 million in damages. "Rubber Plant Emissions Unhealthy, Suit Claims," *Orlando Sentinel*, November 18, 1991, http://articles.orlandosentinel.com/1991-11-18/news/9111180426_1_rubber-plant-pollution-emissions.
15. "Rexene Corporation 1995 Annual Report on Form 10-K, Part 1," Rexene Corporation, 1995, US Security and Exchange Commission, accessed October 15, 2016, https://www.sec.gov/Archives/edgar/data/829218/0000912057-96-004686.txt; Mark Rose, "NAACP Fumin' over Rubber Plant Emissions in West Texas," *The Crisis* 101, no. 4 (February–March 1994).
16. The initial fine of $4.4 million was later reduced to $1.4 million. It represents the largest fine by the state of Texas for environmental contamination since the Texas Clean Air Act of 1965. The five hundred violations still represent the largest number of citations ever given to a Texas industrial site. "75th Anniversary," *Odessa American Online*, accessed October 15, 2016, http://www.oaoa.com/75th_anniversary/article_96695196-5671-11e5-82e5-5b7a0a1e020f.html; "TCEQ WST IHW 30142 Inspection Report MF307610 5-6" and "TCEQ WST IHW 30142 Correspondence MF307609 1–16 (pre 1985)," Microfiche, Archives, Texas Commission for Environmental Quality, Austin.

17. Associated Press, "Officials Say Feud at an End," *Kerrville Daily Times*, March 23, 1997, Kerrville, Texas, 9B; "Protecting the Environment," from oral history interview with Gene Collins, July 8, 2016, Odessa, Texas, Civil Rights in Black and Brown Interview Database, https://crbb.tcu.edu/clips/3814/protecting-the-environment; John E. Matthews, "Industrial Reuse and Recycle of Wastewaters," 1980, Robert S. Kerr Environmental Research Laboratory, Office of Research and Development, US Environmental Protection Agency, Washington, DC. While in the 1990s conversations about oil pollution in Odessa focused on air and water quality, the conversation would change in the 2000s to focus on increased cancer and nervous system disorders associated with chemical exposure. US Securities and Exchange Commission (SEC), "Letter to Stockholders," Rexene Corporation, July 28, 1997, https://www.sec.gov/Archives/edgar/data/829218/0000950134-97-005523.txt.
18. Andrew Buncombe, "Odessa, Texas: Is It the Most Polluted City in America?," *The Independent*, April 1, 2001, http://www.independent.co.uk/environment/odessa-texas-is-it-the-most-polluted-city-in-america-689632.html.
19. For an overview of these relationships, see Fernando Coronil, *The Magical State: Nature, Money, and Modernity in Venezuela* (University of Chicago Press, 1997); Brett Christophers, *Rentier Capitalism: Who Owns the Economy, and Who Pays for It?* (Verso, 2020); Luiz Carlis Bresser-Pereira, *The Rise and Fall of Neoliberal Rentier Capitalism* (Oxford University Press, 2025).
20. Scholars have shown that such systems produced an array of unremarked and extreme hardships for those living and working within them. Greta R. Krippner, *Capitalizing on Crisis: The Political Origins of the Rise of Finance* (Harvard University Press, 2011); G. F. Davis, *Managed by the Markets: How Finance Reshaped America* (Oxford University Press, 2009).
21. For materials theorizing on the links between extractive regimes and American capitalism, see Matt Huber, *Lifeblood: Oil, Freedom and the Forces of Capital* (University of Minnesota Press, 2013); Timothy Mitchell, *Carbon Democracy: Political Power in the Age of Oil* (Verso, 2011); Trish Kahle, *Energy Citizenship: Coal and Democracy in the American Century* (Columbia University Press, 2024).
22. Welfare reform, the rise of 401(k) investments to replace pensions, and the privatization of health care were all efforts to apply market mechanisms to the management of risk and danger.
23. Stanley A. Renshon, "Presidential Address: George W. Bush's Cowboy Politics: An Inquiry," *Political Psychology* 26, no. 4 (2005): 585–614.
24. Alyssa Dizon, "Marker Gives Closure to Denver City 35 Years Later," *Lubbock Avalanche-Journal*, September 18, 2010, https://www.lubbockonline.com/story/news/local/2010/09/19/marker-gives-closure-community/15261618007/.

BIBLIOGRAPHY

ARCHIVES

American Heritage Center, University of Wyoming, Laramie
Archives Center, National Museum of American History, Washington, DC
Briscoe Center for American History, University of Texas at Austin
Hagley Museum and Library, Wilmington, Delaware
Library of Congress, Washington, DC
Midland County Historical Society, Herbert H. Dow Historical Museum, Midland, Texas
Newberry Library Special Collections, Newberry Library, Chicago, Illinois
Permian Basin Petroleum Museum, Odessa, Texas
Railroad Commission of Texas, Austin
Texas Commission for Environmental Quality Archives, Austin
Texas General Land Office, Austin
Texas Tech University, Special Collections/Southwest Collection, Lubbock
University of Colorado, Boulder, Special Collections
Walter Reuther Library, Wayne State University, Detroit, Michigan

PERIODICALS

Abilene Daily Reporter
Abilene Reporter-News
API Facts and Figures
Atlanta Constitution
Austin American Statesman
Brownsville Herald

Chemical and Engineering News
Clifton Record
Corsicana Semi-Weekly Light
Corpus Christi Caller-Times
Dallas Morning News
El Paso Evening Post
El Paso Herald
Galveston Daily News
The Lamp
Longview Daily News
Longview News-Journal
Lubbock Morning Avalanche
Magnolia News
Mexia Weekly Herald
Midlander Magazine
Midland Reporter Telegram
The New Yorker
New York Herald Tribune
New York Times
Houston Post
Pampa Daily News
San Angelo Standard Times
Odessa American
The Odessa News and Ector County News
Oil Weekly
Oil and Gas Journal
Petroleum Refiner
Pittsburgh Press
Texas Monthly
Texaco Star Magazine
TP Voice
Wall Street Journal
Wichita Falls Times-Record-News
World Oil

SECONDARY SOURCES

Abrams, Herbert K. "A Short History of Occupational Health." *Journal of Public Health Policy* 22, no. 1 (2001): 34–80.

"Active Drilling Rigs Zoom to 4-Year High." *World Oil* 178, no. 3 (February 15, 1979): 85–86.

Adams, John A. *Damming the Colorado: The Rise of the Lower Colorado River Authority, 1933–1939*. Texas A&M University Press, 2000.

Aldrich, Mark. "Safety First Comes to the Railroads, 1910–1939." *Railroad History*, no. 166 (1992): 6–33.

BIBLIOGRAPHY

Aldrich, Mark. *Safety First: Technology, Labor, and Business in the Building of American Work Safety, 1870–1939*. Johns Hopkins University Press, 1997.

Allen, Barbara. *Uneasy Alchemy: Citizens and Experts in Louisiana's Chemical Corridor Disputes*. MIT Press, 2003.

Aloni, Omer. *The League of Nations and the Protection of the Environment*. Cambridge University Press, 2021.

Alonzo, Armando. *Tejano Legacy: Rancheros and Settlers in South Texas, 1734–1900*. University of New Mexico Press, 1998.

American Petroleum Institute (API). *Petroleum: The Story of an American Industry*. American Petroleum Institute, 1935.

Anderson, Gary C. *The Conquest of Texas: Ethnic Cleansing in the Promised Land, 1820–1875*. University of Texas Press, 2005.

Anderson, Richard C. "The Contributions of J. A. Udden to an Understanding of Iowa Geology." *Journal of the Iowa Academy of Science* 104, no. 4 (1997): 91–96.

Andrews, Gregg. "Black Working-Class Political Activism and Biracial Unionism: Galveston Longshoremen in Jim Crow Texas, 1919–1921." *Journal of Southern History* 74, no. 3 (2008): 627–68.

Andrews, Thomas. *Killing for Coal: America's Deadliest Labor War*. Harvard University Press, 2010.

API Committee on Public Affairs. *Petroleum Facts and Figures, Centennial Edition*. American Petroleum Institute, 1959.

Arnold, W. C. *Cattle, Cotton, Corn: A History of Central Texas Middle-Class Ranches, 1880–1930*. Texas Tech University Press, 2022.

Bailey, Janis, and Ross Gwyther. "Red and Green: Toward a Cross-Fertilization of Labour and Environmental History." *Labor History* 99 (2010): 1–16.

Banks, James H., and John E. Babcock. *Corralling the Colorado: The First Fifty Years of the Lower Colorado River Authority*. Eakin, 1988.

Beasly, Alex. "Exporting Service: Houston and the Globalization of Oil Expertise, 1945–2008." PhD diss., Yale University, 2015.

Beck, Ulric. *Risk Society: Toward a New Modernity*. Sage, 1992.

Beckert, Sven. *Empire of Cotton: A Global History*. Vintage, 2014.

Bell, M. L., and D. L. Davis. "Reassessment of the Lethal London Fog of 1952: Novel Indicators of Acute and Chronic Consequences of Acute Exposure to Air Pollution." *Environmental Health Perspectives* 109, Suppl. 3 (June 2001): 389–94.

Black, Brian. *Petrolia: The Landscape of America's First Oil Boom*. Johns Hopkins University Press, 2003.

Black, Brian, Karen Merrill, and Tyler Priest, eds. "Oil in American History." *Journal of American History*, 99 (June 2012).

Blanchard, Charles. *The Extraction State: A History of Natural Gas in America*. University of Pittsburgh Press, 2021.

Boatright, Mody C. *Tales from the Derrick Floor: A People's History of the Oil Industry*. University of Nebraska Press, 1982.

Bohme, Susana. *Toxic Injustice: A Transnational History of Exposure and Struggle*. University of California Press, 2014.

Bolling, Raynal C. "The United States Steel Corporation and Labor Conditions." *Annals of the American Academy of Political and Social Science* 42 (1912): 38–47.

Bouk, Dan. *How Our Days Became Numbered: Risk and the Rise of the Statistical Individual*. University of Chicago Press, 2015.
Boyd, William. *The Slain Wood: Papermaking and Its Environmental Consequences in the American South*. Johns Hopkins University Press, 2015.
Brantley, John Edward. *History of Oil Well Drilling*. Gulf Publishing, 1971.
Bresser-Pereira, Luiz Carlis. *The Rise and Fall of Neoliberal Rentier Capitalism*. Oxford University Press, 2025.
Brewster, J. "Record Pecos Deep Wells Make Major Strides." *Drill Bit* 29, no. 6 (1980).
Brown, Kate. *Plutopia: Nuclear Families, Atomic Cities, and the Great Soviet and American Plutonium Disasters*. Oxford University Press, 2013.
Brown, Timothy L. "A Primer for Understanding Texas Water Law." Legislative Reference Library of Texas, 29. Austin, 2006.
Brown, Susan Jane M. " 'The Forest Must Come First': Gifford Pinchot's Conservation Ethic and the Gifford Pinchot National Forest—the Ideal and the Reality." 11 *Fordham Environmental Law Review* 137 (1999).
Burchell, G., C. Gordon, and P. Miller, eds. *The Foucault Effect: Studies in Governmentality*. University of Chicago Press, 1991.
Carlson, Paul H. *Texas Woolybacks: The Range Sheep and Goat Industry*. Texas A&M University Press, 1982.
Carlson, Paul H., and Bruce Glasrud. *West Texas: A History of the Giant Side of the State*. University of Oklahoma Press, 2014.
Casteneda, Christopher, and Clarence M. Smith. *Gas Pipelines and the Emergence of America's Regulatory State: A History of Panhandle Eastern Corporation, 1928–1993*. Cambridge University Press, 1996.
Cawley, R. McGreggor. *Federal Land, Western Anger: The Sagebrush Rebellion and Environmental Politics*. University of Kansas Press, 1993.
Chagnon, Christopher W., et al. "From Extractivism to Global Extractivism: The Evolution of an Organizing Concept." *Journal of Peasant Studies* 49, no. 4 (2022): 760–92.
Childs, William R. "Texas, the Interstate Oil Compact Commission, and State Control of Oil Production: Regionalism, States' Rights, and Federalism During World War II." *Pacific Historical Review* 64, no. 4 (1995): 567–98.
Childs, William R. *The Texas Railroad Commission: Understanding Regulation in America to the Mid-Twentieth Century*. Texas A&M University Press, 2005.
Childs, William R. "The Transformation of the Railroad Commission of Texas, 1917–1940: Business-Government Relations and the Importance of Personality, Agency Culture, and Regional Differences." *Business History Review* 65, no. 2 (1991): 285–344.
Cohen, Lizabeth. *A Consumer's Republic: The Politics of Mass Consumption in Postwar America*. Vintage, 2008.
Christophers, Brett. *Rentier Capitalism: Who Owns the Economy, and Who Pays for It?* Verso, 2020.
Collett, James. *Images of America: Midland*. Arcadia, 2010.
Coronil, Fernando. *The Magical State: Nature, Money, and Modernity in Venezuela*. University of Chicago Press, 1997.
Coulter, Matthew Ware. "Taming the East Texas 'Black Giant': Ernest O. Thompson and Illusions of Independence, 1930–1935." *Southwestern Historical Quarterly* 123, no. 3 (2020): 292–315.

Cowan, Ruth Schwartz. *A Social History of American Technology*. Oxford University Press, 1997.

Cowie, Jefferson. *Stayin' Alive: The 1970s and the Last Days of the Working Class*. New Press, 2010.

Critchlow, Donald. *The Conservative Ascendancy: How the GOP Right Made Political History*. University Press of Kansas, 2007.

Cronon, William. *Nature's Metropolis: Chicago and the Great West*. Norton, 1991.

Cullen, David O'Donald, and Kyle G. Wilkinson, eds. *The Texas Right: The Radical Roots of Lone Star Conservatism*. Texas A&M University Press, 2014.

Cunningham, Sean P. *Cowboy Conservatism: Texas and the Rise of the Modern Right*. University Press of Kentucky, 2010.

Davidson, Chandler. *Race and Class in Texas Politics*. Princeton University Press, 1990.

Davis, G. F. *Managed by the Markets: How Finance Reshaped America*. Oxford University Press, 2009.

DeLay, Brian. *War of a Thousand Deserts: Indian Raids and the US-Mexican War*. Yale University Press, 2009.

De Leon, Arnoldo. "Mexican Americans in the Edwards Plateau and Trans-Pecos Region, 1900–2000." *Southwestern Historical Quarterly* 112 (October 2008): 148–70.

De Leon, Arnoldo. *Tejano West Texas*. Texas A&M University Press, 2015.

Derickson, Alan. "Naphtha Drunks, Lead Colic, and the Smelter Shakes: The Inordinate Exposure of Immigrant Workers to Occupational Health Hazards at the Turn of the Twentieth Century." *Journal of American Ethnic History* 37, no. 2 (2018): 37–61.

Dochuk, Darren. *Anointed with Oil: How Christianity and Crude Made Modern America*. Basic Books, 2019.

Doughty, Robin. *At Home in Texas: Early View of the Land*. Texas A&M University Press, 1987.

Douglas, Mary, and Aaron Wildavsky. *Risk and Culture: An Essay on the Selection of Technological and Environmental Dangers*. University of California Press, 1983.

Durham, Philip, and Everett L. Jones. *The Negro Cowboys*. Bison Books, 1983.

Eagleton, Nancy Ethie. *On the Last Frontier: A History of Upton County, Texas*. Texas Western Press, 1971.

Earl, Richard A., and Robert Czerniac. "Sunbelt Water War: The El Paso–New Mexico Water Conflict." *Social Science Journal* 33, no. 4 (1996): 359–79.

Eastabrook, Thomas. *Labor-Environmental Coalitions: Lessons from a Louisiana Petrochemical Region*. Baywood, 2007.

Edises, Bertram. "Multiplicity of Remedies in the Field of Industrial Accident Law." *California Law Review* 21, no. 5 (1933): 430–59.

Ekbladh, David. *The Great American Mission: Modernization and the Construction of an American World Order*. Princeton University Press, 2011.

Eller, J., D. L. Ford, and E. F. Gloyna. "Water Reuse and Recycling in Industry." *American Water Works Association Journal* 62, no. 3 (1970): 149–54.

Elmore, Bartow. *Citizen Coke: The Making of Coca-Cola Capitalism*. Norton, 2014.

Feagin, Joe R. "The Global Context of Metropolitan Growth: Houston and the Oil Industry." *American Journal of Sociology* 90, no. 6 (1985): 1204–30.

Ferguson, Walter Keene. *Geology and Politics in Frontier Texas, 1845–1909*. University of Texas Press, 2014.

Fiege, Mark. *The Republic of Nature: An Environmental History of the United States.* University of Washington Press, 2012.
Fishback, Price, and Shawn Kantor. *A Prelude to the Welfare State: The Origins of Workers' Compensation.* University of Chicago Press, 2000.
Fishman, Robert. *Bourgeois Utopias: The Rise and Fall of Suburbia.* Basic Books, 1987.
Foley, Neil. "Mexicans, Mechanization, and the Growth of Corporate Cotton Culture in South Texas: The Taft Ranch, 1900–1930." *Journal of Southern History* 62, no. 2 (1996): 275–302.
Foley, Neil. *The White Scourge: Mexicans, Blacks and Poor Whites in Texas Cotton Culture.* University of California Press, 1999.
Ford, Gus L., ed. *Texas Cattle Brands.* Cockrell, 1936.
Foucault, Michel. *Discipline and Punish.* Gallimard, 1975.
Fox, Sarah Alisabeth. *Downwind: A People's History of the Nuclear West.* University of Nebraska Press, 2014.
Frehner, Brian. *Finding Oil: The Nature of Petroleum Geology.* University of Nebraska Press, 2011.
Giacomelli, Joseph. *Uncertain Climes: Debating Climate Change in Gilded Age America.* University of Chicago Press, 2023.
Glasrud, Bruce A., and James C. Maroney. *Texas Labor History.* Texas A&M University Press, 2013.
Goldsteen, Joel B. *Danger All Around: Waste Storage Crisis on the Texas and Louisiana Gulf Coast.* University of Texas Press, 2009.
Gonzalez, Gabriela. *Redeeming La Raza: Transborder Modernity, Race, Respectability, and Rights.* Oxford University Press, 2017.
Gordon, Robert. " 'Shell No!': OCAW and the Labor-Environmental Alliance." *Environmental History* 3, no. 4 (1998): 460–87.
Gorman, Hugh. *Redefining Efficiency: Pollution Concerns, Regulatory Mechanisms, and Technological Change in the U.S. Petroleum Industry.* University of Akron Press, 2001.
Gottlieb, Robert. *Forcing the Spring: The Transformation of the American Environmental Movement.* Island, 1993.
Gould, Lewis L. *Progressives and Prohibitionists: Texas Democrats in the Wilson Era.* University of Texas Press, 1973.
Griffin, John Howard. *Land of the High Sky.* First National Bank of Midland, 1959.
Guttman, Myron P., and Christie G. Sample. "Land, Climate, and Settlement in Texas." *Southwestern Historical Quarterly* 99, no. 2 (October 1995): 137–72.
Hadjicostandi, Joanna. "Historical Growth of African Americans in Odessa, Texas." *National Forum of Multicultural Issues Journal* 12, no. 1 (2015).
Hagstrom, Jerry. *Beyond Reagan: The New Landscape of American Politics.* Norton, 1988.
Hahn, Barbara. *Making Tobacco Bright: Creating an American Commodity, 1617–1937.* Johns Hopkins University Press, 2011.
Haigh, Berte R. *Land, Oil and Education.* Texas Western Press, 1986.
Haltunen, Karen. *Confidence Men and Painted Women: A Study of Middle-Class Culture in America, 1830–1870.* Yale University Press, 1986.
Halvorson, Charles. *Valuing Clean Air: The EPA and the Economics of Environmental Protection.* Oxford University Press, 2021.
Hamalainen, Pekka. *The Comanche Empire.* Yale University Press, 2009.

Hanchett, Thomas. "Financing Suburbia: Prudential Insurance and the Post–World War II Transformation of the American City." *Journal of Urban History* 26, no. 3 (2000): 312–28.

Harper, Douglas, and Helene M. Lawson. *The Cultural Study of Work*. Rowman & Littlefield, 2003.

Helvarg, David. *The War Gains the Greens: The "Wise-Use" Movement, the New Right, and Anti-Environmental Violence*. Random House, 1994.

Hinton, Diana Davids. "Creating Company Culture: Oil Company Camps in the Southwest, 1920–1960." *Southwestern Historical Quarterly* 111, no. 4 (2008): 371–87.

Hinton, Diana Davids, and Roger M. Olien. *Oil in Texas: The Gusher Age, 1895–1945*. University of Texas Press, 2002.

Hochfelder, David. " 'Where the Common People Could Speculate': The Ticker, Bucket Shops, and the Origins of Popular Participation in Financial Markets, 1880–1920." *Journal of American History* 93, no. 2 (2006): 335–58.

Holdren, Nate. *Injury Impoverished: Workplace Accidents, Capitalism, and Law in the Progressive Era*. Cambridge University Press, 2020.

Hookstadt, Carl, et al. "Workmen's Compensation." *Monthly Labor Review* 9, no. 5 (1919): 266–338.

Horan, Caley. *Insurance Era: Risk, Governance, and the Privatization of Security in Postwar America*. MIT Press, 2021.

Horowitz, Roger, ed. *Boys and Their Toys: Masculinity, Class and Technology in America*. Routledge, 2001.

Horowitz, Roger. *Putting Meat on the American Table: Taste, Technology, Transformation*. Johns Hopkins University Press, 2006.

Horton, Finas Wade. "A History of Ector County, Texas." MA thesis, University of Texas, 1950.

Houck, Todd. *The University Lands: Resources and Higher Education in Texas, 1838–1996*. Windy Fox, 2011.

Howe, Charles W. "Water Resources and Regional Economic Growth in the United States, 1950–1960." *Southern Economic Journal* 34, no. 4 (1968): 477–89.

Huber, Matt. *Lifeblood: Oil, Freedom and the Forces of Capital*. University of Minnesota Press, 2013.

Hudnall, James S. "Geology and Economic Importance of the East Texas Field." *Oil Weekly*, July 31, 1931.

Ickes, Harold. *Fightin' Oil*. Knopf, 1943.

Jackson, Kenneth T. *Crabgrass Frontier: The Suburbanization of the United States*. Oxford University Press, 1985.

Jacobs, Meg. *Panic at the Pump: The Energy Crisis and the Transformation of American Politics in the 1970s*. Hill & Wang, 2017.

Jenkins, J. Craig, and Craig M. Eckert. "The Right Turn in Economic Policy: Business Elites and the New Conservative Economics." *Sociological Forum* 15, no. 2 (2000): 307–38.

Johnson, Cedric. *The Neoliberal Deluge: Hurricane Katrina, Late Capitalism, and the Remaking of New Orleans*. University of Minnesota Press, 2011.

Johnson, Robert. *Carbon Nation: Fossil Fuels and the Making of American Culture*. University Press of Kansas, 2014.

Jones, Christopher. *Routes of Power: Energy and Modern America.* Harvard University Press, 2016.

Jordan, Terry G. "A Century and a Half of Ethnic Change in Texas, 1836–1986." *Southwestern Historical Quarterly* 89, no. 4 (1986): 385–422.

Jordan, Terry G. "Early Northeast Texas and the Evolution of Western Ranching." *Annals of the Association of American Geographers* 67, no. 1 (1977): 66–87.

Jordan, Terry G. *Environment and Environmental Perceptions in Texas.* American Press, 1980.

Kahle, Trish. *Energy Citizenship: Coal and Democracy in the American Century.* Columbia University Press, 2024.

Kazis, Richard, and Richard Grossman. *Fear at Work: Job Blackmail, Labor and the Environment.* New Society, 1990.

Kiechel, Melanie. *Smell Detectives: An Olfactory History of Nineteenth-Century Urban America.* University of Washington Press, 2017.

Kim, Seung-Wook, and Price V. Fishback. "Institutional Change, Compensating Differentials, and Accident Risk in American Railroading, 1892–1945." *Journal of Economic History* 53, no. 4 (1993): 796–823.

Klein, Jennifer. *For All These Rights: Business, Labor, and the Shaping of America's Public-Private Welfare State.* Princeton University Press, 2003.

Klein, Jennifer. "The Politics of Economic Security: Employee Benefits and the Privatization of New Deal Liberalism." *Journal of Policy History* 12, no. 1 (2004).

Knowles, Scott Gabriel. *The Disaster Experts: Mastering Risk in Modern America.* University of Pennsylvania Press, 2013.

Kramer, Bruce M., and Patrick H. Martin. *The Law of Pooling and Unitization.* 3rd ed. Matthew Bender, 1970.

Krippner, Greta R. *Capitalizing on Crisis: The Political Origins of the Rise of Finance.* Harvard University Press, 2011.

Krochmal, Max. *Blue Texas: The Making of a Multiracial Democratic Coalition in the Civil Rights Era.* University of North Carolina Press, 2016.

Krochmal, Max, and Todd Moye. *Civil Rights in Black and Brown: Histories of Resistance and Struggle in Texas.* University of Texas Press, 2021.

Lambert, Paul F. *Voices from the Oil Fields.* University of Oklahoma Press, 1984.

Larson, Henrietta M., and Kenneth Wiggins Porter. *History of Humble Oil and Refining Company: A Study in Industrial Growth.* Harper, 1959.

Lathrop, Barnes F. *Migration into East Texas, 1835–1860: A Study from the United States Census.* Texas State Historical Association, 1949.

Leech, Brian James. *The City That Ate Itself: Butte, Montana and Its Expanding Berkeley Pit.* University of Nevada Press, 2018.

Lemangier, Stephanie. *Living Oil: Petroleum Culture in the American Century.* Oxford University Press, 2014.

Leopold, Les. *The Man Who Hated Work and Loved Labor: The Life and Times of Tony Mazzocchi.* Chelsea Green, 2007.

Lerner, Steve. *Sacrifice Zones: The Front Lines of Toxic Chemical Exposure in the United States.* MIT Press, 2010.

Levy, Jonathan. *Freaks of Fortune: The Emerging World of Capitalism and Risk in America.* Harvard University Press, 2012.

Libecap, Gary, and James L. Smith. "The Economic Evolution of Petroleum Property Rights in the United States." *Journal of Legal Studies* 31, no. S2 (June 2002): S589–S608.

Libecap, Gary D., and Steven N. Wiggins. "The Influence of Private Contractual Failure on Regulation: The Case of Oil Field Unitization." *Journal of Political Economy* 31, no. S2 (June 2002): S589–S608.

Lichtenstein, Nelson. *State of the Union: A Century of American Labor*. Princeton University Press, 2002.

Lifset, Robert D. "A New Understanding of the American Energy Crisis of the 1970s." *Historical Social Research/Historische Sozialforschung* 39, no. 4 (150) (2014): 22–42.

Limerick, Patricia Nelson. *The Legacy of Conquest: The Unbroken Past of the American West*. Norton, 1987.

Lloyd, Henry Demarest. *Wealth Against Commonwealth*. Harper, 1894.

Lowman, Al. "Bell Cord Rutherford: Cowboy Quixote of the West Texas Plains; Or, Some Shards from Our Storytelling Past." *Southwest Historical Quarterly* 104, no. 4 (2001): 495–513.

Lubken, Uwe, and Christof Mauch. "Uncertain Environments: Natural Hazards, Risk and Insurance in Historical Perspective." *Environment and History* 17, no. 1 (2011): 1–12.

Luckingham, Bradford. *The Urban Southwest: A Profile History of Albuquerque, El Paso, Phoenix, Tucson*. Texas Western Press, 1982.

Lynch, Gerald. *Roughnecks, Drillers, and Tool Pushers*. University of Texas Press, 1991.

Mackintosh, Barry. "Harold L. Ickes and the National Park Service." *Journal of Forest History* 29, no. 2 (1985), https://npshistory.com/publications/jfh-v29n2-78-84.pdf.

MacLaury, Judson. "The Job Safety Law of 1970: Its Passage Was Perilous." *Monthly Labor Review* 104, no. 3 (March 1981): 18–24.

Mangan, Frank. *The Pipeliners: The Story of El Paso Natural Gas*. Guynes, 1977.

Manganiello, Christopher J. *Southern Water, Southern Power: How the Politics of Cheap Energy and Water Scarcity Shaped a Region*. University of North Carolina Press, 2017.

Maroney, James C. "The Texas-Louisiana Oil Field Strike of 1917." In *Essays in Southern Labor History*, edited by Gary M. Fink and Merl E. Reed. Greenwood, 1976.

Marshall, J. Howard, II. *Done in Oil: An Autobiography*. Edited by Robert L. Bradley Jr. Texas A&M University Press, 2000.

Marshall, Ray. "Independent Unions in the Gulf Coast Petroleum Refining Industry—the Esso Experience." *Labor Law Journal* 12 (1961): 823–40.

Martin, Robert L. *The City Moves West: Economic and Industrial Growth in Central West Texas*. University of Texas Press, 1969.

McCarthy, Tom. "The Coming Wonder? Foresight and Early Concerns About the Automobile." *Environmental History* 6, no. 1 (2001): 46–74.

McFarlane, Wallace Scot. "Oil on the Farm: The East Texas Oil Boom and the Origins of an Energy Economy." *Journal of Southern History* 83, no. 4 (2017): 853–88.

McGirr, Lisa. *Suburban Warriors: The Origins of the New American Right*. Princeton University Press, 2001.

McPhee, Andy. *The Donora Death Fog: Clean Air and the Tragedy of a Pennsylvania Mill Town*. University of Pittsburgh Press, 2023.

Meikle, Jeffrey L. "Material Doubts: The Consequences of Plastic." *Environmental History* 2, no. 3 (1997): 278–300.

Meinig, Donald. *The Interpretation of Ordinary Landscapes: Geographical Essays*. Oxford University Press, 1979.

Melosi, Martin. *Effluent America: Cities, Industry, Energy, and the Environment*. University of Pittsburgh Press, 2001.

Melosi, Martin V. "Energy and Environment in the United States: The Era of Fossil Fuels." *Environmental Review: ER* 11, no. 3 (1987): 167–88.

Merrill, Karen R. *The Oil Crisis of 1973–1974: A Brief History with Documents*. St. Martin's, 2007.

Merrill, Karen. "Texas Metropole: Oil, the American West, and U.S. Power in the Postwar Years." *Journal of American History* 99, no. 1 (June 2002): 197–207.

Miller, H. C. *The Function of Natural Gas in the Production of Oil*. American Petroleum Institute, 1929.

Miller, Thomas L. *The Public Lands of Texas, 1519–1970*. University of Oklahoma Press, 1972.

Mitchell, Don. *They Saved the Crops: Labor, Landscape, and the Struggle over Industrial Farming in Bracero-Era California*. University of Georgia Press, 2012.

Mitchell, Timothy. *Carbon Democracy: Political Power in the Age of Oil*. Verso, 2011.

Mitchell, W. J. T. *Landscapes and Power*. University of Chicago Press, 2002.

Modisett, Bill, ed. *Historic Midland*. Historical-Publishing Network Lammert Publications, 1998.

Mohun, Arwen P. "Constructing the History of Risk: Foundations, Tools, and Reasons Why." *Historical Social Research/Historische Sozialforschung* 41, no. 1 (155) (2016): 30–47.

Mohun, Arwen. *Risk: Negotiating Safety in American Society*. Johns Hopkins University Press, 2013.

Montgomery, Carl T., and Michael B. Smith. "Hydraulic Fracturing: History of an Enduring Technology." *Journal of Petroleum Technology* 62, no. 12 (2010): 26–40.

Montire, Chad. *Making a Living: Work and the Environment in the United States*. University of North Carolina Press, 2008.

Moore, Richard R. *West Texas After the Discovery of Oil*. Pemberton, 1971.

Moreton, Bethany. *To Serve God and Walmart: The Making of Christian Free Enterprise*. Harvard University Press, 2009.

Mormino, Gary R. "Sunbelt Dreams and Altered States: A Social and Cultural History of Florida, 1950–2000." *Florida Historical Quarterly* 81, no. 1 (2002): 3–21.

Morrow, Norman L. "The Industrial Production and Use of 1,3-Butadiene." *Environmental Health Perspectives* 86 (1990): 7–8.

Moses, Julia. *The First Modern Risk: Workplace Accidents and the Origins of European Social States*. Cambridge University Press, 2018.

Murrah, David J. *C. C. Slaughter, Rancher, Banker, Baptist*. University of Texas Press, 1981.

Myres, Samuel D. *The Permian Basin: Era of Discovery*. Permian, 1973.

Myres, Samuel D. *The Permian Basin: Era of Advancement*. Permian, 1977.

Nash, Gerald. *United States Oil Policy, 1890–1964: Business and Government in Twentieth-Century America*. University of Pittsburgh Press, 1968.

Needham, Andrew. *Power Lines: Phoenix and the Making of the Modern Southwest*. Princeton University Press, 2014.

Nelson, Scott. *A Nation of Deadbeats: An Uncommon History of America's Financial Disasters*. Vintage, 2013.
Nickerson, Michelle, and Darren Dochuk, eds. *Sunbelt Rising: The Politics of Space, Place, and Region*. University of Pennsylvania Press, 2011.
Noble, Charles. *Liberalism at Work: The Rise and Fall of OSHA*. Temple University Press, 1986.
Nye, David. *Technologies of Landscape: From Reaping to Recycling*. University of Massachusetts Press, 2000.
Olien, Roger M., and Diana Davids Hinton. *Oil Booms: Social Change in Five Texas Towns*. University of Nebraska Press, 1982.
Olien, Roger M., and Diana Davids Hinton. *Oil and Ideology: The Cultural Creation of the American Petroleum Industry*. University of North Carolina Press, 2000.
Olien, Roger M., and Diana Davids Hinton. *Wildcatters: Texas Independent Oilmen*. Texas A&M University Press, 2007.
Orlean, Susan. "A Place Called Midland." *The New Yorker*, October 16, 2000, https://www.newyorker.com/magazine/2000/10/16/a-place-called-midland, 128.
Ornish, Natalie. *Pioneer Jewish Texans*. Texas A&M University Press, 2011.
Orren, Karen. *Corporate Power and Social Change: The Politics of the Life Insurance Industry*. Johns Hopkins University Press, 1974.
Orrenius, Pia M., Jesús Cañas, and Michael Weiss, eds. *Ten-Gallon Economy: Sizing up Economic Growth in Texas*. Palgrave Macmillan, 2015.
Page, Joseph A. "Consumer Involvement and the Consumer Product Safety Act." *Hofstra Law Review* 2 (1974): 605–18.
Parmet, Harbert. *George Bush: The Life of a Lone Star Yankee*. Transaction, 2010.
Patterson, Jimmy. *A History of Character: The Story of Midland, Texas*. Abell-Hanger Foundation, 2014.
Perales, Monica. *Smeltertown: Making and Remembering a Southwest Border Community*. University of North Carolina Press, 2010.
Perlstein, Rick. *Before the Storm: Barry Goldwater and the Unmaking of the American Consensus*. Hill & Wang, 2001.
Phillips, Kevin B. *The Emerging Republican Majority*. Anchor, 1969.
Phillips, Sarah T. *This Land, This Nation: Conservation, Rural America, and the New Deal*. Cambridge University Press, 2007.
Porter, Theodore. *Trust in Numbers*. Princeton University Press, 1995.
Pratt, Joseph, Martin Melosi, and Kathleen Brosnan, eds. *Energy Capitals: Local Impact, Global Influence*. University of Pittsburgh Press, 2014.
Priest, Tyler. "Labor's Last Stand in the Refinery: The Shell Oil Strike of 1962–1963." *Houston History* 4, no. 2 (2008).
Priest, Tyler, and Michael Botson. "Bucking the Odds: Organized Labor in Gulf Coast Oil Refining." *Journal of American History* 99, no. 1 (June 2012): 100–110.
Prindle, David F. *Petroleum Politics and the Texas Railroad Commission*. University of Texas Press, 1980.
Quam-Wickham, Nancy. "'Cities Sacrificed on the Altar of Oil': Popular Opposition to Oil Development in 1920s Los Angeles." *Environmental History* 3, no. 2 (1998): 189–209.
Quam-Wickham, Nancy. "An 'Oleaginous Civilization': Oil in Southern California." *Southern California Quarterly* 97, no. 3 (2015): 283–95.

Quam-Wickham, Nancy. "Rereading Man's Conquest of Nature: Skills, Myths, and the Historical Construction of Masculinity in Western Extractive Industries." In *Boys and Their Toys: Masculinity, Class and Technology in America*, edited by Roger Horowitz. Routledge, 2001.

Randall, Stephen J. "Harold Ickes and United States Foreign Petroleum Policy Planning, 1939–1945." *Business History Review* 57, no. 3 (Autumn 1983): 367–87.

Ratner, Michael, and Carol Glover. "U.S. Energy: Overview and Key Statistics." Congressional Research Service, Washington, DC, June 27, 2014, https://fas.org/sgp/crs/misc/R40187.pdf.

Reisner, Marc. *Cadillac Desert: The American West and Its Disappearing Water*. Penguin, 1993.

Remes, Jacob A. C. *Disaster Citizenship: Survivors, Solidarity, and Power in the Progressive Era*. University of Illinois Press, 2016.

Resnikoff, Jason. *Labor's End: How the Promise of Automation Degraded Work*. University of Illinois Press, 2022.

Revathi, I. "African Americans' Struggle for Environmental Justice and the Case of the Shintech Plant: Lessons Learned from a War Waged." *Journal of Black Studies* 31, no. 6 (July 2001): 777–89.

Rice, Bradley R., and Richard M. Bernard, eds. *Sunbelt Cities: Politics and Growth Since World War II*. University of Texas Press, 1984.

Roche, Jeff. *The Political Culture of the New West*. University Press of Kansas, 2008.

Rogers, Donald W. *Making Capitalism Safe: Workplace Safety and Health Regulation in America, 1880–1940*. University of Illinois Press, 2009.

Roosevelt, Franklin D. *The Public Papers and Addresses of Franklin D. Roosevelt*. Macmillan, 1941.

Rosen, Christine M., and Joel A. Tarr, eds. "Special Issue Devoted to the Environment and the City." *Journal of Urban History* 20, no. 3 (1994).

Rosenberg, Nathan. "Technological Change in the Machine Tool Industry, 1840–1910." *Journal of Economic History* 23, no. 4 (1963): 414–43.

Rundell, Walter, Jr. *Oil in West Texas and New Mexico: A Pictorial History of the Permian Basin*. Texas A&M University Press, 1982.

Ryan, Robert H., and Leonard G. Schifrin. *Midland: The Economic Future of a Texas Oil Center*. University of Texas Bureau of Business Research, 1959.

Sabin, Paul. "Crisis and Continuity in U.S. Oil Politics, 1965–1980." *Journal of American History* 99, no. 1 (2012): 177–86.

Sabin, Paul. *Crude Politics: The California Oil Market, 1900–1940*. University of California Press, 2004.

St. John, Rachel. *Line in the Sand: A History of the Western US/Mexico Border*. Princeton University Press, 2011.

Salas, Miguel Tinker. *The Enduring Legacy: Oil, Culture, and Society in Venezuela*. Duke University Press, 2009.

Schulman, Bruce, and Julian E. Zelizer. *Rightward Bound: Making America Conservative in the 1970s*. Harvard University Press, 2008.

Scott, James C. *Seeing Like a State: How Certain Schemes to Improve the Human Condition Have Failed*. Yale University Press, 1998.

Sellars, Nigel Anthony. *Oil, Wheat and Wobblies: The Industrial Workers of the World in Oklahoma, 1905–1930*. University of Oklahoma Press, 1998.

Sellers, Christopher. "Factory as Environment: Industrial Hygiene, Professional Collaboration and the Modern Sciences of Pollution." *Environmental History Review* 18, no. 1 (1994): 55–83.

Shifflett, Crandall. *Coal Towns: Life, Work, and Culture in Company Towns of Southern Appalachia, 1880–1960*. University of Tennessee Press, 1995.

Silver, Beverly J. *Forces of Labor: Worker's Movements and Globalization Since 1870*. Cambridge University Press, 2003.

Smith, Michael Berry, and Carl T. Montgomery. *Hydraulic Fracturing*. CRC Press, 2015.

Smith, Julia Cauble. "Santa Rita Oil Well." In *Handbook of Texas Online*. Published June 15, 2010. http://www.tshaonline.org/handbook/online/articles/doso1.

Steinberg, Ted. *Acts of God: The Unnatural History of Natural Disaster in America*. Oxford University Press, 2000.

Sterling, Ross S., and Ed Kilman. *Ross Sterling, Texan*. University of Texas Press, 2007.

Stern, Roger J. "Oil Scarcity Ideology in US Foreign Policy, 1908–97." *Security Studies* 25, no. 2 (May 2016): 214–57.

Sugrue, Thomas. *The Origins of the Urban Crisis: Race and Inequality in Postwar Detroit*. Princeton University Press, 1997.

Switzer, Jacqueline Vaughn. *Green Backlash: The History and Politics of Environmental Opposition in the U.S.* Lynne Rienner, 1997.

Szeman, Imre, and Dominic Boyer. *Energy Humanities: An Anthology*. Johns Hopkins University Press, 2017.

Taft, Philip. "Independent Unions and the Merger." *Industrial and Labor Relations Review* 9, no. 3 (April 1956): 433–46.

Tarr, Joel A. "Toxic Legacy: The Environmental Impact of the Manufactured Gas Industry in the United States." *Technology and Culture* 55, no. 1 (2014): 107–47.

Tarr, Joel A., and Jeffrey K. Stine, eds. "Special Issue on Technology, Pollution, and the Environment." *Environmental History Review* 18, no. 1 (1994).

Taylor, Keeanga-Yamahtta. *Race for Profit: How Banks and the Real Estate Industry Undermined Black Homeownership*. University of North Carolina Press, 2019.

Templer, Otis W. "Texas Ground Water Law: Inflexible Institutions and Resource Realities." *Ecumene* 10 (April 1978).

Theriot, Jason P. "The Strategic Petroleum Reserve: U.S. Energy Security and Oil Politics, 1975–2005." *Technology & Culture* 49, no. 4 (2008): 1103–4.

Thomas, Terry L., et al. "Mortality Patterns Among Workers in Three Texas Oil Refineries." *Journal of Occupational Medicine* 24, no. 2 (1982): 135–41.

Thomasson, Melissa A. "From Sickness to Health: The Twentieth-Century Development of the Demand for Health Insurance." *Journal of Economic History* 60, no. 2 (2000): 504–8.

Truett, Samuel. *Fugitive Landscapes: The Forgotten History of the U.S. Mexico-Borderlands*. Yale University Press, 2008.

Turner, James Morton. "'The Specter of Environmentalism': Wilderness, Environmental Politics, and the Evolution of the New Right." *Journal of American History* 96, no. 1 (2009): 123–48.

Tyler, Ron, ed. *The New Handbook of Texas*, Vol. 4. Texas State Historical Society, 1996.

Viehe, Fred W. "The Social-Spatial Distribution in the Black Gold Suburbs of Los Angeles, 1900–1930." *Southern California Quarterly* 73, no. 1 (1991): 33–54.

Vitalis, Robert. *America's Kingdom: Mythmaking on the Saudi Oil Frontier.* Stanford University Press, 2006.

Volanto, Keith. *Texas, Cotton, and the New Deal.* Texas A&M University Press, 2004.

Watts, Michael J. "A Tale of Two Gulfs: Life, Death, and Dispossession Along Two Oil Frontiers." *American Quarterly* 64, no. 3 (2012): 437–67.

Weaver, Bobby. *Oilfield Trash: Life and Labor in the Oil Patch.* Texas A&M University Press, 2010.

Wells, Christopher W., ed. *Environmental Justice in Postwar America.* University of Washington Press, 2018.

Wells, Dan M., Robert M. Sweazy, and George A. Whetstone. "Long-Term Experiences with Effluent Reuse." *Water Pollution Control Federation Journal* 51, no. 11 (1979): 2641–48.

White, Richard. *Railroaded: The Transcontinentals and the Making of Modern America.* Norton, 2011.

Wiencek, Henry Alexander. *Oil Cities: The Making of North Louisiana's Boomtowns, 1901–1930.* University of Texas Press, 2024.

Williams, John. *The Untold Story of the Lower Colorado River Authority.* Texas A&M University Press, 2016.

Williamson, Harold F., Ralph L. Andreano, and Carmen Menezes. "The American Petroleum Industry." In *Output Employment and Productivity in the United States After 1800,* edited by Dorothy S. Brady. American Petroleum Institute, 1966.

Williamson, Jeffrey G. *Trade and Poverty: When the Third World Fell Behind.* MIT Press, 2011.

Witt, John Fabian. "The Transformation of Work and the Law of Workplace Accidents, 1842–1910." *Yale Law Journal* 107, no. 5 (1998): 1467–502.

Wolbert, George S. *American Pipe Lines: Their Industrial Structure, Economic Status and Legal Implications.* University of Oklahoma Press, 1952.

Wooding, John, Charles Levenstein, and Beth Rosenberg. "The Oil, Chemical and Atomic Workers International Union: Refining Strategies for Labor." *International Journal of Health Services* 27, no. 1 (1997): 125–38.

Worcester, Don. *The Texas Longhorn: Relic of the Past, Asset for the Future.* Texas A&M University Press, 1987.

Wright, Richard B. "Urban Centers of West Texas." In *West Texas: A History of the Giant Side of the State,* edited by Paul H. Carlson and Bruce A. Glasrud. University of Oklahoma Press, 2007.

Wunder, John R. *Working the Range: Essays on the History of Western Land Management and the Environment.* Greenwood, 1985.

Yergin, Daniel. *The Prize: The Epic Quest for Oil, Money, and Power.* Free Press, 2008.

Yoakum, Henderson K. *History of Texas: From Its First Settlement in 1685 to Its Annexation to the United States in 1846.* Redfield, 1855.

Zamora, Emilio. *Claiming Rights and Righting Wrongs in Texas: Mexican Workers and Job Politics During World War II.* Texas A&M University Press, 2009.

Zamora, Emilio. *The World of the Mexican Worker in Texas.* Texas A&M University Press, 2000.

Zaretsky, Natasha. *No Direction Home: The American Family and the Fear of National Decline, 1968–1980.* University of North Carolina Press, 2007.

INDEX

Printed and bound by CPI Group (UK) Ltd, Croydon, CR0 4YY
12/10/2026
14980082-0001